# Deleuze and the Contemporary World

## Deleuze Connections

'It is not the elements or the sets which define the multiplicity. What defines it is the AND, as something which has its place between the elements or between the sets. AND, AND, AND – stammering.'

Gilles Deleuze and Claire Parnet, *Dialogues*

**General Editor**
Ian Buchanan

**Editorial Advisory Board**
Keith Ansell-Pearson
Rosi Braidotti
Claire Colebrook
Tom Conley
Gregg Lambert
Adrian Parr
Paul Patton
Patricia Pisters

**Titles in the Series**
Ian Buchanan and Claire Colebrook (eds), *Deleuze and Feminist Theory*
Ian Buchanan and John Marks (eds), *Deleuze and Literature*
Mark Bonta and John Protevi (eds), *Deleuze and Geophilosophy*
Ian Buchanan and Marcel Swiboda (eds), *Deleuze and Music*
Ian Buchanan and Gregg Lambert (eds), *Deleuze and Space*
Martin Fuglsang and Bent Meier Sørensen (eds), *Deleuze and the Social*
Constantin V. Boundas (ed.), *Deleuze and Philosophy*

# Deleuze and the Contemporary World

Edited by Ian Buchanan
and Adrian Parr

Edinburgh University Press

© in this edition, Edinburgh University Press, 2006
© in the individual contributions is retained by the authors

Edinburgh University Press Ltd
22 George Square, Edinburgh

Typeset in 10.5/13 Sabon
by Servis Filmsetting Ltd, Manchester, and
printed and bound in Great Britain by
MPG Books Ltd, Bodmin, Cornwall

A CIP record for this book is available from the British Library

ISBN-10 0 7486 2341 8 (hardback)
ISBN-13 978 0 7486 2341 9 (hardback)
ISBN-10 0 7486 2342 6 (paperback)
ISBN-13 978 0 7486 2342 6 (paperback)

The right of the contributors
to be identified as authors of this work
has been asserted in accordance with
the Copyright, Designs and Patents Act 1988.

# Contents

*For Tom Conley*

# Acknowledgements

With thanks to Jackie Jones, Carol Macdonald and Michael Zaretsky for their help and support. Support in part for this project has been provided by the Savannah College of Art and Design Presidential Fellowship.

Introduction

# Deleuze and the Contemporary World

*Ian Buchanan and Adrian Parr*

In *Nietzsche and Philosophy*, Deleuze says that you can never know a philosopher properly until you know what he or she is against. To know them at all, you have to know what puts fire in their soul, what makes them take up the nearly impossible challenge of trying to say anything at all. Too many people are content to say Deleuze, like Nietzsche, was *against* Hegel without ever asking why. And those who do trouble themselves to ask this question are too often satisfied with a merely philosophical answer. But if Deleuze found Hegel's philosophy intolerable it was not simply because he thought that the dialectic was a badly made concept, or that he objected to a metaphysics predicated on negation. These are the complaints of a sandbox philosopher and Deleuze was certainly not that. Hegel's philosophy was intolerable to Deleuze because in his eyes it offers a slave's view of the world (Deleuze 1983: 10). Worse, it is a model of thought that seems to participate in the legitimation of the very system that enslaves us by installing the master–slave dialectic at the centre of our ratiocination, making it seem like this is the only choice we have, effectively denying us in advance the option of asking our own questions and forming our own problematics. But this critique is only meaningful (for example, authentically critical) to the extent that it is read in terms of Deleuze's conception of philosophy's purpose, which is precisely Marxian to the extent that, like Marx, they hold that the point of philosophy is not simply to understand society, but to change it.[1]

One answer to the question of what Deleuze and Guattari are against, then, is this: the axiomatic. The axiomatic is the latest form of social organisation, which for Deleuze and Guattari always means the organisation of the flows of desire. For them, desire is a kind of cosmic energy that is constantly being deformed into the desire-for-something; but, in their view, its true form is that of production itself.[2] It is, in other words, a process rather than a thing. Desire is the force in the universe that brings things together, but does so without plan or purpose and the results are always uncertain. It may lead to the formation of new compositions, but it might also lead to decomposition. As such, desire is an ambivalent force – without it, we shrivel up and die, but if it isn't carefully harnessed it can tear us apart. Deleuze and Guattari's handling of the concept is similarly ambivalent: on the one hand, they are constantly demanding that desire be unbound from the various shackles of guilt, repression and shame, but on the other hand they caution that this process needs to be done slowly and with care. We need *just enough* of those shackles of guilt, repression and shame to keep us human.

The organisation of desire occurs on all levels of society, from the mundane to the world-historical. Obviously, at the mundane level, desire is subjected to literally countless constraints, most of them quite innocuous. And as the example of the extremely mundane activity of hand-washing will illustrate readily enough, the molar can always be discerned in the molecular. Insofar as we wash our hands because of a concern for hygiene, or in deference to a religious ritual, that mundane activity is the means by which we express our fidelity to the social matrix we think of ourselves as belonging to. Whether it is because we accept the scientific rationale for washing our hands or because we are obedient to the edicts of faith, our actions signify belonging. By the same token, we don't hesitate to castigate others for failing to follow the routine; indeed, it provokes feelings of disgust and rage if we learn, for instance, that someone hasn't washed their hands after using the toilet, especially if they are handling our food. On the macro scale, however, desire has been subjected to relatively few world-historical types of organisation. Throughout history, there have been only three main types of social organisation: (1) the primitive tribe or band, (2) the state, and (3) the axiomatic. Deleuze and Guattari differentiate these organisations according to the different ways in which they codify the objects and practices of everyday life to channel desire into socially useful activities and corporate entities.

> If it is true that we are not using the word axiomatic as a simple metaphor, we must review what distinguishes an axiomatic from all manner of codes, overcodings and recodings: the axiomatic deals directly with purely functional elements and relations whose nature is not specified, and which are immediately realised in highly varied domains simultaneously; codes, on the other hand, are relative to those domains and express specific relations between qualified elements that cannot be subsumed by a higher formal unity (overcoding) except by transcendence and in an indirect fashion. (Deleuze and Guattari 1987: 454)

Axioms are operative statements of a primary type; they do not derive from or depend upon other statements. They function as the component parts of the various assemblages of production, circulation and consumption that comprise the capitalist system in full. Their principal function is to regulate flows – of money, people, raw materials, commodities, and so on. Flows can be the subject of several axioms at once, but they can also lack axioms of their own, whereby they are either contained by the consequences of other axioms, or they remain 'untamed'. Axioms may take the form of laws, but more often they appear as contracts, trade agreements, policy statements, governance protocols, and so on. The Marshall Plan for the post-war reconstruction of Europe is an example of an axiom, as would be Brazil's import-substitution programme of the 1970s and the seemingly perennial Global War on terror. Axioms are in effect order-words by another name; they are the slogans that underpin and give reason to the heterogeneous raft of laws, policies and regulations that give daily life in the contemporary world its structure, consistency and its essential nature. In what they refer to as a 'summary sketch', Deleuze and Guattari identify seven 'givens' that taken together constitute the *l'universe axiomatique*.

## Addition, Subtraction

Axioms can be added and withdrawn at will. The general tendency in capitalism is to add axioms in response to changing circumstances; but in certain cases, particularly in totalitarian regimes, the opposite tendency is the rule.

> What makes the axiomatic vary, in relation to States, is the distinction and relation between foreign and domestic markets. There is a multiplication of axioms most notably when an integrated domestic market is being organised to meet the requirements of the foreign market. (Deleuze and Guattari 1987: 462)

These opposing tendencies converge in crisis form in the third-world when debt-ridden totalitarian regimes try to reorganise in order to stave off red-lining by first-world credit agencies. If totalitarianism is defined by the withdrawal of axioms, or what might also be conceived as the reduction of the state to its bare minimum, then developments in the third-world suggest that not only are the conditions ripe for a massive proliferation of totalitarian regimes, but in a real sense they are in the grip of a totalitarianism from without. The austerity conditions imposed by the IMF, World Bank, WTO and indeed the White House itself, have the hallmarks of classic totalitarianism.

At the behest of these allegedly benevolent agencies domestic markets are forcibly deregulated, government spending is slashed, wages are pared to the bone, to create structural conditions – disproportionately – favourable to foreign investment (the axiom of 'access') whence salvation is supposed to come. The effect of the loss of these internal structures is that third-world nations are denied the very same supports first-world nations, such as Japan and Germany, but also the US, a notoriously protectionist market, used to claw their way forward. The first-world effectively uses its financial muscle to kick away the ladder the third world might use to get out of its infamous poverty trap (Davis 2004: 19). As Mike Davis notes, the principal cause of the continued downward spiral of pauperisation in the third-world is precisely the retreat of government (Davis 2004: 19). The domestic economy is sacrificed for the sake of foreign profit-taking. In the twentieth century, it was internal dictators that created these conditions; today it is globalisation. The gap separating totalitarianism and fascism is narrow. The latter uses war to rescue its economy. The US policy of giving credit to needy countries so they can buy arms is already pushing a number of countries in this direction.

When not pointing the finger at demography, these agencies, the World Bank and WTO in particular, tend to blame poverty on bad governance, rather than the structural inequalities of globalisation, citing lack of trust and reciprocity at a grassroots level as the major impediment to growth.[3] Under these auspices the concept of 'social capital' has known an unparalleled rise in fortune. The fiction underpinning this thinking is that communitarian attitudes, if they are properly fostered, will stem rapacious profit-taking and enable social justice to flourish. What should be obvious, but seems to have escaped notice, is that social capital is effectively a form of social and labour discipline: its precise aim is to create conditions safe for foreign investment. Community development is really a codeword for what financial analysts call 'risk treatment', that is, it identifies and tries to attenuate the 'human factor' as the principal cause of the failure of aid programmes. If villagers were more community-minded they would be less likely to embezzle aid funds, so this reasoning goes, the irony being that it creates a paradoxical situation in which laissez-faire capitalists find themselves promoting socialism to protect their investment, all the while singing the praises of the 'free market'. The creation of co-operative markets in peasant villages is then taken to be a sign of success rather than yet another instance of micro-exploitation and informalisation of labour rampant in the third world (Davis 2004: 24).

As important as the emergence of the various 'fair trade' initiatives have been in ameliorating the impoverishing structural inequality between first- and third-world countries, their very existence stands in the way of a clear-eyed view of the universality of this situation. It effectively amounts to an instance of what Roland Barthes astutely described as 'rhetorical inoculation', the small concession that immunises against a more systematic criticism (Barthes 1972: 164). By admitting that in certain circumstances the market system isn't always fair, those who benefit most from this system try to duck the fact that it is the system itself that is iniquitous. Starbucks' agreement to pay slightly over-market for its coffee beans is an attempt to blind us to the reality that this situation – third-world as market garden for the first – is the cause of the problem in the first place. The lack of diversity in the domestic sectors of the coffee growing nations places them in a very vulnerable position, their livelihood literally hingeing on the whim of first worlders. It also prevents them from expanding their agricultural (much less their industrial) base because they cannot afford to grow less lucrative, but ultimately more nutritive crops. So countries like Brazil have to import food, despite having an enormous primary industries sector.

## Saturation

'Capitalism is indeed an axiomatic, because it has no laws but immanent ones. It would like for us to believe that it confronts the limits of the Universe, the extreme limit of resources and energy' (Deleuze and Guattari 1987: 463). But the reality is that the only limits it confronts are of its own making. And even as it confronts these limits it repels them, or displaces them, thus avoiding the moment when the system would actually have to change. The oil industry offers an instructive case in point. In spite of scaremongering, from both the Left and the Right, there is no shortage of oil. Oil shortages – or at least the threat of oil shortages – are expedient political weapons for both sides: the green-hued left use it as leverage to foster a more eco-friendly outlook and to encourage greater investment in research and development to find a replacement energy source; meanwhile the hawkish right use it to argue that imperialism is necessary to protect 'energy security' and the first-world lifestyle. And there is a plethora of positions in between. Yet, the fact is, even if China and India continue to escalate their rate of oil consumption, oil isn't going to run out in the short or medium term. Current estimates are that proven reserves are sufficient to last us another 150 to 500 years (one hopes that this will be time enough for a replacement energy source to be standardised).

Some theorists, like Yeomans, have argued that what there is a shortage of is cheap oil. Cheap oil is oil that can be extracted and processed at low cost. If one looks at the various potential oil sources in the world, from Canadian shale oil, to North Sea oil and gas, to Texas, and the Middle East, it is Middle East oil that is cheapest by a big margin. Whereas extracting oil from oil sands can cost upwards of $14 a barrel and is environmentally messy, Iraqi oil costs a mere $1.50 a barrel and is relatively clean or at least far enough away not to attract much attention from the NIMBY set. The difference in profit potential is obvious. While this puts the Middle East oil producing countries in a strong position in the market place, if they do not keep oil prices down then they make presently uneconomical oil reserves attractive and risk losing market share which is effectively what happened in the years following the 'oil shock' of early 1970s.

> As Saudi oil minister Sheik Yamani said in 1981, 'If we force Western countries to invest heavily in funding alternative sources of energy, they will. This will take them no more than seven to ten years and will result in their reduced dependence on oil as a source of energy to a point which will jeopardise Saudi Arabia's interests'. (Yeomans 2004: 105)

In most of the West this is precisely what happened in the 1970s. Fuel efficiency suddenly becomes a watchword everywhere, even in the US with its notorious lack of energy thrift. By the same token, the so-called 'oil shock' was in fact a boon for producers and retailers alike, so from the point of view of the accumulation of capital it was anything but a disaster.[4] As such, this version of the oil shortage argument is not, finally, persuasive.

The inverse – or, oversupply – argument is more compelling. 'The history of oil in the 20th century is not a history of shortfall and inflation, but of the constant menace – for the industry and the oil states – of excess capacity and falling prices, of surplus and glut' (Retort 2005: 14). In other words, the real oil crisis is not an external crisis or 'extreme limit' of vanishing resources, but an entirely internal crisis of the volatility of prices. On this argument, the Gulf Wars have been fought to stabilise prices and regularise profit-taking. Blood is not being spilled for oil, as such, which at least has a certain materiality, but for the utterly nebulous and by nature completely ephemeral base points on the stock exchange. In the end, as Retort have argued, it is not even the price of oil that matters, so much as the sustainability of the triangular trade of oil, weapons and military base construction, that has grown around the oil industry – fighting over oil concessions, building military bases to protect oil interests, are ultimately just as profitable as dealing in oil, at least when viewed from the perspective of the domestic US market. With so many new players in the oil and guns business, it has become impossible to regulate the market by the old-fashioned oligarchic means. Hence, the necessity of war. War is the last resort of the axiomatic, which usually has much more powerful instruments at its disposal.

## Models, Isomorphy

In principal, insofar as all states are domains for the realisation of capital within a single, integrated world market, they are isomorphic. Although this isomorphy implies a degree of homogeneity between the states, at least on an operational level ('the highway code, the circulation of commodities, production costs, etc.'), this only holds true insofar as there is a general 'tendency toward a single integrated domestic market' (Deleuze and Guattari 1987: 464). At a deeper level, however, there can be a real heterogeneity between states without them ceasing to be isomorphic because the fact of the worldwide market leaves them no option but to conform.

> The general rules regarding this are as follows: the consistency, *the totality* (*l'ensemble*), *or unity of the axiomatic* are defined by capital as a 'right' or relation of production (for the market); *the respective independence of the axioms* in no way contradicts this totality but derives from the divisions or sectors of the capitalist mode of production; *the isomorphy of the models*, with the two poles of addition and subtraction, depends on how the domestic and foreign markets are distributed in each case. (Deleuze and Guattari 1987: 464)

Deleuze and Guattari identify three kinds of isomorphy corresponding to three bipolarities that constitute the contemporary world. The first refers to the states in the centre of the capitalism world-system: the US, the member-nations of the EU, Australia, Canada, and so on. Although their various models of governance are different when compared in strict detail, they are isomorphic with respect to the capitalist world-system. Obviously, too, organisations like WTO, NAFTA, WEF, and so on have as their precise goal the machining of this isomorphy. The nations in the centre do not become homogeneous via this process; indeed, the opposite is true – in the guise of tourism and niche marketing, the cash-value of difference has long been recognised – but their relations of product do become increasingly well integrated. The second bipolarity is fading significance in the contemporary world: the grand bureaucracies of what used to be known as the second world, namely the USSR and PRC, have effectively relinquished what Deleuze and

Guattari call their 'heteromorphy' in favour of a more streamlined iso-morphy. Even so, one can still find countries whose mode of production and relation of production do not conform to the Washington 'consensus', but continue to integrate themselves with the world market all the same. One could point to the planned economy of North Korea or the bizarrely feudal economy of Saudi Arabia as instances of this. The third bipolarity is the familiar distinction between centre and periphery (North–South), which Deleuze and Guattari describe as a 'polymorphy': here capital acts as the relation of production in non-capitalist or not necessarily capitalist modes of production.

## Power

Whether the US is the lone or remaining superpower is not the crucial issue – militarism defined as a peace more terrifying than war amounts to a single smooth space of war reigning over the globe and it doesn't matter whether there are opposing parts or not. It is not whether the US is at loggerheads with North Korea or Syria that is the issue, but rather that diplomacy between states is defined by the presence or absence of a 'credible threat'. For the US, withdrawing a trade agreement is just as devastating, perhaps more so, than sending in the marines; likewise OPEC nations can do more damage by driving up oil prices than by blowing up tall buildings in New York. States no longer appropriate the war machine; they are a component of it.

The San Francisco-based 'gathering of antagonists to capital and empire', Retort, has argued that the invasion of Iraq can only be properly understood in light of the 'Battle in Seattle' and, more especially, the troubling display of third-world insubordination at Doha and Cancún where 'an in-house insurgency of 20 nations refused to endorse the massive US-EU subsidies to North Atlantic agriculture and the WTO rules crafted to prevent the South from protecting itself' (Retort 2005: 16).[5] Commentators who have drawn comparisons between the second Gulf War and the Vietnam War generally do so on the basis of outcomes, real and predicted. The lack of gratitude on the part of the liberated Iraqis and their failure spontaneously to Americanise coupled with uncontrolled insurgency in most parts of the country has led many to mutter the fateful word long associated with Vietnam, namely 'quagmire'. To put it in Deleuze and Guattari's terms, the US, but by this one really means the entire integrated being of first-world capital, has been thrust up against a limit-point. The whole world is holding its breath waiting to see if it is a real or an absolute limit . . .

## The Included Middle

The very operation of the axiomatic – namely, its restless search for new models of realisation – creates problems it cannot solve.

> The more the worldwide axiomatic installs high industry and highly industrialised agriculture at the periphery, provisionally reserving for the centre the so-called postindustrial activities (automation, electronics, information technologies, the conquest of space, overarmament, etc.), the more it installs peripheral zones of underdevelopment inside the centre, internal Third Worlds, internal Souths. (Deleuze and Guattari 1987: 469)

In search of new sources of capital, capital willingly invades the underdeveloped regions of the world so it can build and operate factories unburdened with high taxes and labour and environmental restrictions; equally willingly, it consigns to the scrap heap entire industries and the jobs and lives dependent upon them in the first-world if the profit and loss statement no longer appeals to the shareholders. Capitalism has never had any interest in enriching all – indeed unequal exchange is indispensable to its functioning. 'Even a social democracy adapted to the Third World surely does not undertake to integrate the whole poverty-stricken population into the domestic market; what it does, rather, is to effect the class rupture that will select the integratable elements' (Deleuze and Guattari 1987: 468). Today, in the first-world, we can witness this strategy at work behind the rhetoric of the so-called 'deserving poor'. The included middle refers to the rump of citizens of capitalism it deems unnecessary to save.

## Minorities

What is a minority? It certainly isn't an affair of numbers – indeed those who number among the minority are frequently in the majority if we take a purely numerical view of things. The world's poor outnumber the rich by an extremely wide margin, yet theirs is the minor voice. The combined wealth of the 500 richest people in the world exceeds the GDP of the entire continent of Africa, and is greater than the combined incomes of the 'poorest half of humanity' (George Monbiot, cited in Cook 2004: 232). A handful of people whose total wealth has to be measured in the trillions are numerically speaking quite obviously in the minority; they are a very select group indeed. Yet the power they wield in consequence of their tremendous wealth makes it nonsense to describe them as a minority. In contrast, the three billion people constituting the poorest half of humanity have so little power singly or collectively that it is no error of judgement to describe them as a minority. So why do Deleuze and Guattari speak of the minority as being vested with the power of the nondenumerable?

For Deleuze and Guattari, the nondenumerable refers to the power to ask one's own questions, to form one's own problematics, and, more particularly, to define the conditions under which a satisfactory answer or response to these questions and problems might be obtained. Today, after so many centuries of suffering and silence, it is the indigenous peoples of the world who are showing the rest of us how potent this power can be. If the 1960s took inspiration from Che Guevara in the Sierra Maestra, as Jameson records in his capsular cultural history of the period, then the 1990s took inspiration from Subcomandante Marcos in the Chiapas. For many, the road to Seattle began in the mountains of south-east Mexico when the Zapatistas launched their movement.[6] The figure of Che as militant and utopian was a potent one for the Left in the 1960s, but as Jameson argues, the failures of the guerilla movements in Peru and Venezuela effectively robbed it of its utopian energy. The guerilla lost his appeal and there followed a profound 'disinvestment of revolutionary libido and fascination on the part of the First World Left' (Jameson 1988: 203). The headline-grabbing violence of the Red Army Faction and the Baader-Meinhof Gang disillusioned many on the Left and the very idea of militancy was jettisoned. Subsequently, the figure of the guerilla fighter was appropriated by the Right and transformed fatefully into the image of the terrorist, effectively depriving the Left of its ideological claim on the right to bear arms.[7] Thus a new figure was needed and that is how we should understand the Zapatistas. Subcomandante Marcos put it thus in an interview with Gabriel García Márquez and Roberto Pondo:

> A soldier is an absurd person who has to resort to arms in order to convince others, and in that sense the movement has no movement if its future is military. If the EZLN perpetuates itself as an armed military structure it is headed for failure. Failure as an alternative set of ideas, an alternative attitude to the world. The worst that could happen to it, apart from that, would be to come to power and install itself there as a revolutionary army. For us it would be a failure. (Marcos 2001: 70)

The Zapatistas' movement began with eleven demands – work, land, shelter, food, health, education, independence, freedom, democracy, justice and peace – but eventually expanded to fifteen with the addition of security, anti-corruption, information and environmental protection. They claimed the right of dissent and rebellion, but chose to practise democracy rather than wage war for it (Weinberg 2000: 201). Using the electronic media to full advantage, the Zapatistas sowed powerful slogans of the password type into the global political subsoil. Among the many rallying slogans the Zapatistas have put into circulation, the one that has gained the most traction in the first-world is undoubtedly the one Naomi Klein has made the centrepiece of her recent utopian cry to reclaim the commons: 'one world with many worlds in it'. This, for Klein, defines the stakes of the present struggle. It means fighting against the logic of centralisation, consolidation and homogenisation dear to what she calls McGovernment, the purveyors of the 'happy meal of cutting taxes, privatizing services, liberalizing regulations, busting unions' (Klein 2001: 89). It means giving local communities 'the right to plan and manage their schools, their services, their natural settings, according to their own lights' (Klein 2001: 89).

As charming as this picture of a world freed from the predatory claws of capitalism is, it misses its target inasmuch as it defines capitalism as denying us the right to plan and manage our schools and so on. In fact, the sad truth is most neo-liberal governments would be quite happy to hand over management of schools to local communities, seeing this as one easy way of cutting overheads and appearing to do something good at the same time. The real problem is that the axiomatic is able to treat all forms of organisation as its model of realisation. This is something it has only lately perfected, as Naomi Klein's book on the rise of the logo documents. We didn't lose control of our schools so much as give it up in the name of profit, or rather its insidious other: efficiency. Education, health, life; these are the non-denumerable in their very essence, yet we have seen the neo-liberals transform them into denumerables, for which a balance-sheet approach can be taken. If one must frame this discussion in the language of rights, then it is the right to determine what can and cannot be a model of realisation that must first be obtained. The lesson the Zapatistas have passed on to us is that we should start with government itself!

## Undecidable Propositions

The Left's response to Seattle and Porto Alegre has been mixed, ranging from the fervent enthusing of anarchists like David Graeber to the cooler considerations of Michael Hardt. These two positions, which by no means exhaust the range of responses or even map out its extremes, typify the two dominant kinds of responses Seattle and Porto Alegre have been met with: either their sheer existence is enough, or more organisation is needed really to make things change. How would Deleuze and Guattari respond? One can speculate that Deleuze and Guattari would

have approved, perhaps with a few reservations concerning fascist reterritorialisation, as they did in May 1968. The anarchism evident in Seattle
would no doubt have pleased them too. As is evident in their remarks
on 'Saturation', Deleuze and Guattari do not view the potential development 'of a worldwide labour bureaucracy or technocracy' as an
improvement on capitalism (Deleuze and Guattari 1987: 464). Indeed,
they list it as a danger to be warded off by focusing on precise and highly
localised struggles.

There is no consensus on what to call the flashpoints of dissent we associate metonymically with Seattle and Porto Alegre – the media-applied
label 'anti-globalisation movement' has stuck, despite being an obvious
misnomer (these movements are global in their outlook and in their range
of concerns and make use of all the available globalising technology at
their disposal). But as Emir Sader puts it, new formations are difficult to
recognise in the new contexts they create for themselves (as Borges might
have said, revolutionaries like all great artists create their own precursors)
and to continue to try to read them against the background of former
movements misses the point of their very existence (Sader 2002: 94). The
overwhelming complaint about Porto Alegre is that it is difficult to see
how it will co-ordinate its efforts. By contrast, following Deleuze and
Guattari, we might equally argue that it is their lack of organisation and
their spreading of disorganisation that capitalism cannot tolerate – what
it wants is for dissent to be organised. The 'Turtles and Teamsters' catch-
cry of the 'Battle in Seattle' neatly summarises Deleuze and Guattari's
thesis concerning the revolutionary: connections not conjugations: 'Every
struggle is a function of all these undecidable propositions and constructs
*revolutionary connections* in opposition to the *conjugations of the
axiomatic*' (Deleuze and Guattari 1987: 473).

As Alexander Cockburn and Jeffrey St Clair wrote in their report on
the 'Battle in Seattle', it was a triumph despite what latter-day doomsay-
ers said in the months that followed the 'five days that shook the world'
(28 November 1999 to 3 December) because it placed the protesters'
'issues squarely on the national and indeed global political agenda'
(Cockburn and St Clair 2000: 1). Until then international trade meetings
were relatively inconspicuous affairs whose agenda were reported, if it at
all, in the dry tones of economists. After Seattle, this changed. The first
casualty was their physical invisibility – following Seattle meetings of
WTO, IMF, NAFTA, WEC and so on became extremely high profile.
Subsequent meetings in Washington, Prague, Genoa and Melbourne
were similarly disrupted, though none nearly so effectively as in Seattle.
The security forces learned from Seattle. DC spent $1 million in new riot

equipment and $5 million in overtime to secure the city for the April 2000 meeting of the IMF and the World Bank. Unlike Seattle, the protesters weren't able to halt the meeting much less shut the city down. Yet in its own way this was a victory for the protesters because the cost of providing security at these meetings escalated so much that it became almost impossible to contemplate staging them. By the same token, the meetings did not continue to go unanswered, the World Social Forum being the most important response. Significantly, though, the agenda of these trade talks ceased to be reported and indeed thought about in purely economic terms – the economic gained a face and a body. The axiomatic was shown to be the cruel, callous system that it is and though this did not bring it to a halt it created a landscape in which hitherto silenced minorities could begin to pose new problems.

As Cockburn and St Clair acknowledge, the effects of the 'Battle in Seattle' can be compared to the long summer of the 'events of May'.

> You can take the state by surprise only once or twice in a generation. May/June, 1968, took the French state by surprise. The French state then took very good care not to have that unpleasant experience repeated. The same reaction by the state's security apparatus happened after Seattle, which represented a terrible humiliation on a global stage for the US government. (Cockburn and St Clair 2000: 9–10).

The heady optimism of this activist moment which stretched from late November 1999 to September 2001 is difficult to recollect in the present era, and that is perhaps the most damaging effect of the collapse of the Twin Towers. As John Sellers, the director of Ruckus Society, one of the more active organisations present in Seattle, commented:

> People all over the world were so inspired by Seattle, partly because it was the most heavily televised protest in history . . . but also because most people had no idea that there was real dissent here in the United States. But when they saw tens of thousands of people in the streets, and the facade of democracy peel away to reveal the armed storm troopers with shields, grenades and gas, wielding chemical weapons against unarmed crowds, it really drove home the fact that there are all kinds of different opinions in this country, and that there can be a true, sweeping social movement in the United States. (Sellers 2001: 85)

Since 9/11, however, such molecularising images of political dissent have effectively vanished; to be replaced by the molarity of mourning.

What is most striking about the global mood change is that whereas the images of US brutality towards its own citizens were shocking in 1999, they now seem pallid in the face of its brutality towards the citizens of

Iraq and Afghanistan. But that isn't quite right either, because it misses the fact that then it was still possible to think in terms of police action as a violation of civil liberties. And although they had already taken a severe belting during the so-called war on drugs which peaked under self-confessed pot-smokers Clinton and Gore, civil liberties are suffering an even greater thrashing under Bush in the name of homeland security. The images of Seattle were also shocking because, as Cockburn and St Clair point out, they gave the world its first glimpse of America's highly militarised police force (Cockburn and St Clair 2000: 100). Visored black helmets, kevlar body-armour and assault rifles replaced the thin blue line as the image of peaceableness, which is as eloquent a testimony to the change in temperature of the times as one could hope for. A Cold War abroad and a Hot War at home.

## What Gives?

In the opening chapter to this volume – 'Treatise on Militarism' – Ian Buchanan takes up a number of these issues to develop a picture of militarism in the contemporary world.

Nicholas Thoburn offers a complementary analysis which seeks to identify the limits of Hardt and Negri's Deleuze-inspired theses. Critiquing their concept of the 'multitude' Thoburn introduces us to the problem of political composition in the context of communist politics, addressing the minor politics operating through the vacuoles of non-communication. He asks: how can politics be rescued from the musty corners of self-referentiality and begin to engage the social once more? This is by and large a problem of minor political expression, contends Thoburn, depending on whether communication is couched in terms of information-transfer or collective enunciation. The first plays straight into the hands of populist forms of mass communication. The second is more attuned to productivity than a specific political message. Thoburn is critical of the political subject and the whole notion of an independent social body; the latter, he says, is a position Hardt and Negri's concept of the multitude supports.

Kenneth Surin's '1,000 Political Subjects' proposes that in a world where transcendental guarantees no longer hold sway we need to seek out a new basis for solidarity. This is important if politics is to have any *raison d'être*, exposing us to alternatives to the current situation. In order to do this he revitalises the notion of the Citizen Subject that Foucault cast into the ocean, calling for a new conception of belonging that is based upon Deleuze and Guattari's concept of singularity. Drawing examples from

Kurdish separatism to the value laden categories of 'Englishness', Surin details the benefits of the concept of singularity for new ways of assigning identities: he advocates for description in place of identification. Hence, rather than consider someone else as 'being' English or American or Kurdish, he puts forward the helpful suggestion that we may in fact lean upon descriptions so as to open 'being' up to difference.

Rosi Braidotti adds to this project of how to reconfigure dominant national identities. Implicit within the European unification project, she says, is the vision for a post-nationalist sociopolitical space. This space, Braidotti likens to a space of becoming-minoritarian, the reason being that European unification points to a shift in identity, one that she proposes can produce a more ecophilosophical sense of multiple belonging. Ultimately, this shift in consciousness will result in dramatic changes in how 'whiteness' is conceived and experienced. From here she goes on to outline the political and methodological implications of the structural invisibility European whites have previously enjoyed. The influx of migrants and the blending of various cultures in contemporary Europe work to break down ethnic and nationalist categories of identification. Braidotti warns, though, that this move away from unified identity positions will be a painful process, albeit a necessary one if Europe is going to start dis-identifying with previous Eurocentric nationalist models.

The problem of national identity also figures strongly in Verena Conley's chapter 'Borderlines'. Using Deleuze and Guattari's concepts of the rhizome and smooth space, Conley investigates the connection between the nation-state and the citizen, exploring how alternative social spaces can be produced. She is critical of smooth space, in particular the amenability of such spaces to the flows of capital, flows that often undermine social wellbeing more than enhance it. As such, Conley calls for a 'qualified' understanding of smooth space, that when combined with the rhizomatic connections working to open up and transform territories, can actually help us understand borderlines differently. She argues that the current situation of border politics, whereby the state apparatus functions through a mechanism of inclusion and exclusion, only ends up immobilising sociality. Yet the state need not be fixed to its territorial borders, for at the limit of borderlines rhizomatic lines generate new pathways and it is along these that change ensues. It is not just a territorial change occurring at the level of the earth that Conley speaks of here, but a change at the level of language, affect and desire. What is pivotal in her analysis, then, is not just the liberation of social desire but of psychic desire as well.

Paul Patton turns our attentions to internal colonisation and decolonisation, understood to mean the colonisation of indigenous peoples who continue to live on their traditional homelands but are held captive by the colonial state. Using Deleuze's theory of events and his concept of deterritorialisation, developed together with Guattari, Patton considers the legal colonisation of Aboriginal societies in order to reflect upon the event of colonisation. An event, outlines Patton, is not be confused with a physical body, rather it is an expression of 'particular configurations and movements of bodies' that vary from occasion to occasion. In this way, as Parr outlines in her essay, the event and history are not one and the same occurrence, insofar as the event escapes the linear organisation of history. Patton provides a detailed study of the historico-political event of colonisation, that functions according to a principle of *terra nullius* (a territory that was believed by white settlers to be legally empty regardless of whether or not indigenous peoples still inhabited the land). The *Mabo* case in Australia is a good example of a legal event that not only inaugurated groundbreaking legal changes but carried with it radical social implications as well.

Adrian Parr also engages with Deleuze and Guattari's rather innovative understanding of desire, using it to examine how the past is territorialised through mainstream culture and politics. Thinking about different forms of Holocaust remembrance in the context of Austrian national historiography and Israeli national identity, the case studies she examines reveal how the Holocaust functions as a reactionary ground of identification. She then considers the different yet inter-related roles culture and politics play in the context of memory and historiography. It is from here she extends her analysis of the Holocaust to consider the more complex movement of memory in terms of desiring-production drawing upon Deleuze's distinction between spiritual and material memory, all the while interweaving this analysis with Deleuze and Guattari's discussions of genealogical history.

Laurence Silberstein highlights the importance of the concepts of desire, deterritorialisation and reterritorialisation to how we rethink and concomitantly reconfigure the sociocultural boundaries of the Zionist project in Israel. What Silberstein advocates is a doubled becoming-Israeli and an Israeli-becoming, which he understands in terms of changing the dominant structures of both the Israeli state and how Zionism is produced and circulated through the Israeli sociocultural sphere. Using the example of Arab Israeli novelist Shammas, Silberstein points out that Shammas both deterritorialises the Hebrew language – owned by Jews and the primary signifier of Jewish identity – only to reterritorialise it as the language of Israeli national identity. Rather than striving for equality within Israeli Jewish culture, Shammas chooses to redirect and change

Israeli culture beyond the majoritarian Zionist premise that 'being Israeli' equates with 'being Jewish'. When infused with the Deleuzian concept of becoming, Silberstein points out that a post-Zionist critique of how Israeli national identity is formed in terms of a Jewish people and nation can open up new directions for Israeli subjectivity.

Like Parr, Eugene Holland also sets his attentions on Deleuze and Guattari's concept of desire as it figures in schizoanalysis. Holland chooses the schizoanalytic method to explore how economic and familial determinations in a modern capitalist society reinforce one another and state politics along with it. Holland makes the spirited argument that the sovereign state is long gone and what prevails in its place is the biopower state. The state no longer enforces order through death and terror, now the biopower state represses death in order fully to exploit the production of surplus that capital in turn appropriates in order to generate more capital. This is what Holland calls the 'Death-State'. He goes on to demonstrate the connection between the Death-State and the current 'war on terrorism', bringing to our attention the convergence between capital, state and family. The Death-State, he outlines, is a form of fascism that through fear isolates individuals from one another and this comes at the expense of the overall social good of the community. Here fascism rears its ugly head operating at the level of mass desire: the libidinal investment in the protective order of the Fatherland at the expense of the nurturing Motherland. This over-investment in the Fatherland, argues Holland, is inherently pathological and fascistic.

In her analysis of First, Second and Third Cinema, Patricia Pisters also looks to history; combining Marxist and Deleuzian theoretical positions. In a Marxist vein the definition she provides for Second and Third Cinema is that it aspires to raise political consciousness by addressing the struggles and contradictions of history. She then extends Deleuze's thesis that free indirect discourse is the time-image, to propose that free indirect discourse not only operates in the time-image, it also appears in the movement-images of First Cinema. In what may appear for some to be a rather anti-Deleuzian methodology, she embraces the subtle dialectics of Deleuze at work in the concept of the 'event'. She proposes, as Buchanan and Jameson do, that we 'neutralise' the past if we refuse to engage in any historicising activities whatsoever. Her understanding of dialectics here leans heavily upon the definition that Buchanan provides in his book *Deleuzism*, that being a way of distancing the 'present as an event from itself' (Buchanan 2000). From here she goes on to expose the politics of film, arguing that contemporary cinema is less concerned with representing a unified conception of 'the people' than it is with speech-acts that operate as free indirect discourse in reality. In this way, film cuts its way through reality as it combines diverse histories, all the while revealing the complexity of these.

As Patton outlines in his chapter, the structure of the virtual is that of the problem: regardless of how virtual conditions may be determined, or specified, the nature of the virtual itself can never be fully captured. This is not to suggest, though, that the virtual lacks materiality though it is immanent. The virtualisation of a contemporary world as it increasingly becomes networked is an issue in which cybertheory and cybernetics share an interest. Tracing the development of cybertheory from cybernetics and information theory, John Marks draws out the utopian vision of cybertheory as it divorces information from materiality. But is the concept of the virtual that Deleuze and Guattari develop the same as that espoused by cybertheory? They certainly have a common focus when it comes to challenging and disturbing conceptions of a clearly unified body, as well as a shared interest in non-centric modes of organisation, but there is much about how cybertheory uses Deleuze and Guattari that is not just conceptually weak but worse still strips the critical impetus out of the concept. It is in their focus on material complexity in the context of their concept of the virtual that Deleuze and Guattari dramatically part ways with cybertheory. Contrary to cybertheory, they do not advocate a disembodied vision of the virtual. Furthermore, the virtual, as Deleuze and Guattari understand it, is not the dematerialised antithesis of the actual. The critical impetus of their theory of the virtual lies in what Rajchman calls the 'intelligence of the virtual' in thought, and what cybertheory does in its bastardisation of the concept is, in fact, depoliticise it.

All in all, the following collection of essays uses Deleuzian concepts to describe, analyse, critique and evaluate the tone, timbre and rhythm of the contemporary world. Typically, problems of solidarity, militarism, citizenship, immigration, history and memory, minorities, colonisation and resistance occur again and again throughout the sociopolitical arena. In this book the Deleuzian conceptual apparatus functions like a conduit through which we can rethink and offer theoretical alternatives to many of the problems manifest throughout our world. There is therefore a cross-pollination of viewpoints in the volume that could be said to produce a rhizomatic vision and response to the world in which we currently live. That said, though, all the essays here have been chosen because they push Deleuzism to the limit and in their combination they encourage us to take risks in our thinking and to disturb our comfort zones. As Claire Colebrook announces in the final chapter 'The Joy of Philosophy' comes from facilitating 'styles of thinking that will do violence to cliché'.

Summing up the underlying current of this volume, Colebrook investigates the sociability of philosophical thinking. She argues that the singularity of perception is what brings us into connection with the inhuman and this is what opens the self up to difference and becoming. She is highly critical of the utilitarian principles operating at the heart of the contemporary world and she urges us to consider the importance of the activity of thinking beyond utility. More importantly, the affirmation of thought lies in thinking those very forces that push life beyond the human condition. The becoming-imperceptible of thought that Deleuze's philosophical project advances resists colonising life with an anthropocentric model of thought or a utilitarian focus on ends. The upshot of advancing an image of thought that does not reinforce the image of a representing self is that we begin to understand thought pragmatically. That being, the manner in which thought is productive of different orientations in the world.

# References

Badiou, A. (2000), *Deleuze: The Clamour of Being*, trans. L. Burchill, Minneapolis: University of Minnesota Press.

Barthes, R. (1972), *Mythologies*, trans. A. Lavers, London: Jonathan Cape.

Buchanan, I. (2000), *Deleuzism: A Metacommentary*, Durham: Duke University Press.

Buchanan, I. (2002), 'Deleuze and Hitchcock: Schizoanalysis and *The Birds*', *Strategies: Journal of Theory, Culture and Politics* 15 (1): 105–18.

Certeau, Michel de (1997), *The Capture of Speech and Other Political Writings*, trans. T. Conley, Minneapolis: University of Minnesota Press.

Cockburn, A. and St Clair, J. (2000), *Five Days That Shook the World: Seattle and Beyond*, London: Verso.

Cook, C. (2004), *Diet for a Dead Planet: How the Food Industry is Killing Us*, New York: The New Press.

Davis, M. (2004), 'Planet of Slums', *New Left Review* 2 (26): 5–34.

Deleuze, G. (1983), *Nietzsche and Philosophy*, trans. H. Tomlinson, London: Athlone.

Deleuze, G. and Guattari, F. (1983), *Anti-Oedipus: Capitalism and Schizophrenia*, trans. R. Hurley, M. Seem and H. R. Lane, Minneapolis: University of Minnesota Press.

Deleuze, G. and Guattari, F. (1987), *A Thousand Plateaus: Capitalism and Schizophrenia*, trans. R. Hurley, 31 M. Seem and H. R. Lane, Minneapolis: University of Minnesota Press.

Deleuze, G. (1989), *Cinema 2: The Time-Image*, trans. H. Tomlinson and R. Galeta, Minneapolis: University of Minnesota Press.

Deleuze, G. (1990), *The Logic of Sense*, trans. M. Lester and C. Stivale, London: Continuum.

Deleuze, G. and Guattari, F. (1994), *What is Philosophy?*, trans. H. Tomlinson and G. Burchell, New York: Columbia University Press.

Gowan, P. (1999), *The Global Gamble: Washington's Faustian Bid for World Dominance*, London: Verso.

Graeber, D. (2002), 'For a New Anarchism', *New Left Review* 13: 61–73.

Jameson, F. (1988), *The Ideologies of Theory*, vol. 2, Minneapolis: University of Minnesota Press.

Jameson, F. (1997), 'Marxism and Dualism in Deleuze', in Ian Buchanan (ed.), *A Deleuzian Century?* (1997), (a special edition of) *The South Atlantic Quarterly* 96 (3). Durham: Duke University Press, pp. 393–416.

Jameson, F. (2002), *A Singular Modernity: Essay on the Ontology of the Present*, London: Verso.

Klein, N. (2001), 'Reclaiming the Commons', *New Left Review* 9: 81–9.

Marcos, (2001), 'Punch Card and Hourglass', *New Left Review* 9: 69–79.

Marx, K. (1976), *Capital*, vol. 1, trans. B. Fowkes, London: Penguin.

Retort (2005), 'Blood for Oil?', *London Review of Books* 27 (8): 12–16.

Rorty, R. (2004), 'Post-Democracy', *London Review of Books*, 26 (7): 10–11.

Sader, E. (2002), 'Beyond Civil Society', *New Left Review* 17: 87–99.

Sellers, J. (2001) 'Raising a Ruckus', *New Left Review* 10: 71–85.

Weinberg, N. (2000), *Homage to Chiapas: The New Indigenous Struggles in Mexico*, London: Verso.

Yeomans, M. (2004), *Oil: Anatomy of an Industry*, New York: The New Press.

Žižek, S. (1991), *Looking Awry: An Introduction to Lacan through Popular Culture*, Cambridge: MIT Press.

Žižek, S. (2004), *Organs without Bodies: On Deleuze and Consequences*, London: Routledge.

## Notes

1. Consequently, we reject Badiou's (2000) claim that Deleuze's philosophy is not critical, but this is not the place to lay out in full all the arguments against this very severe judgement. However, it should be clear from what follows though that the 'problematic' form of philosophy is explicitly conceived as a critical engagement with the present. It is not, in other words, a case by case philosophy as Badiou claims, but an ongoing attempt to create a concept adequate to the problem of the everyday itself in all its complexity.

2. The schizoanalytic argument is simple: desire is a machine, a synthesis of machines, a machinic arrangement – desiring machines. The order of desire is the order of *production*; all production is at once desiring-production and social production. (Deleuze and Guattari 1983: 296)

3. Demography is not merely a third-world 'evil' – social security privatisation pundits use it to argue that the government can't afford to support so many pensioners.

4. Peter Gowan (1999: 21) argues that the 1970s oil shock was in fact orchestrated by the US. On the one hand, it was a means of tightening its grip around the throats of its erstwhile allies, Japan and Europe, which were far more dependent on Middle East oil than the US. On the other hand, it strengthened the position of the US dollar as the default global currency (putting an end once and for all to the idea of a return to a Bretton Woods style financial system); and, just as importantly, created an ocean of petrodollars to be recycled through US banks, thus improving liquidity.

5. Retort consists of: Iain Boal, T. J. Clark, Joseph Mathews and Michael Watts.

6. Graeber (2002: 63) argues for a direct connection between the Zapatistas and the anti-globalisation protests in Seattle.

7. On this point, as Jameson (1988: 203) reminds us, it needs to be underscored that however one feels about terrorism as a political means, from an ideological perspective it is a concept of the Right and should be refused in that form.

# Chapter 1

# Treatise on Militarism

## Ian Buchanan

The 2004 US presidential election caused hearts to sink everywhere in the world. Time will tell if this is to be another American century, as the Vulcans in Washington intend, or a Chinese century, as some are already predicting, but in the short term at least the re-election of Bush is discouraging for those with hopes that it might be a World or Multilateral century, to say the least.[1] The bloody insurgency in Iraq only strengthened the position of the 'War President', who rallied the electorate to 'stay the course in Iraq', giving him greater licence to continue his campaign of terror there and by implication elsewhere. At the time of the election the death toll of US soldiers was nearing a thousand with the number injured seven times that. To which toll one must add the haunting fact that of the 500,000 plus US servicemen and women who served in the First Gulf War some 325,000 are now on disability pensions suffering a variety of acute maladies generally attributed to the toxic cocktail of radiation from depleted uranium munitions and other pollutant chemicals from the hundreds of oil fires they were exposed to during their tour of duty. Those who fight in Iraq today can scarcely look forward to a healthier future given that it is effectively twice as irradiated now as it was in 1991.[2] Yet still the minority who voted, voted in the main for the man who put these soldiers in harm's way; but then it isn't as though John Kerry was promising to bring the troops home, or offered any real solutions to the insurgency problem. By declining to take a genuinely dissenting stand on the war, Kerry put himself in the invidious position of being simply the other party that wanted to be tough on terror and of course nobody bought it. As important as Tom Frank's *What's the Matter with Kansas?* (2004) is as an explanation of conservatism in the heartland of the US, it doesn't answer this question – why did the war on terror fail to ignite anti-Bush sentiment?[3] More to the point, why was it impossible to vote against the war?

The situation described above is militarism at its hegemonic peak – you cannot decide between going to war or not, only which is the most desired (least worst?) way of handling the conduct of a war whose legitimacy seems not to matter and whose exigencies are such that one could not withdraw from it now even if that was wanted. As a senior adviser at the French Institute for International Relations has observed: 'If America simply pulled out [of Iraq] now, other countries would find themselves in the strange position of having to put pressure on the Americans to stay, having previously begged them not to risk invasion without a United Nations resolution' (cited in Arrighi 2005: 58). This is because the non-involvement of the US in world affairs is in some ways more perilous than its active engagement. A rapid withdrawal from Iraq, for example, a withdrawal not preceded by (at least) the installation of a moderately stable puppet regime, would leave the world's major oil reserves vulnerable to opportunistic take-over and control by other powers interested in seizing the hegemonic high ground. Militarism creates problems it claims only militarism can solve, but its solutions are only so many more problems that, too, seem insoluble except to militarism. The US cannot turn back the clock and retreat to its pre-World War II stance of 'Fortress America'; its manifold interventions into the domestic politics of other countries (all the while eschewing such practices and forbidding others – with the signal exception of Israel – to follow their example) have created the very 'arc of instability' it now has reason to be concerned about. Like it or not, it is locked into its role as 'Garrison America' (Cumings 2003).

Militarism, in Deleuze and Guattari's terms, is always coming up against its limits and at the same time constantly repelling those limits. It has always been with us, but like the dark shadow of a tumorous growth on an x-ray film it isn't always visible, nor is its nature always obvious. What we have witnessed in the last three decades is a profound mutation in militarism that has almost without our knowing it changed the meaning of war – war, I will argue, following Deleuze and Baudrillard, has a new object. The idea that war should be considered a logical and necessary extension of politics was first given expression by Clausewitz, but he was merely putting into philosophical form what was already accepted thinking for government: arms are a legitimate means of achieving political goals. Militarism is not always as unabashed about its existence, not to say its intentions, as it is now when – as Debord so presciently put it – it has 'its own inconceivable foe, terrorism' to bedazzle a frightened, confused and misinformed public (Debord 1990: 24). But out of the limelight does not mean out of the picture; militarism has not been officially questioned since the end of World War I when disarmament had its last genuine hurrah.[4] World War II, which caught the US, and the UK in particular, under-armed and under-prepared for conflict, eliminated in a stroke the very concept of disarmament – strategic arms limitation and force reduction are essentially fiscal notions, decisions made in the interests of preserving a militarist posture in the face of rising costs, not disarmament. Neither should we delude ourselves that anti-war is anti-militarism. As we shall see, the very opposite is true.

In the aftermath of 9/11, it is generally thought that a paradigm shift in the nature of militarism has occurred, and as the violence in the Middle East continues with no sign of abatement (the running sore that is the Israel/Palestine conflict, the smouldering fires of Iraq and Afghanistan and the gathering storm in Iran all bode ill for a peaceful future) any doubt that a new era of 'hot' war has been ushered in tends to vanish. What is less certain, however, at least from a philosophical perspective, is the conceptual nature of the change. Those who demur that the present era is substantially different enough to warrant the label 'new' do so on the grounds that what we are seeing today is merely the continuation of an older struggle, or struggles, as it might be better to say given the tangled mess of multiple rivalries and resentments on both sides. Obviously, many of the struggles fuelling the present war are legacies of World War II, the Yalta summit in particular (many of course predate that by hundreds of years).[5] On this score, I am persuaded by Immanuel Wallerstein's thesis that the First and Second World Wars should be treated as a single thirty-year struggle for global hegemony between Germany and the US, but it seems to me the militarism we are faced with today is different from the one spawned in 1945 in the aftermath of victory; the militarism of today no longer thinks in terms of winning and losing – it has another agenda (Wallerstein 2003: 14–15). So even if the origins of the present crisis are to be found in the wash-up of World War II, as Wallerstein and many others have rightly argued, the nature of the response to this crisis is not similarly located there.

Historians generally agree that the Vietnam War put paid to that 'victorious' mode of militarism the US knew following World War II when it was briefly the lone nuclear power.[6] Following its demoralising defeat at the hands of a comparatively puny third-world country, however, even the idea that it was a superpower was questioned. Amongst the decision-makers in Washington there took hold a moribund and risk-averse mentality that came to be called the 'Vietnam Syndrome'. This syndrome allegedly explains the US's failure to act on a number of occasions when it might have been prudent – or, as perhaps would have been the case in Cambodia, humanitarian to do so – culminating in the embarrassing mishandling of the Teheran Embassy siege in the last days of Jimmy Carter's administration. It also explains the tactics used on those occasions when the US has acted, as in Clinton's decision initially to restrict the engagement in the Balkans to airpower alone and use aerial bombardment where deft geopolitical negotiation was needed. On this occasion, as has now become routine, an alleged ethical imperative combined powerfully with a rhetoric of 'surgical strikes' and 'smart bombs' to stall protest and garner support from even those who ought to have known better.[7] As Giovanni Arrighi puts it, since getting its nose bloodied in Vietnam, the US has generally avoided conflict in circumstances similar to those that led to the *débâcle* in Indo-China. Instead, it has 'either fought wars by proxy (Nicaragua, Cambodia, Angola, Afghanistan; supporting Iraq in the war against Iran), or against militarily insignificant enemies (Grenada, Panama), or from the air, where US high-tech has absolute advantage (Libya)' (Arrighi 2005: 52). Taken at face value, this would seem to confirm the existence of the 'Vietnam Syndrome', but this assumes that wars should be limited to single, defined engagements with clear-cut outcomes and that they cannot be conceived as fuzzy, ill-defined encounters. But I would argue the 'Vietnam Syndrome' is a convenient cover story, not a genuine explanation of US foreign policy.

What makes anyone think, for instance, that a peaceful settlement to the Israel/Palestine conflict (as much a potential Vietnam as Iraq) is on the US agenda? Countless commentators have pointed out that the US backing of Israel can but inflame the Middle East situation as though this was news to the ones responsible, or, more to the point, as though winning or losing, peace or war, are the only options open to US foreign policy. Isn't the answer staring us right in the face: perpetual unrest is the solution that present action is achieving. And the same is obviously true in Iraq. Failed states, or TFCs to use the US State Department's less charitable shorthand (TFC stands for totally fucked-up countries) are preferable to the aims of US business than states that won't trade on its terms. Indeed, in most cases, a forensic analysis of the reason a failed state has become a TFC leads directly to the US.[8] The 'Vietnam Syndrome' is an optical illusion, both a cover story for the US military and a wish-fulfilment on the part of those who would like to see an end to US imperialism.[9] In philosophical terms, the 'Vietnam Syndrome' was the negative needed by militarism to resurrect itself. What the military realised in Vietnam was that the US public will not tolerate a high casualty rate amongst its own troops unless there is a pressing need. While saving freedom might be construed as a pressing need, stopping communism in a country most people hadn't heard of before the war started couldn't.

Lacking ideological support, the US military publicly adopted a zero-casualty approach to its 'elective wars' (to continue with the surgical trope) and banked on technology to achieve it. This rhetoric suits the military-industrial complex too since plainly it can be used to justify the monstrous cost of weapons development in precisely the same terms. The anti-war sentiment ignited by the Vietnam conflict played a large part in securing public acceptance for this strategy in spite of the escalating costs it entailed. The US showed it was anti-war only to the extent that war put its people in harm's way, but had no strong opinion on the matter when it was merely a question of unloading deadly ordnance from a high altitude on faceless peoples far from the homeland. In other words, the US reliance on airpower is misconstrued as an avoidance of war; it is rather the preferred mode of war. If it could avoid the use of ground troops altogether it undoubtedly would.

Technology has become the solution to what is essentially an ideological problem: the US population isn't willing to commit its collective body to the US's military causes.[10] By the same token, as I will discuss more fully in a moment, the development and sale of military technology is a central plank in the US's geopolitical business strategy. It quite literally armed its two most recent opponents – Afghanistan and Iraq. In a classic case of militarism appearing as the only solution to militarism's problems, the insurgency problem in Iraq is to be answered by the superior surveillance capability of the US, which with its satellite technology can simply pluck conversations out of the air. This is, of course, belied to a very great extent by the public outing of the medieval methods used in Abu Ghraib to extract information from prisoners. But even there, sleep-deprivation and sexual humiliation is dressed up in pseudo-scientific language to give it the appearance of being technologically determined. The spin-doctoring that has gone into talking up the capabilities of the new class of so-called 'smart' weapons as well as hiding their many weaknesses is worthy of Madison Avenue.[11] Its ultimate effect has been to persuade the American people that technology has made them invulnerable. Thus war has entered the age of intelligent machines and unintelligent government.[12]

The present conflict proves beyond any shadow of a doubt that the US will not hesitate to embroil itself in a potentially Vietnam-like conflict if the conditions are ripe. I have read reports that US soldiers based in Iraq are writing 'Is this Vietnam yet?' on their helmets; sadly they're not asking the right question. Given the admission that the insurgency problem may never be resolved, it plainly *is* another Vietnam. If this isn't the view of the Hawks in Washington who orchestrated the war, then it begs the question: what makes the present conflict *not* another Vietnam in the eyes of its architects? The answer is a combination of existential chest-beating and naked self-interest. Corey Robin, writing in the *London Review of Books*, puts it this way:

> [The] neo-cons were drawn into Iraq for the sake of a grand idea: not the democratisation of the Middle East, though that undoubtedly had some appeal, or even the conquest of the world, but rather the idea of themselves as a brave and undaunted army of transgression (Robin 2005: 13)

The neo-cons realised that to put the Vietnam Syndrome to rest they would not require a clear-cut victory in Iraq, as the Powell doctrine stipulated. Indeed, it is hard to believe the neo-cons are so stupid as actually to think that a clear-cut victory was possible irrespective of their public declarations to the contrary. After all, these are more or less the same group of Vulcans who reasoned in 1991 that taking Baghdad was a bad idea because it would lead to years of insurgency. Their change of heart has to be explained another way. What they realised is that what is important geopolitically is the occasional demonstration of a willingness to act forcefully regardless of cost so that every minor power will look upon what is happening in Iraq – this time – and conclude there but for the grace of Bush go I. As Žižek might put it, the Vulcans understand well that a little bit of reality is needed from time to time to sustain the fantasy of 'full spectrum dominance'.

Full spectrum dominance is a fantasy to the extent that the most generous evaluations of US military strength deem it capable of – at most – two simultaneous engagements of the scale of the 2003 invasion of Iraq. In other words, in spite of all its tough talk, it could not simultaneously tackle the six named enemies in the so-called 'axis of evil' without visiting ruin upon itself. Indeed, most commentators doubt it could even sustain engagement on two fronts, for instance, Iraq and North Korea. These estimates are premised on the model of a limited war with clear-cut objectives and in those terms are doubtless accurate. What I'm suggesting is that the US knows this, but this isn't a game it is playing. It knows that even if it cannot win a full-scale war with Iraq *or* North Korea it can nonetheless unleash enough destruction on its enemy to make the toll of even challenging them too high to risk. In the Cold War, when the principal enemy was a superpower also this doctrine was known as mutually assured destruction (MAD) and it was said that this was the price of peace. The certainty of total annihilation in the event of a nuclear war was the ideological umbrella sheltering us from that very eventuality. The era we have entered now is one of self-assured destruction – SAD. I mean this in two ways – for the US it is its very self-assuredness (hubris) that will ultimately lead to its destruction; while for its hapless enemies, challenging the US to a shooting war is to assure destruction is rained upon them.

War not only has a new object, it has a new body without organs as well. To justify SAD, a rhetoric of the conditional has emerged at the highest levels –if we wait until a smoking gun is found, then it might be a mushroom cloud that we get and that will be too late – while at the administrative levels soldiers and generals are entreated to act swiftly on the evidence before them, rather than wait for authorisation from above. Not acting has been made to seem worse than acting, regardless of how egregious the action might be. A new species of ethics has been created that takes literally the idea of 'greater good' as meaning good for the greater number of people. If, this ethics asks, one prisoner knows where a nuclear bomb is set to go off then what action is not justified to extract that information given that perhaps a million lives might be at stake? Indeed, if one innocent civilian happens to be locked up, even tortured, but by virtue of the security vigilance that action implies countless other innocent lives are saved, then surely that action is justified? Such questions cannot even be answered, much less responded to with anything approaching a judgement. It can never be ethically right to kill to save lives, but neither can it be ethically right not to act to save lives when the means are at hand to do so.

How have the Hawks persuaded themselves that the SAD doctrine does not apply to them? To put it another way: what are the conditions under which the US will engage in a potentially protracted foreign war? What are the conditions it needs suddenly to strike this active posture? The short answer is 9/11; this provides the mandate needed to act, but it neither explains the acts taken in its name nor accounts for the way in which those acts have been carried out. Behind the smokescreen of the 'Vietnam Syndrome', the US has taken on board two hard lessons learned in Vietnam which now shape its foreign policy: (1) It can win battles, but it can't necessarily win wars, (2) It can afford battles, but it can't pay for wars. Both these lessons were heeded by Bush the elder, who pointedly decided not to take Baghdad though it was there for the taking precisely because he didn't want an expensive quagmire.[13] It is tempting to think Bush the younger is simply Bush the dumber and that's the reason why he felt emboldened to go where Daddy dare not, but I believe there is an even more sinister explanation: naked self-interest. Whereas Daddy figured out how to get someone else to pay for the battles that needed to be fought to dislodge Saddam's forces from Kuwait, he didn't solve the problem of how to pay for a long war so he avoided it. Neither did the son solve the problem, but he figured out how to get the loser to line the pockets of the victor and transform a costly war into a privateer's mother lode.[14] Reconstruction is the surplus value of war. At least it is supposed to be. But it is still to yield dividends because Iraq is not yet safe for capitalism.

If, as Chalmers Johnson suggests, the US military has gone Hollywood, then war has gone Wall Street.[15] Profit is put before everything.[16] But this may well be what brings the whole edifice crashing down, because the war is not paying for itself and probably never will. The doctrinal Wall Street aversion to taxation which Bush adheres to has left him with only two other options to finance his 'global gamble' (to use Peter Gowan's apt phrase) – he can either continue to borrow from foreign sources, or exploit the 'seignorial privileges' the US enjoys by virtue of its dollar being the de facto global currency (Arrighi 2005: 67; Gowan 1999: 19–38). This gamble is doubly risky because in many respects US military power is its financial power – not just its greater ability to spend on military hardware, but also its ability to flex its market muscle and either dump its subsidised produce on unprotected markets or slap hefty tariffs on imported goods. Obviously, it cannot maintain its world-dominating expenditure on military hardware if it loses its economic edge. But, as Retort argues, things are even more complicated than that: on its view, the US's financial position is heavily dependent on its militarist posture. As it puts it, the control of oil is only one of the stakes in the current Gulf War conflict. Just as important are the arms sales to third-world countries and the lucrative construction contracts that go with the development of military capacity. 'The invasion of Iraq was about Chevron and Texaco, but it was also about Bechtel, Kellog, Brown and Root, Chase Manhattan, Enron, Global Crossing, BCCI and DynCorp' (Retort 2005: 16).

But we still haven't articulated what turned out to be the greatest change to militarism. This occurred in the late stages of the Vietnam War, past the point when anyone – even the president of the United States – could say there was a worthwhile military reason to continue the fight, apart from the need to defend the credibility of the fighting forces. The last years of the war saw the first truly conspicuous outing of what has now become standard procedure, the use of airpower as a substitute for diplomacy.[17] At the time it was narrated as being a necessary complement to diplomacy to ensure proper attention at the bargaining table, but its effect was to make the North Vietnamese dig their heels in harder. And yet the US persisted in spite of its obvious failure as a tactic, convinced no doubt that there had to be a limit to the willingness of the people of North Vietnam to endure the terrible toll of death its B52s were able to lay upon them. Ho Chi Minh's bravado claim that Vietnam had struggled against

China for a thousand years before winning its freedom, and had carried the fight to the French for 150 years, and therefore felt unthreatened by the US who had only been on their soil a mere fifteen years plainly fell on deaf ears in Washington. The net result was a peace deal no better than what was on the table in 1968, with the loss of a further 20,492 American lives and many thousands more Vietnamese and Cambodian lives (Hitchens 2002: 23). It is generally assessed as a military and diplomatic failure, but this is where I think history is being a little hasty. The determination that it was the credibility of the fighting forces that was at stake in the final years of the war is a convenient cover story, but not all that convincing.

For Wallerstein (2003), the Vietnam War represented a rejection by the third-world of the 'Yalta accord', the less than gentlemanly agreement between the two superpowers, the USA and the USSR, to divide the planet into spheres of interest (the USA grabbing two-thirds and the USSR a third). He treats America's willingness to invest all its military strength in the struggle and more or less bankrupt itself in the process as testament to the felt geopolitical significance of the conflict. And yet, as he puts it, it was still defeated. While I accept the first part of his thesis, I disagree with his conclusion because I think the very premise on which it rests lost its validity in the course of the war. A pragmatically conceived intervention designed to stop the spread of revolutionary communism became the US military's own equivalent of a 'cultural revolution' as it underwent a profound rethinking of its mode of acting in the world.[18] I do not mean to claim as military revisionists have done that Vietnam was actually a victory for the USA (the right wing rhetoric on this, so resonant of the early days of the Nazi party, is that the government and the people back home betrayed the soldiers on the front line and didn't allow them to win).[19] With Baudrillard, I want to argue that there occurred a paradigm shift during the course of that protracted and bitter struggle which resulted in the concepts of victory and defeat losing their meaning.

> Why did this American defeat (the largest reversal in the history of the USA) have no internal repercussions in America? If it had really signified the failure of the planetary strategy of the United States, it would necessarily have completely disrupted its internal balance and the American political system. Nothing of the sort occurred.
> Something else, then, took place. (Baudrillard 1994: 36)

Baudrillard's answer to this question is that war ceased to be real; it ceased to be determined in terms of winning and losing and became instead 'simulation', a pure spectacle no less terrifying or deadly for its lack of reality. The consequences of this metaphysical adjustment are shocking and go a long way towards explaining the rise of terrorism in recent years. As Andrew Bacevich writes, it is not only the superpowers like the US that have relinquished the concept of victory. It is as though war itself has jettisoned it as so much extra baggage.

> The typical armed conflict today no longer pits like against like – field army v. field army or battle fleet v. battle fleet – and there usually is no longer even the theoretical prospect of a decisive outcome. In asymmetric conflicts, combatants employ violence indirectly. The aim is not to defeat but to intimidate and terrorise, with women a favoured target and sexual assault often the weapon of choice. (Bacevich 2005: 26)

The B52 pilot unloading bombs on an unseen enemy below knows just as well as the suicide bomber in Iraq that his actions will not lead directly to a decisive change, that in a sense the gesture is futile; but, he also knows, as does the suicide bomber, that his actions will help create an atmosphere of fear that, it is hoped, will one day lead to change. Deprived of teleology, war thrives in an eternal present.

Terror is not merely the weapon of the weak, it is the new condition of war, and no power can claim exception status. For Clausewitz and his spiritual tutor Machiavelli the only rational reason to wage war is to win where winning means achieving a predetermined and clearly prescribed goal. Britain's colonial wars are an obvious case in point. The self-serving claim that Britain acquired its empire in a fit of absence owes its sense to the fact that it never set out to gain its eventually quite considerable empire (it was at least geographically true, albeit not historically true, that the sun never set on the British Empire, encompassing as it did territories in virtually every region of the world) all at once, as Hitler and Hirohito were later to do, but built it one territory at a time over a two-century-long period. Through a sequence of limited wars it was able to deploy its limited means to obtain colossal riches. World War I essentially started out in the same way. Germany's goal was to secure a European empire before it was too late, but barbed wire, heavy artillery and the machine-gun put paid to that ambition and instead of a quick war returning a specific prize there irrupted a global conflagration that was to consume the wealth and youth of Europe. As Wallerstein argues, the true victor of World War I wasn't Britain or France, but American industry, and by extension the true loser wasn't Germany and its allies but Europe itself. Eric Hobsbawm has defined the twentieth century as the age when wars of limited means and limited aims gave way to wars of limited means and *unlimited* aims (Hobsbawm 1994: 29–30). The twenty-first century appears to be the age of wars of unlimited means and no precise aim.

This, according to Deleuze and Guattari 'is the point at which Clausewitz's formula is effectively reversed'. When total war – for instance, war which not only places the annihilation of the enemy's army at its centre but its entire population and economy too – becomes the object of the state-appropriated war machine, 'then at this level in the set of all possible conditions, the object and the aim enter into new relations that can reach the point of contradiction' (Deleuze and Guattari 1987: 421). In the first instance, the war machine unleashed by the state in pursuit of its object, total war, remains subordinate to the state and 'merely realises the *maximal conditions*' of its aims. Paradoxically, though, the more successful it is in realising the state's aims, the less controllable by the state it becomes. As the state's aims grow on the back of the success of its war machine, so the restrictions on the war machine's object shrink until – scorpion-like – it effectively subsumes the state, making it just one of its many moving parts. In Vietnam, the state was blamed for the failure of the war machine precisely because it attempted to set limits on its object. Its inability adequately to impose these limits not only cost it the war, but in effect its sovereignty too. Since then the state has been a puppet of a war machine global in scope and ambition. This is the status of militarism today and no-one has described its characteristics more chillingly than Deleuze and Guattari:

> This worldwide war machine, which in a way 'reissues' from the States, displays two successive figures: first, that of fascism, which makes war an unlimited movement with no other aim than itself; but fascism is only a rough sketch, and the second, postfascist, figure is that of a war machine that takes peace as its object directly, as the peace of Terror or Survival. The war machine reforms a smooth space that now claims to control, to surround the entire earth. Total war is surpassed, toward a form of peace more terrifying still. (Deleuze and Guattari 1987: 421)

It is undoubtedly Chalmers Johnson who has done the most to bring to our attention the specific make-up of what Deleuze and Guattari call here the worldwide war machine (Johnson 2000, 2004). His description of a global 'empire of bases' is consistent with Deleuze and Guattari's uptake of Paul Virilio's concept of the 'fleet in being'. This is the paradoxical transformation of the striated space of organisation into a new kind of 'reimparted' smooth space 'which outflanks all gridding and invents a neonomadism in the service of a war machine still more disturbing than the States' (Deleuze and Guattari 1987: 480). Bases do not by themselves secure territory but, as is the case with a battle fleet, their mobility and their firepower mean they can exert an uncontestable claim over territory that amounts to control. This smooth space surrounding the earth is, to put it back into Baudrillard's terms, the space of simulation. The empire of bases is a virtual construct with real capability. Fittingly enough, it was Jean Baudrillard who first detected that a structural change in post-World War II militarism had taken place. In *Simulacra and Simulation* he argues that the Vietnam War was a demonstration of a new kind of will to war, one that no longer thought in terms of winning or losing, but defined itself instead in terms of perseverance (Baudrillard 1994: 37). It demonstrated to the US's enemies, clients and allies alike, its willingness to continue the fight even when defeat was certain, or had in a sense already been acknowledged (the US strategy of 'Vietnamising' the war which commenced shortly after the Tet offensive in 1968, and become official policy under Nixon, was patently an admission that the war couldn't be won – in the short term it was Johnson's way of putting off admitting defeat until after the election so as to give Hubert Humphrey some chance of victory; in the longer term it was a way of buying time for a diplomatic solution) (Kolko 1994: 321). It was a demonstration of the US's reach, of its ability to inflict destruction even when its troops were withdrawing and peace talks (however futile) were under way. It also demonstrated to the American people that the fight *could* be continued as the troops were withdrawn, a factor that, as I've already pointed out, would become decisive in reshaping militarism as an incorporeal system.

It was also a demonstration to the American domestic population that the country's leaders were willing to continue to sacrifice lives to prove this point.[20] The contrary view, that Nixon wanted to end the war sooner but was unable to do so because domestic politics didn't allow it, in no way contradicts this thesis. If anything it confirms it because if true it would mean, as Deleuze and Guattari have said of fascism 'at a certain point, under a certain set of conditions' the American people *wanted* Vietnam, and, as they add: 'It is this perversion of the desire of the masses that needs to be accounted for' (Deleuze and Guattari 1983: 29). While there can be no doubt Vietnam was an unpopular war that was eventually brought to a halt by popular pressure, it is a sobering thought to remind oneself that it was a war that lasted some ten years. If one takes 1967 as the decisive turning point in popular opinion, the moment when protest against the war became the prevailing view and support for it dwindled into a minority murmur, then one still has to take stock of the fact that it took a further six years for US troops to be fully withdrawn.[21] The kind of sustained popular pressure that brought the Vietnam War to a close has not yet even begun to build in the US in spite of the fact that the death toll has passed 1,700 (as of August 2005).

Wars are spectacles in the traditional sense of being events staged to convey a specific message, but also in the more radical or postmodern sense that spectacle is the final form of war, the form war takes when it takes peace as its object. Hence, the military's facilitation of the media (this backfired to a large degree in Vietnam, but the lessons learned then are put to good use today). Ultimately, though, as Baudrillard rightly argues, the 'media and official *news services* are only there to maintain the illusion of an actuality, of the reality of the stakes, of the objectivity of the facts' (Baudrillard 1994: 38). Chillingly, this is no longer an incisive criticism of the state, but its explicit outlook. In a conversation with a 'senior adviser' to President Bush, *New York Times Magazine* reporter Ron Suskind was told:

> We're an empire now, and when we act, we create our own reality. And while you're [i.e., the media] studying that reality – judiciously, as you will – we'll act again, creating other new realities, which you can study too, and that's how things will sort out. (cited in Danner 2005a: 73)

The creation of that reality – or what Tony Blair more pointedly referred to as the 'political context' for action – was, as Mark Danner has conclusively shown, the true purpose behind the spurious charge that Iraq had Weapons of Mass Destruction (WMD). Planning for the Iraq war began as early as 21 November 2001, when Rumsfeld was ordered by Bush to explore military options for removing Saddam Hussein by force. The decision to execute these plans was made in mid-July 2002 – the only issue left to be decided at that point was how to justify it to the public. Not without some hesitation, the WMD card was played – it was a risky move because if the weapons inspectors were able to demonstrate that Iraq had in fact destroyed its WMDs then it would look like the UN process had worked. If Iraq could be made to look non-compliant, secretive and cunning, as was the case, then the failure to find WMDs could be explained away as evidence of preparation for war (Danner 2005a: 70).

Ironically, as Hans Blix himself realised, the worst-case scenario for Iraq was not to be found hiding weapons, but the very opposite – 'It occurred to me', Blix wrote, 'that the Iraqis would be in greater difficulty if . . . there truly *were* no weapons of which they could "yield possession"' because then they'd have no way of proving compliance (Danner 2005a: 73). By not having any WMDs to give up, they couldn't prove they didn't have any to begin with, nor could they demonstrate their good faith in wanting to get rid of WMDs. From this perspective,

North Korea is clearly correct in its surmise that it is better off having WMDs because not only is not having them no deterrent to invasion, it seems not having them is a positive invitation for invasion because it denies the targeted country the diplomatic 'out' of giving them up and conspicuously demonstrating to a world audience that a political solution is being actively pursued. Far from being a last-ditch effort to save peace and prevent war, the UN weapons inspection gambit was a calculated stratagem to make war possible. The US reluctance to involve the UN had nothing to do with its claimed inefficiencies and everything to do with its likely success. What the US could not allow, if it wanted its war plans to proceed, was for the weapons inspection teams to reveal – in Blix's words – that 'the UN and the world had succeeded in disarming Iraq without knowing it' (Danner 2005a: 73). Therefore, right from the start the whole process had to be cast as a failure, or more particularly as wasting precious time that might at any moment see those WMDs used against US targets. This then became the basis for the 'preventive war' rhetoric.

The justification for war was stage-managed with the consummate skill of a corporate brand manager. The White House chief of staff Andrew Card even put it that way to the *New York Times*, referring to the building of a case for war as a product roll-out (cited in Danner 2005a: 72). At least since the start of World War II, when the Nazis dressed dead Polish soldiers in German uniforms and displayed their corpses to the world as justification for war, almost all modern wars have resorted to such media-friendly theatrical 'events'. A simulated event is needed to prove that no dissimulation has been involved in justifying the war. Chomsky's analyses of current trends in US imperialism lend further weight to this thesis that wars are spectacles by undercutting their reality in a different, more concrete fashion. As he argues, 'preventive' wars are only fought against the basically defenseless.[22] Chomsky adds two further conditions that chime with what we have already adduced: there must be something in it for the aggressor, for instance, a fungible return not an intangible moral reward, and the opponent must be susceptible to a portrayal of them as 'evil', allowing the victory to be claimed in the name of a higher moral purpose and the actual venal purpose to be obscured (Chomsky 2003: 17). At first glance, waging war to prevent war appears to be as farcical as fucking for virginity, but that is only if we assume that the aim of the war is to prevent one potential aggressor from striking first. Or, rather, given that it is alleged that the putative enemy, Al Qaeda and its supposed supporters, took first blood (the Rambo reference is of course deliberate), we are asked to believe the current war is being fought to prevent a second, more damaging strike. The obsessive and suitably grave references to Weapons of Mass Destruction by the various mouth-pieces of the Bush regime (Rumsfeld, Wolfowitz, Rice, but also Blair and Howard) are plainly calculated to compel us to accept that any such second strike will be of biblical, or worse, Hollywood proportions.

As one joke put it, the Americans could be certain that Iraq had at least some Weapons of Mass Destruction because they had the receipts to prove it. The grain of truth in this joke reveals the true purpose of the war – it was a demonstration to all of America's clients that it wouldn't tolerate 'price-gouging'. Obviously I am speaking metaphorically here, but the fact is that Saddam's Iraq was a client of the US, it purchased arms and consumer goods and sold oil at a carefully controlled price. Why this arrangement suddenly became so unsatisfactory is subject to a great deal of speculation which centres on two basic theories: (1) when Iraq switched from the dollar to the euro it posed an intolerable threat to the stability of the US currency, (2) the US is positioning itself to monopolise oil ahead of growing Chinese demand. Either way, if one wants a metaphor to describe US imperialism it wouldn't be McDonald's, a com-paratively benign operator, but the predatory retail giant Wal-Mart.[23] In other words, today's wars are fought to demonstrate will. The age of gunboat diplomacy – when gunboats were used to open up markets and impose favourable market conditions for the foreign traders – has given way to the age of gunboat commerce, an era in which war does not precede commerce, but is integral to it.[24]

When war changed its object it was able to change its aim too, and it is this more than anything that has saved 'real' war from itself. Baudrillard's later work on the spectacle of war misses this point: through becoming spectacles the fact that real wars (for example, territorial wars) are no longer possible has not diminished their utility – the US isn't strong enough to take and hold Iraq, but it can use its force to demonstrate to other small nations that it can inflict massive damage and lasting pain on anyone who would dare defy it. Baudrillard's lament that the real Gulf War never took place can only be understood from this viewpoint – although he doesn't put it in these words, his insight is essentially that war in its idealised form is much more terrifying than peace. Again, although Baudrillard himself doesn't put it this way, the conclusion one might draw from the paradigm shift in war's rationalisation elucidated above – from pragmatic object (defeating North Vietnam) to symbolic object (defend-ing the credibility of the fight forces) – is that war has become 'postmod-ern'. This shift is what enables the US, ideologically, to justify war in the absence of a proper object and indeed in the absence of a known enemy.

The Bush regime's 'war on terror' is the apotheosis of this change: the symbolic (terror) has been made to appear instrumental (terrorism), or more precisely the symbolic is now able to generate the instrumental according to its own needs.

This is the moment when the war machine becomes militarism, the moment when doxa becomes doctrine. What is a war machine? The answer to this question must always be, it is a concept. But because of the way Deleuze and Guattari create their concepts, by abstracting from the historical, there is always a temptation to treat the war machine as primarily descriptive. More importantly, the war machine is only one element in a complex treatise which is ultimately a mordant critique of the present. Deleuze and Guattari's analysis proceeds via a threefold hypothesis: (1) the war machine is a nomad invention that does not have war as its primary object, war is rather a second-order objective, (2) the war machine is exterior to the state apparatus, but when the state appropriates the war machine its nature and function changes, its polarity is effectively reversed so that it is directed at the nomads themselves, (3) it is only when the war machine has been appropriated by the state that war becomes its primary object (Deleuze and Guattari 1987: 418). Deleuze and Guattari are careful to clarify that their main purpose in assigning the invention of the war machine to the nomads is to assert its historical or 'invented' character. Their implication is that the nomadic people of the steppes and deserts do not hold the secret to understanding the war machine. We need to look past the concrete historical and geographical character of the war machine to see its eidetic core. Clearly, it is not 'the nomad who defines this constellation of characteristics'; on the contrary, 'it is this constellation that defines the nomad, and at the same time the essence of the war machine' (Deleuze and Guattari 1987: 422–3).

In its nomad origins, the war machine does not have war as its primary objective. Deleuze and Guattari arrive at this conclusion by way of three questions. First of all they ask: is battle the object of war? Then they ask if war is the object of the war machine. And finally they ask if the war machine is the object of the state. The first question requires further and immediate clarification, they say, between when a battle is sought and when it is avoided. The difference between these two states of affairs is not the difference between an offensive and defensive posture. And while it is true that at first glance war does seem to have battle as its object whereas the guerrilla has non-battle his object, this view is deceiving. Dropping bombs from 10,000 metres above the earth, firing missiles from a distance of hundreds of kilometres, using unpiloted drones to scout for targets, using satellite controlled and guided weapons, are the actions of a war-machine that has no interest at all in engaging in battle. The truism that the Viet Cong frustrated the US Army in Vietnam by failing to engage them in battle should not be taken to mean the US Army sought battle and the enemy did not. The Viet Cong frustrated the US Army by failing to succumb to its non-battle strategies and forced them into seeking battles with an elusive army with a better understanding of the terrain. If operation 'Rolling Thunder', or any of the many other battle-avoiding stratagems the US attempted had worked, they would not have sought battle at all.[25] Ironically, too, as Gabriel Kolko points out, the more strategic the US tried to make its offensive operations, for example, the more it tried to disengage from face-to-face encounters on the battlefield, the more passive its posture became because of its escalating logistical support requirements and increasing reliance on high maintenance technology (Kolko 1994: 193).

By the same token, it is clear that the guerilla armies of the Viet Cong did in fact seek battle, but did so on their own terms. As Mao said, the guerilla strikes where the other is weak and retreats whenever the stronger power attacks, the point being that the guerilla is constantly on the look-out for an opportunity to engage the enemy.[26] Battle and non-battle 'are the double object of war, according to a criterion that does not coincide with the offensive and the defensive, or even with war proper and guerrilla warfare' (Deleuze and Guattari 1987: 417). For this reason the question has to be pushed further back to ask if war is even the object of the war machine? Too often the answer to this question is automatically 'yes', but this reflects a precise set of historical circumstances and not an essential condition. It is true, throughout history, that nomads are regularly to be found in conflict situations, but this is because history is studded with collisions between war machines and the states and cities which would grind them into the dust. War is thrust upon the war machine, but its actual occupation is quite different. It could even be said to be peaceful were we not suspicious of that term. And as I have already argued, it is when the war machine takes peace itself as its object that it enters its most terrifying phase.

# References

Anderson, P. (2005), 'Arms and Rights: Rawls, Habermas and Bobbio in an Age of War', *New Left Review* 31: 5–40.
Arrighi, G. (2005), 'Hegemony Unravelling – 1', *New Left Review* 32: 23–80.
Bacevich, A. (2005), 'Debellicised', *London Review of Books* 27 (5): 25–6.
Baudrillard, J. (1994), *Simulacra and Simulation (The Body, In Theory: Histories of Cultural Materialism)*, trans. S. Glaser, Michigan: University of Michigan Press.

Baudrillard, J. (1995), *The Gulf War Did Not Take Place*, trans. P. Patton, Sydney: Power Institute.
Buchanan, I. (2001), 'Deleuze and American (Mythopoeic) Literature', *Southern Review* 34 (2): 72–85.
Chomsky, N. (2003), *Hegemony or Survival: America's Quest for Global Dominance*, Sydney: Allen and Unwin.
Cumings, B. (2003), *North Korea: Another Country*, New York: The New Press.
Cumings, B, Abrahamian, E. and Maoz, M. (2004), *Inventing the Axis of Evil: The Truth about North Korea, Iran and Syria*, New York: The New Press.
Danner, M. (2005a), 'The Secret Way to War', *New York Review of Books* LII (10): 70–4.
Danner, M. (2005b), 'What are you Going to Do with That?', *New York Review of Books* LII (11): 52–6.
Debord, G. (1990), *Comments on the Society of the Spectacle*, trans. M. Imrie, London: Verso.
DeLanda, M. (1991), *War in the Age of Intelligent Machines*, New York: Zone Books.
Deleuze, G. and Guattari, F. (1983), *Anti-Oedipus: Capitalism and Schizophrenia*, trans. R. Hurley, M. Seem and H. R. Lane, Minneapolis: University of Minnesota Press.
Deleuze, G. and Guattari, F. (1987), *A Thousand Plateaus: Capitalism and Schizophrenia*, trans. B. Massumi, Minneapolis: University of Minnesota Press.
Deleuze, G. and Scherer, R. (1998), 'The UNclean War', trans. T. Murphy, *Discourse*, 20 (3): 170–1.
Frank, T. (2004), *What's the Matter with Kansas?* New York: Metropolitan Books.
Gowan, P. (1999), *The Global Gamble: Washington's Faustian Bid for World Dominance*, London: Verso.
Hitchens, C. (2002), *The Trial of Henry Kissinger*, London: Verso.
Hobsbawm, E. (1994), *Age of Extremes: The Short Twentieth Century 1914–1991*, London: Michael Joseph.
Johnson, C. (2000), *Blowback: The Costs and Consequences of American Empire*, London: Little, Brown and Co.
Johnson, C. (2004), *The Sorrows of Empire: Militarism, Secrecy, and the End of the Republic*, New York: Metropolitan Books.
Klein, N. (2004), 'Baghdad Year Zero', *Harper's Magazine*, September.
Kolko, G. (1994), *Anatomy of a War: Vietnam, the United States, and the Modern Historical Experience*, 2nd edn, New York: The New Press.
Mann, M. (2003), *Incoherent Empire*, London: Verso.
Parenti, C. (1999), *Lockdown America: Police and Prisons in the Age of Crisis*, London: Verso.
Parenti, C. (2004), *The Freedom: Shadows and Hallucinations in Occupied Iraq*, New York: The New Press.
Piven, F. Fox (2004), *The War at Home: The Domestic Costs of Bush's Militarism*, New York: The New Press.
Retort (2005), 'Blood for Oil?', *London Review of Books* 27 (8): 12–16.
Robin, C. (2005), 'Protocols of Machism', *London Review of Books* 27 (10): 11–14.
Wallerstein, I. (2003), *The Decline of American Power*, New York: The New Press.
Yeomans, M. (2004), *Oil: Anatomy of an Industry*, New York: The New Press.

## Notes

1. *New York Times* pronounced the coming of the Chinese century in July 2004 (cited in Arrighi 2005: 79).

2. By 'twice' I mean twice over – what the new actual level of radiation is compared to pre-invasion levels I don't actually know. Given that we know that more depleted uranium ammunition has been used in the most recent Gulf War than was used in the first Gulf War it is reasonable to assume the situation has deteriorated.

3. In one sense, Frank's (2004) answer is precisely that the war was not as significant to the voters in Kansas, particularly the religious right, as other more morally urgent issues such as abortion. If true, one would still want some account of how this myopic outlook could continue to prevail in the face of a rising death toll and declining prosperity.

4. On this point, it has to be observed, however, that the comprehensive Allied victory in World War II and the effective détente that followed did make it difficult for the Hawks in the Pentagon to justify continued expansion of the US's military capacity. But as 'Acheson was to say later, "Korea came along and saved us."' (cited in Arrighi 2005: 25). See also Cumings et al. 2004: 38. Military expenditure increased exponentially following defeat in Vietnam. After Vietnam, no administration could afford to be soft on military spending (if they lost spending $30 billion a year, they could hardly afford to spend less in the future is the presiding logic) (see Kolko 1994: 356).

5. Long durée historians of the future may well conclude that the most historically consequential meeting that took place following the German surrender was the one between Roosevelt and Saudi King Ibn Saud. As Matthew Yeomans (2004: 15–18) argues, this meeting sowed the seeds of US predominance in the region.

6. The common consensus that Afghanistan was the USSR's 'Vietnam' tends to confirm this.

7. See Anderson (2005) for a critique of the support given to the US's military actions of the past two decades by Rawls, Habermas and Bobbio.

8. I take the term TFC from Danner 2005b: 52.

9. It should be clear, then, that I don't share Frances Fox Piven's (2004: 121) optimistic view that the Iraq conflict will induce a return of the Vietnam Syndrome.

10. Michael Mann (2003) extends this point and argues that the US is incapable of supporting an empire because it has proved much less adept than Britain in getting its 'allies' to fight its wars on its behalf.

11. As Deleuze wrote in response to the first Gulf War: 'Did the Americans themselves believe that they could wage precise, rapid war without innocent victims?' (Deleuze and Scherer 1998: 170).

12. Written as it is from the perspective of a robot, the complex and ambiguous element of desire is lacking in Manuel DeLanda's *War in the Age of Intelligent Machines* making it less useful for our purposes than one might have supposed from the title. For DeLanda, an arms race can be understood as a feedback loop within a closed system. But to put it this way is to take no account of desire – it doesn't explain why we should want to pursue that path. Deleuze and Guattari do not assume we are automata; on the contrary, as desiring individuals we have a range of choices before us. Our desire has to be rendered susceptible to capture. This was the basic purpose of the first volume: the diatribe against psychoanalysis had as its purpose the analysis of the way Oedipus operates to seduce desire into monitoring itself. DeLanda's closed system approach is false in another way as well. For Deleuze and Guattari technology is the product of a lifeworld. Metallurgy is not merely a trade, or technique, it is an entire way of life.

13. As Christian Parenti (2004: 15) rightly reminds us, Dick Cheney in his capacity as secretary for defence during the first Gulf War used precisely this word in defence of the decision not to take Baghdad.

14. For a dispiriting account of just how buccaneering American capital is in Iraq today see Parenti (2004: 35–57).
15. Chalmers Johnson (2000, 2004) has shown the old model of the military that did everything itself (for example, the 'studio system') has given way to a vast interlocking network of private enterprises ('Hollywood' as it is today).
16. The justification for war is brazenly Wall Street too, inasmuch that the conception of freedom it propounds is only the meagre stuff entailed in its free market ideology. As the troops were preparing for war, the military's procurements people were busily recruiting post-war reconstruction privateers. Come to Iraq, they said, and make your fortune. So far that particular promise hasn't quite panned out as scripted.
17. It was not the first time such tactics had been used by the US. And indeed, it was not the first time such tactics had been deployed – that dubious honour may well belong to Winston Churchill who used it in the 1920s to secure British oil interests in then Mesopotamia. But, as I suggest here, it was the first time airpower was openly rationalised as an aid to diplomacy. Now we know, as Christopher Hitchens (2002: 10–15) has shown, that its actual aim was the opposite: it was meant to thwart the peace process so as to ruin Hubert Humphrey's chances of succeeding Johnson as president. My thanks to Jennifer Gaynor from the University of Michigan for drawing my attention to this.
18. I use 'cultural revolution' here in the sense that Jameson has given the term, namely to describe the often painful process of changing a way of thinking. I specify the 'spread of revolutionary communism' because as Baudrillard (1995: 85) points out, the Vietnam War stopped when a bureaucracy had replaced the revolution.
19. As I have argued elsewhere (see Buchanan 2001), the theme of betrayal is the basis of what is essentially a redemption narrative in *Rambo*.
20. That this position chimed with the government's position on welfare, which was to become similarly hard-hearted, is scarcely likely to be a coincidence. The current regime has shown the truth of this. As Frances Fox Piven (2004: 89) has recently pointed out, in contrast to the Johnson administration, the Bush II regime has offered nothing to its domestic population to ease the burden of war. In fact, it seems hell-bent on brutalising the people at home too as it clamps down on welfare and intensifies surveillance.
21. In 1967 more Americans opposed sending troops to Vietnam than supported. By 1973, the ratio of opposition to support was 2:1. Officially, the last US troops pulled out of South Vietnam in March 1973, but the US maintained a military presence in the form of 'advisers', embassy staff and CIA operatives right up until April 1975 when the North Vietnamese tanks rolled into Saigon (Kolko 1994: 172).
22. By defenceless Chomsky means not only that the country in question has less military capacity than the US, which is true of *every* country on earth, but also that its terrain offers no natural resistance to US weapons-systems. Iraq is a perfect case in point – its empty, flat desert terrain is ideally suited to blitzkrieg tactics. By contrast, Afghanistan's mountainous terrain is highly resistant to this kind of warfare, as the failed campaign to capture Bin Laden in Tora Bora proved.
23. Did not the Bush–Cheney campaign manager glibly describe the US action in Iraq as getting it 'ready for Wal-Mart'? (cited in Retort 2005: 13).
24. Brecht once asked: who is the bigger criminal, the bank robber or the banker? In Iraq today that question would have little meaning. The bankers are the ones who do the robbing. As Private England and her colleagues were administering electric shock treatment to the genitals of prisoners in Abu Ghraib, so Paul

Brenner and his CPA team were administering shock therapy to the Iraqi economy. While we pretended to be shocked about the former, we barely raised an eyebrow at the latter. As Naomi Klein (2004) has pointed out, these two forms of shock treatment are not entirely unrelated. Inasmuch as the current aim of the occupying forces is to make Iraq a safe place to do business, one may well be justified in concluding they are directly related. It is an open question as to which of these two treatments are producing the greatest amount of blowback, but one can be sure that is precisely what they are doing.

25. Christian Parenti (1999: 18) confirms this by showing how the US utilised refined techniques of non-battle on the homefront in the development of its policing of inner city crime – control the population, control the resources are the watchwords of non-battle.

26. De Certeau's description of everyday life in terms of strategy and tactics bears this out: the tactical is defined by *kairos*, the ability to seize a moment and turn an unfavourable set of circumstances to its own benefit. Strategy, meanwhile, which for de Certeau is typified by Foucault's account of discipline, is defined by its immobility.

# Chapter 2

# Vacuoles of Noncommunication: Minor Politics, Communist Style and the Multitude

## Nicholas Thoburn

Remarking on the place of Deleuze's thought in contemporary political circles, Slavoj Žižek has recently suggested that: 'Deleuze more and more serves as the theoretical foundation of today's anti-globalist Left' (Žižek 2004: xi).[1] This situation, however, is not cause for celebration on Žižek's part. Following Alain Badiou, Žižek argues that the current leftist reading of Deleuze is little more than an anarcho-desiring cliché that is ultimately complicit with the postmodern orientations of contemporary capitalism. Indeed, he writes that: 'There are, effectively, features that justify calling Deleuze the ideologist of late capitalism' (Žižek 2004: 185). This assessment is not quite of Deleuze in total, but of a 'popular image' of Deleuze; an image formed of a certain Marxism, a particular reading of Deleuze's ontology, and an aspect (albeit a key one) of Deleuze's own work – a Deleuze 'guattarized' in his work with Guattari (Žižek 2004: 20). It is evident that for Žižek a prominent manifestation of this popular image of an anti-globalist Deleuze is Hardt and Negri's *Empire*, where there is a clear meeting of Deleuzian figures of becoming, multiplicity, control and so on, with Marxian formulations of labour, capital and communism. Though Žižek initially endorsed *Empire* on the dust-jacket as a 'rewriting of *The Communist Manifesto* for our time', he now sees it as a 'pre-Marxist' work that conceals 'its lack of concrete insight' in 'Deleuzean jargon of multitude, deterritorialization, and so forth' (Žižek 2001: 192). It is not unhelpful that Žižek has raised issues with the way Deleuze has emerged as a political figure in the contemporary situation. The trouble with his diagnosis, however, is that he too readily allows *Empire* to be an expression of Deleuze's politics. In so doing he fudges the points of difference between Deleuze and Negri (sometimes allowing a critique of Hardt and Negri to stand in for a critique of Deleuze) and refrains from examining the diverse forces and politically productive possibilities of this conjuncture.

This paper takes Žižek's sense of a contemporary nexus between Deleuze, Negri and the anti-globalist left as a point of departure to consider the productivity of Deleuze for communist politics, in what is, in part, an alternative reading of this nexus. Starting from Deleuze's rather enigmatic proposition of the need for 'vacuoles of noncommunication' to counter the regimes of communication in control societies, the paper considers how Deleuze and Guattari's 'minor politics' can be used to understand the generation of political community. Stressing the relation between forms of expression and the composition of collectivity, minor politics is presented in a fashion that challenges a model of inclusive and popular political subjectivity, and orients attention to the particular, situated processes of political composition, or 'foci of creation', and the styles of expression that result. This framework is employed to engage with the model of political subjectivity, the 'multitude', developed by Hardt and Negri and their problematic tendency toward generalising categories and popular modes of address. The discussion then turns to the Italian Marxist current of *operaismo* and *autonomia*, the milieu of emergence for much of Negri's recent work, to see how a more minor model of expression can be seen in communist cultures – something based less on the elaboration of a subject position than on a diffuse process of problematisation and invention.[2]

In an interview first published in 1990, Negri questions Deleuze on the possibility that new technologies may enable a politics based on a fluid communication between minorities. In response Deleuze proposes that the centrality of information and communication technology to control societies is such that speech and communication are 'thoroughly permeated by money', and that rather than develop a politics based on 'minorities speaking out' or 'universals of communication', politics might orient around a certain creative 'non-communication': 'We've got to hijack speech. Creating has always been something different from communicating. The key thing may be to create vacuoles of noncommunication, circuit breakers, so we can elude control' (Deleuze 1995: 175). It is forms of resistance associated with computer hacking and piracy that Deleuze has in mind, but this image raises a crucial concern for politics – that of the appropriate mode of expression for thought and practice that seeks to effect radical change in a time when communication, with its mechanisms of identity-formation and command (Terranova 2004), has become central to capitalist dynamics. How can political expression – and all that it entails in terms of the generation and circulation of knowledge, the formation of community, and the production of political intensity – take the form of a creative non-communication? One way to consider this question is through the specific mode of political creation Deleuze and Guattari develop in their account of minor literature and politics.

For Deleuze and Guattari the question of the form of political communication is inseparable from that of the composition of subjectivity and collectivity. As they elaborate in their account of minor politics, it can be approached through three aspects – minority, deterritorialisation, and authorship.[3] First, minor politics marks a challenge to political models founded on the representation or delineation of a subject or an identity, whether in the form of a 'people' or a self-declared marginal. These 'molar' models are premised on the fetishisation of an already present identity that exists in a nurturing social environment. Minor politics, on the other hand, operates, as Deleuze and Guattari put it, in the 'choked passages', 'cramped spaces' and 'impossible' positions of 'small peoples' and 'minorities' who lack or refuse coherent identity – those who, constrained by a wealth of determining social relations, exist under and affirm the condition that 'the people are missing' (Deleuze 1989: 216).

The affirmation of this subjectless condition is such that, alongside a perceptual sensitivity to very real cramped minority conditions (and Deleuze and Guattari are clear that politics tends to emerge amongst those who are readily perceivable as minorities within a culture), in minor politics there is also a certain 'willed poverty' – a continual deferral of subjective plenitude – such that 'one strives to see [the boundary] before it is there, and often sees this limiting boundary everywhere' (Deleuze and Guattari 1986: 19; Kafka, cited in Deleuze and Guattari 1986: 17). This deferral not only serves to open minor politics to everybody who would experience the molar standard as restrictive, but also acts as a mechanism to induce continuous experimentation. For, rather than allow the solidification of particular political and cultural routes, forms and subjectivities, such 'willed poverty' operates to draw thought and practice back into a milieu of contestation, argument, and engagement, and forces ever-new forms of experimentation from the intimacy of cramped experience.

Second, the minor political focus on cramped space is far from a resigned turn to the local or particular, since here, without self-secure delineated identity, even the most personal, particular concern is infused with a wealth of social relations and forces that determine its values. The experimentation of politics thus takes the form not of a self-expression through a set of autonomous concerns and languages, but of an engagement with, or 'deterritorialisation' of the social relations that traverse particularities. The intensification of the particular is hence always an opening toward the social: 'The individual concern thus becomes all the more necessary, indispensable, magnified, because a whole other story is vibrating within it' (Deleuze and Guattari 1986: 17).

Third, this mutual enfolding of the social and the particular has ramifications for the mode of minor authorship, what Deleuze and Guattari describe as a 'collective enunciation'. If in minor composition 'everything takes on a collective value' this is not because the minor author is an 'ethnologist of his people', where the author expresses or represents the conditions and truths of a particular group as a fully present constituency (Deleuze and Guattari 1986: 17; Deleuze 1989: 222). Instead, minor authorship is the elaboration and proliferation of the collective intrigue as it is expressed in particular moments by particular authors distributed across the milieu. The author is driven by the concerns of the limited community but also by the relations that cross it and that lead it elsewhere. As such, and in fully materialist fashion, minor authors are not subjects but impersonal singularities, events, composite 'foci of creation' (Deleuze 1998: 42). Moments of minor creativity thus tend to emerge less in completed, coherent works than in what Kafka (1999: 148) describes as the 'incessant bustle' of the unfinished, open forums of 'magazines' and 'schools', spaces that are traversed or even constituted by changing borderlines or anomalous points that incorporate and amplify difference in the community. The constitutive bustle dictates that there can be no easy demarcation between conceptual production, personal styles, particular intrigues, or geopolitical events, and there is, as Kafka (1999: 150) notes, plenty of space for polemic, or as Guattari puts it: 'It's not a question of creating agreement; on the contrary, the less we agree, the more we create an area, a field of vitality' (Guattari 1998: 196). The vital environment of minor literature is thus described by Kafka as one where the constitutive 'cellar' of a literature is brought to the fore:

> Insults, intended as literature, roll back and forth. What in great literature goes on down below, constituting a not indispensable cellar of the structure, here takes place in the full light of day, what is there a matter of passing interest for a few, here absorbs everyone no less as a matter of life and death. (Kafka 1999: 150)

Reading Deleuze's vacuoles of non-communication through this lens of minor politics, one is left with an image of political communication that is very different from that premised on the clean, unambiguous transfer of information from one party to another, be that of a universal language or political theory, or a process of minorities speaking out about their self-evident situation. Deleuze's vacuoles suggest a certain kind of breakdown, refusal, or unworking (to use Nancy's expression) of this model

of information, and at the same time the generation of a variously tex-
tured, affective, stuttering form of expression that is immanent to the creation of particular relations, collectivities, practices and styles. As
Guattari puts it, the point of minor political expression is not to create a
language or theory as a 'universal tool' that should 'communicate' a
message to a social body – political writing, rather, is concerned with the
question of 'efficiency', or particular productivity (Guattari 1995: 38–9):

> I do not believe in universal literature or philosophy but rather in the virtues
> of minor languages. So the question becomes rather simple, either a minor
> language connects to minor issues, producing particular results, or it
> remains isolated, vegetates, turns back on itself and produces nothing . . .
> [T]heoretical expressions . . . should function as tools, as machines, with
> reference neither to an ideology nor to the communication of a particular
> form of subjectivity . . . Think about May 1968. There was no ideological
> transmission, but rather the repercussion of events. (Guattari 1995: 37–8)

This resistance to the model of political communication as information-
transfer raises the problem of popularity. From the perspective of minor
politics, the successful communication of a message in popular fashion to
a mass audience may actually be a sign of a reduction in political intensity inasmuch as it manifests a diminution in particular invention in
favour of the composition of a generic collectivity shorn of its borderlines,
complexities and points of crisis. This in part explains the distrust of popularity and the foregrounding of a certain 'failure' amongst the minor
authors Deleuze most privileges: Kafka, Melville and Beckett. As Cesare
Casarino (2002) shows, Melville, for example, considered success in the
mass market as requiring a literary form that he despised. As he writes in
a letter to his father-in-law: 'So far as I am individually concerned, &
independent of my pocket, it is my earnest desire to write those sort of
books which are said to "fail".' And, in another letter: 'What I feel most
moved to write, that is banned, – it will not pay. Yet, altogether, write the
*other* way I cannot. So the product is a final hash, and all my books are
botches' (Melville, cited in Casarino 2002: 68).[4] But this critique of mass
communication or popular appeal is not an élitist model, however 'difficult' the literary or theoretical constructions minor politics may generate
(Guattari 1995: 37–8). It is the popularity of any particular formulation
that is put into question for fear of the constitution of an easy literary or
political community – as an author or concept becomes elevated above
the political milieu, transformed into cliché and consumed as a universal
message by an already constituted social group – that betrays the intensive mechanisms and processes of intimately situated textual and political experimentation. Minor politics is a 'popular' politics, 'the people's

concern' (Deleuze and Guattari 1986: 18), but it is the popular as milieu of emergence, as the diffuse striving for a people to come in the midst of a willed poverty that wards off achieved identity.

The question remains as to how much minor politics presents an account of the generation of cultures that can be seen as 'communist'. One could cite a number of moments from the communist movement that resonate with the features of minor politics recounted above: Marx's refusal of subjective plenitude in his account of the proletariat and his emphasis in *The Eighteenth Brumaire of Louis Bonaparte* on the exhaustive reworking of social experience as constitutive of proletarian cultures; Marx and Engels' refusal in *The Communist Manifesto* to present the Communist Party as a distinct group apart from the plane of social forces and struggle and Marx's persistent distrust of political groupings and the cult of personality; the critique of the author in left communist politics as exemplified by Amadeo Bordiga and his refusal to attribute a name to his works, or the recent experiments in multiple names around the Luther Blissett and Wu Ming projects. One could also note that Deleuze and Guattari (1986: 18) stress that the criteria of a proletarian literature are difficult to establish without the 'more objective' concept of minor literature, or that Kafka's understanding of the 'literature of small peoples', contrary to Casanova's (2004) recent critique of the minor literature thesis on the basis of Kafka's nationalism, is not unrelated to his interest in communist and anarchist politics. But it is more useful to see how minor politics can be used as a means of understanding particular moments of communist writing and composition, to put the concept to use, and it is to this that I want to turn in a reading of Hardt and Negri's 'multitude' – probably the most influential of contemporary political figures.

Negri has, to say the least, had a complex political career, arising from his involvement in the 1960s and 970s in Italian *operaismo* and *autonomia* and the clashes with the Italian state during its 'strategy of tension' – *Empire* and *Multitude*, more than most books, are the products of a long and complex series of political situations and encounters that are readily perceivable from a minor perspective. Yet at the same time they work as rather self-coherent and popular texts somewhat abstracted from their constitutive environments. If the *New York Times* was able, albeit in a cynical gesture, to call *Empire* theory's 'next big idea', in England even New Labour types found something to affirm in it – this is Mark Leonard, then of the Foreign Policy Centre think tank, in his review of the book:

Unlike the British and German left, Italian Marxism has always placed great emphasis on individual emancipation. It echoes some of New Labour's thinking – for example, John Prescott's 'quality of life indicators', measuring everything from pollution to childcare and working hours. (Leonard 2001: 37)

The problem is not in itself the popularity of *Empire* and *Multitude*, but the way that the style and conceptual constructions of these books lend themselves to, or even encourage, this inclusive popularity – something that is characterised more by a generic inclusion in a subject position than by the diffuse, rhizomatic production that is the quality of minor political environments. A number of features could be isolated to account for the popularity of *Empire*, not least its use of (and dust-jacket endorsement by) key post-colonial theorists of the Anglo-American academy, its self-presentation as a kind of transcendence of Foucault, Deleuze and *operaismo*, and a certain image of political commitment that Negri's name conjures in the academy. But a key feature of the appeal of *Empire* derives from the nature of its political subject, the 'multitude'.[5]

Whereas Deleuze, in accord with my first point about minor politics, insists that capital tends to become immanent to the mobilisation of life such that political subjectivity – if one can call Deleuze's impersonal arrangements of invention that – exists in the midst of complex and mutable regimes of control on the condition that 'the people are missing', Hardt and Negri tie the multitude – at times in an almost millennial fashion (Quinby 2004) – to the emergence of a self-organising immaterial mode of labour that tends toward autonomy from capital (Hardt and Negri 2000: 294; Hardt and Negri 2004: 335–6).[6] It is, I would argue, precisely this open, inclusive subjectivity and the affective pull of a certain avant-garde position that comes with it that accounted for much of the popularity of the book across divergent constituencies.[7] In a recent interview Hardt draws attention to this, and interestingly raises the possibility that such popularity had its problems. He says that: '[I]n a certain way, *Empire* is not a very politically-defined book. Insofar as one is describing the new form of power, it can appeal to people with many different political orientations; it can support many different political tendencies', and continues by suggesting that such a compendium of divergent political supporters is less possible in the reception of *Multitude* since here he and Negri are 'talking about an alternative', and 'that's where you divide ways' (in Hardt, Smith and Minardi 2004: n.p.). Hardt would seem, then, to be affirming a more situated, engaged form of research and writing. And indeed, on the face of it *Multitude* appears to be a more explicitly political work. As such, one may expect it to generate less wide-ranging support and operate at the more intimate, situated level of political composition.

However, though it fleshes out the category of the multitude (especially around the politics of 'the common') and explores a number of political currents, movements and events, the book develops an even stronger inclusive narrative of an emerging political subject.[8]

The result of this is that rather general, overarching concepts are employed to characterise or represent this subject en masse – concepts like love, democracy, global citizenship – that work by amassing complex and varied phenomena under their name, that have a propensity to operate like slogans, and that tend to discourage an attention to the multiplicity, conflict and alternate trajectories of social arrangements. Consideration, that is, is paid less to the intimate processes of deterritorialisation of social relations – the plane of minor politics – than to the elaboration of a rather universal theory of the multitude. It is telling, then, that Hardt and Negri begin the book by writing that it does not offer an answer to the question 'What is to be done? or propose a concrete programme of action' (an orientation that, though problematic in its vanguardist inclination, still looks toward specific, practical tasks and interventions) but seeks to 'rethink the most basic political concepts, such as power, resistance, multitude, and democracy' (Hardt and Negri 2004: xvi).

The correlate of the inclusive and generalising categories and millennial narratives is that the textual style of *Empire* and *Multitude* takes the form of a straightforward communication of a message to an audience, as the authors seek to 'convince' the reader of their argument (Hardt and Negri 2004: xviii). Indeed, *Multitude* is self-consciously formed in an explicitly inclusive and popular style – at the start of the book Hardt and Negri state that: 'We have made every effort to write this in a language that everyone can understand' (Hardt and Negri 2004: xvii). In responses to *Multitude* this pitch to a popular audience has tended to be affirmed as a progressive, 'non-academic' mode of writing (Brown and Szeman 2005: 373). Any challenge to this apparently laudable aim of making a text accessible is, of course, potentially subject to the charge of élitism. Yet, what tends to happen in such approaches (that are, of course, common in radical literature) is that political works are left devoid of the complexity and materiality that are part of the constitutive process of minor political reading and engagement, as one is encouraged, in Jameson's words, to 'salute a readymade idea effortlessly in passing' (cited in Helmling 2001: 36). In the case of *Multitude*, the effect is that rather than a product of the intimate, intensive 'cellar' of the magazines and schools of a minor political environment, the book has more of a feel of being pitched to the leftist equivalent of the audience for Fukuyama's *The End of History and the Last Man* or Friedman's *The*

*Lexus and the Olive Tree*[9] in the large market of popular books on anti-capitalism.[10]

Drawing back from *Empire* and *Multitude*, one can see a more minor style or mode of expression in *operaismo*, *autonomia* and aspects of Negri's work, and it is to this that I want to turn. It was a key principle of *operaismo*, based on the perspective of the refusal of work, that its politics was premised less on a substantial identity than on the minor political position that 'the people are missing'. Mario Tronti, for example, argued that 'when the *working class* politically refuses to become *people*, it does not close, but opens the most direct way to the socialist revolution' (Tronti 1973: 116). Crucially, this marked not an affirmation of the presence of the working class as autonomous subject, but a recognition, following Marx, that the working class is itself constituted in capital and fully permeated by capitalist relations. Thus, and it is noteworthy that Deleuze and Guattari make use of the passage in discussion of minority processes, Tronti writes: 'To struggle against capital, the working class must fight against itself insofar as it is capital' (cited in Deleuze and Guattari 1988: 571). As such, *operaismo* emerged in a rather cramped space. Owing to the dominance of the large communist (PCI) and socialist (PSI) parties, the early *operaisti* found themselves surrounded by the disabling culture of orthodox and then eurocommunist Marxism. But they were unable, due to the influence of the party in radical workers' culture, to make a clean break. One of the ways out of this cramped condition was to return to Marx, and break from orthodoxy under cover of Marxian terminology. As well as producing important work on Marx – particularly on the nature of technology, the critique of objectivist categories in Marxism, the social factory, and the subjectivity of the proletariat – this process developed quite clearly in terms of a deterritorialisation of the major language of orthodoxy in something of a Marxist patois. As Yann Moulier puts it:

[D]oubtless by the same token that Althusser ventured into the French Communist Party under cover of scientific Marxism and Spinoza, the adherents of *operaismo* proceeded to use formulae that would not have shocked the old Stalinist communists. One could even say that part of the strange character of *operaismo* in the years 1964 to 1971 lies in this paradoxical way of saying in the very language of the Communist Party things which are so contrary to its whole theoretical foundation as to imitate its internal rupture. (Moulier 1989: 20–1)

As a result the texts of *operaismo* are characterised by a rather dry, terse, quite obsessive manner that is far from the model of communication as clean information-transfer; as Moulier remarks: '[T]he aridity or the obscurity of this form of Marxism . . . is like no other manifestation we have known' (Moulier 1989: 5). Yet it is, of course, this quality that marks the strange beauty and intensity of this work as a collective, minor literature – a quality that emerges from the apparently petty concerns in aspects of Marx, the proliferation of self-published journals (what Kafka might call the 'little diaries') where research was generated and disseminated,[11] the polemic and small points of conflict, the relay between militant activity, research and theory, the way the theoretical intrigues linked up to and emerged from social problematics and political events, the politicisation of needs, the relation of writing to minority formations (from southern migrants in the 1960s factories, to the unwaged labour of housework, the cultural formations of proletarian youth) and so on, as what would be the 'cellar' of a major literature here pushed to the foreground as the plane of composition.

If they operated through a kind of deterritorialisation of orthodox Marxism, *operaismo* and *autonomia* at the same time emphasised the need to form a political language that was particular to workers' experience and, as *autonomia* developed, to the minorities that constituted the working class. Hence one sees the lexical invention of categories and perspectives like 'auto-valorisation', the '*emarginati*', 'wages for housework', 'auto-reduction', each seeking to account for particular phenomena and maintain an operationality for the various political milieux – to function, as Guattari was seen above to require of a minor politics, as 'tools' and 'machines' in the production of political effects. In the hands of groups like Collective A/traverso and their Radio Alice (with whom Guattari had some involvement) the question of communication was specifically politicised in a fashion that Meaghan Morris (1978) has characterised as a certain 'semiological delinquency' (as against the clear and concise language of the PCI) and that bears relation to Deleuze's image of vacuoles of non-communication.[12] Radio Alice experimented with a mixing-up of political, personal, communicative and affective registers through music, discussion programmes, phone-ins, poetry and political co-ordination, seeking to make language 'unproductive', 'tactile' and to draw out, as they put it, the 'unstated' and the 'uncanny' in a direct challenge to the 'simplification', 'mathematicisation' and 'codification' of communication associated with 'techno-scientific' intellectual labour (Collective A/traverso 1980: 130–1):

> The system of production that is based upon the reduction of all aspects of human life to abstract work, exchangeable against wages, could not separate itself from the logic of language. Human language had to be reduced by capitalism to a simple instrument of production, and thus first codified, confined within the canons of comprehensibility, and it therefore had to root

out all contradiction, and – given that contradiction lay in the existence of the subject/class – root out the subject. (Collectif A/traverso 1977: 109–10; my translation)

This issue of communication and the complexity of political language is addressed by Negri too, in response to a question about the difficulty of his language in this period and the consequent problems rank and file militants might have in using it. Significantly, and in contrast to *Multitude*, he draws attention to the disaggregated and differentiated nature of audiences, the relation between different forms of theoretical production and political situation, and a certain productivity of difficulty as against the simplistic slogans of the PCI:

> Certainly, the language is occasionally obscure. But it was far more obscure 20 years ago. At that time we had to find ways of inserting Marxist and revolutionary debates into the official labour movement, and since at the same time we had to avoid being expelled and marginalised, we found a hermetic style of language. The bureaucrats did not understand it, and underestimated the power of what we were saying. But since then things have changed a lot. Nowadays revolutionary students are far more able to understand the language that I and my friends use, rather than the 'clear and distinct' language of the ideological falsifications of the official parties.
>
> Our language is difficult, but distinct. It speaks of things. Theirs is clear, but not distinct: they speak of nothing. Our language is difficult: but our comrades study it, as they study the classics of Marxism, the critique of political economy and many other things. (Negri 1988: 206)

Something of this point is also made by Maurizio Viano in his preface to Negri's (1991) *Marx beyond Marx*. In raising the possibility of an objection to Negri's writing on the basis of its difficulty, Viano argues that it is a bourgeois or humanist fallacy that assumes that a book should be consumed similarly by the spectrum of social subjects, a fallacy rooted in the notion of a fully present universal humanity, or, one could say, a fully present, molar people. Viano suggests instead that Negri's language is a 'homage to difference' rooted in a cultural environment that was opposed to the repetition of the regular refrains and meanings of 'normal' political discourse. *Autonomia*, Viano argues, was self-consciously positioned at the margins of the system of symbolic reproduction and comprised many different parallel and divergent expressions, an 'atonality' developed against the tonal repetitions of the ' "natural", common-sensical logic which is paradoxically common to Right, Left and Center' (in Negri 1991: xxxiv).

To conclude, this chapter has taken Žižek's diagnosis of a contemporary conjunction of Deleuze, Hardt and Negri, and the anti-globalist left as its point of departure to consider the styles of composition and expression of a minor, communist politics. The framework of minor politics both raises problems with Hardt and Negri's understanding of the multitude as a tendentially autonomous and inclusive social body and the generalising categories and popular mode of expression that is its correlate, and shows how alternative developments and trajectories can be seen in Negri's work and the wider environment of *operaismo* and *autonomia*. The argument concerning the problems with communication and popularity could sound a little strange in the context of the development of a communist politics. The point, however, is not to affirm an arcane political style for its own sake but to recognise that politics has a specific mode of composition and expression. Minor politics is less about the formation of a political subject and the development of universal tools of theory in a language 'that everyone can understand' – an apparently laudable aim that in practice can leave a text shorn of its productive relation with material environments – than about the generation of intimate, engaged and particular problematics in diffuse foci of creation, what Deleuze might call 'vacuoles of noncommunication'. One hopes that these intensify, multiply and consolidate at a popular level, but a widespread social formation will not occur through an act of popular recognition or inclusion in a set of political concepts and narratives. There is, of course, a crucial need to develop theories adequate to the forces and relations that traverse the social multiplicity – forces that could be named through concepts like biopolitical production, Empire, immaterial labour and multitude – but the minor political elaboration of these categories requires that they are drawn into a milieu of contestation arising from particular and multiform situations, as Hardt and Negri themselves affirm when they write of *Empire*: 'Ours is the kind of book that asks to be criticized' (Hardt and Negri 2001: 236).

# References

Balakrishnan, G. (2000), 'Virgilian Visions', *New Left Review* 5: 142–8.

Beasley-Murray, J. (2002), 'Towards an Unpopular Cultural Studies: The Perspective of the Multitude', in S. Godsland and A.M. White (eds) (2002), *Cultura Popular: Studies in Latin American Popular Culture*, Oxford: Peter Lang, pp. 27–45.

Bourdieu, P. (1993), *The Field of Cultural Production: Essays on Art and Literature*, ed. R. Johnson, Cambridge: Polity Press.

Brown, N. and Szeman, I. (2005), 'What Is the Multitude? Questions for Michael Hardt and Antonio Negri', *Cultural Studies* 19 (3): 372–87.

Buchanan, I. (2003), 'The Utility of *Empire*', *Continuum: Journal of Media and Cultural Studies*, 17(4): 379–85.

Casanova, P. (2004), *The World Republic of Letters*, trans. M. B. DeBevoise, London: Harvard University Press.

Casarino, C. (2002), *Modernity at Sea: Melville, Marx, Conrad in Crisis*, London: University of Minnesota Press.

Collectif A/traverso (1977), *Radio Alice, Radio Libre*, Paris: Jean-Pierre Delarge.

Collective A/traverso (1980), 'Radio Alice – Free Radio', trans. R. Gardner and S. Walker, *Semiotext(e): Italy: Autonomia – Post-political Politics* 3 (3): 130–4.

Del Re, A. (2005), 'Feminism and Autonomy: Itinerary of Struggle', in T. S. Murphy and A. K. Mustapha (eds) (2005), *The Philosophy of Antonio Negri*, London and Ann Arbor: Pluto Press, pp. 48–72.

Deleuze, G. (1989), *Cinema 2: The Time-Image*, trans. H. Tomlinson and R. Galeta, London: Athlone.

Deleuze, G. (1995), *Negotiations: 1972–1990*, trans. M. Joughin, New York: Columbia University Press.

Deleuze, G. (1998), 'On the New Philosophers and a More General Problem: An Interview with Deleuze', trans. B. Augst, *Discourse* 20 (3): 37–43.

Deleuze, G. and Guattari, F. (1986), *Kafka: Toward a Minor Literature*, trans. D. Polan, London: University of Minnesota Press.

Deleuze, G. and Guattari, F. (1988), *A Thousand Plateaus: Capitalism and Schizophrenia*, vol. 2, trans. B. Massumi, London: Athlone.

Guattari, F. (1995), *Chaosophy*, ed. S. Lotringer, New York: Semiotext(e).

Guattari, F. (1998) 'Pragmatic/Machinic: Discussion with Félix Guattari (19 March 1985)', in C. J. Stivale (1998), *The Two-Fold Thought of Deleuze and Guattari: Intersections and Animations*, London: Guilford, pp. 191–224.

Hardt, M. and Negri, A. (2000), *Empire*, London: Harvard University Press.

Hardt, M. and Negri, A. (2001), 'Adventures of the Multitude: Response of the Authors', *Rethinking Marxism* 13 (3/4): 236–43.

Hardt, M. and Negri, A. (2004), *Multitude: War and Democracy in the Age of Empire*, New York: Penguin.

Hardt, M., Smith C. and Minardi, E. (2004), 'The Collaborator and the Multitude: An Interview with Michael Hardt, *The Minnesota Review* 61–2, http://www.theminnesotareviw.org/ns61/hardt.htm accessed 20 September 2004.

Helmling, S. (2001), *The Success and Failure of Fredric Jameson: Writing, the Sublime, and the Dialectic of Critique*, Albany: SUNY.

Kafka, F. (1999), *The Diaries of Franz Kafka, 1910–23*, ed. M. Brod, trans. J. Kresh and M. Greenberg, London: Penguin.

Leonard, M. (2001), 'The Left should Love Globalisation', *New Statesman* 14 (658): 36–7.

Morris, M. (1978), 'Eurocommunism vs. Semiological Delinquency', in P. Foss and M. Morris (eds) (1978), *Language, Sexuality and Subversion*, Sydney: Feral Publications, pp. 47–76.

Morris, M. (1996), 'Banality in Cultural Studies', in J. Storey (ed.) (1996), *What is Cultural Studies? A Reader*, London: Arnold, pp. 147–67.

Moulier, Y. (1989), 'Introduction', in A. Negri (1989), *The Politics of Subversion: A Manifesto for the Twenty-First Century*, trans. P. Hurd, Cambridge: Polity Press, pp. 1–44.

Negri, A. (1988), *Revolution Retrieved: Selected Writings on Marx, Keynes, Capitalist Crisis and New Social Subjects (1967–83)*, London: Red Notes.

Negri, A. (1991), *Marx beyond Marx: Lessons on the Grundrisse*, trans. H. Cleaver, M. Ryan and M. Viano, London: Pluto Press.

Quinby, L. (2004), 'Taking the Millennialist Pulse of *Empire*'s Multitude: A Genealogical Feminist Diagnosis', in P. A. Passavant and J. Dean (eds) (2004), *Empire's New Clothes: Reading Hardt and Negri*, London: Routledge, pp. 231–51.

Saccarelli, E. (2004), '*Empire*, Rifondazione Comunista, and the Politics of Spontaneity', *New Political Science*, 26(4): 569–91.

Terranova, T. (2004), *Network Culture: Politics for the Information Age*, London: Pluto Press.

Thoburn, N. (2003), *Deleuze, Marx and Politics*, London: Routledge.

Tronti, M. (1973), 'Social Capital', *Telos* 17: 98–121.

Turchetto, M. (2003), 'The Empire Strikes Back: On Hardt and Negri', *Historical Materialism* 11(1): 23–36.

Wright, S. (2002), *Storming Heaven: Class Composition and Struggle in Italian Autonomist Marxism*, London: Pluto Press.

Žižek, S. (2001), 'Have Michael Hardt and Antonio Negri Rewritten the *Communist Manifesto* for the Twenty-First Century?', *Rethinking Marxism* 13 (3/4): 190–8.

Žižek, S. (2004), *Organs without Bodies: On Deleuze and Consequences*, London: Routledge.

## Notes

1. This paper was first presented at the *Experimenting with Intensities* conference at Trent University, May 2004. I would like to thank Constantin Boundas for that opportunity. I am grateful, too, to the editors of this volume for their helpful comments.

2. For an incisive and detailed analysis of *operaismo* and *autonomia* see Wright (2002). This historical Marxist current is, of course, not the contemporary Left that Žižek refers to, but its formulations have had some influence here and as such – without wanting to stretch things too far – the place of *operaismo* in this paper, as well as being part of a minor political engagement with Negri, can function for my purposes as the third term in the Deleuze, Negri, anti-globalisation nexus that Žižek identifies.

3. I have considered these processes of minor political composition in more depth in Thoburn (2003).

4. The shunning of popularity is not necessarily a political manoeuvre, having, as Bourdieu (1993) precisely elucidates, its own place in the production of literary symbolic capital via the assertion of the autonomy of creative activity amongst certain agents in the field of cultural production. The point I am making vis-à-vis minor politics is that, as Casarino shows in discussion of Melville, the critique of popularity here has a particular relation to the elaboration of political forms and forces in a fashion that recognises its immersion in social relations, including those of the market.

5. I would not want to downplay the importance of the concept of 'Empire' to the popular appeal of the book in the context of the dominance of theories of 'globalisation', but I would argue that even here the standpoint of the multitude as counter-subject to Empire affectively drove much of the interest in this category.

6. In making their argument Hardt and Negri of course employ many of the Deleuzian figures that I am using here to make a different case. In discussion of a related point Ian Buchanan has remarked that: '[W]hile it is true that Hardt and Negri are inspired by (and borrow a great deal from) Deleuze and Guattari, their conclusions could not be more different' (Buchanan 2003: 380).

7. For an insightful discussion of some of the practical political problems with Hardt and Negri's tendency to subsume the varied and often divergent elements of contemporary anti-globalisation in the category of the multitude, see Saccarelli (2004).

8. This is most evident in the chapter on 'Resistance' where, despite warnings against reading the argument in mechanistic and evolutionary terms, they propose that 'each new form of resistance is aimed at addressing the undemocratic qualities

of previous forms, creating a chain of ever more democratic movements' (Hardt and Negri 2004: 68).

9. Balakrishnan (2000) and Turchetto (2003) have remarked upon *Empire*'s resemblance to these totalising visions of the post-Cold War world situation.

10. This is especially pronounced in the English edition of *Multitude* which, alongside an endorsement by Naomi Klein, carries the injunction on the dust-jacket to 'Join the many. Join the empowered. Join the . . . Multitude'. There are, of course, many encouraging signs in the emergence of this market in anti-capitalist literature, but it is important to recognise the way it can also tie in with a mode of seduction and consumption based on what Meaghan Morris (1996) in her critique of populism in 1980s Cultural Studies sees as an 'emotional simplification' that tends to produce an abstract subject of resistance and a generic mass audience that is more associated with publishing booms than it is with the affectively complex process of situated and engaged political research. For a critique of populism that makes use of Morris' article in elaborating alternate, non-populist trajectories in the multitude (ones based on an account of the multitude as an ambivalent political constituency) see Beasley-Murray (2002).

11. In some fascinating comments on her experience of *autonomia*, Alisa Del Re talks about the processes of production of political works in this time – in a way that clearly resonates with the minor model of authorship – as a 'collective intelligence' that 'worked in a way that made people in themselves almost interchangeable, even if each person had a particular expressive and educational capacity' (Del Re 2005: 58).

12. Radio Alice, the subject of the recent film *Lavorare con lentezza*, was one of the most prominent 'free radio' stations of the movement, broadcasting from an old military transmitter in Bologna from February 1976 until it was shut down by armed police under the charge of 'military coordination' during the social unrest of March 1977.

# Chapter 3

# 1,000 Political Subjects . . .

## Kenneth Surin

Is it possible for a compatibility to exist between Althusser's well-known doctrine of the interpellation of the subject by the ideological apparatuses of the state and the theses regarding the assemblages of the state propounded by Deleuze and Guattari in *A Thousand Plateaus*?[1] Is there, more generally, a recognisable political subject whose ontological shape and character is limned in *A Thousand Plateaus*, even as it is 'undone' by Deleuze and Guattari? And is there a fundamental connection between this subject and the traditional metaphysical-epistemological subject that is also unravelled in *A Thousand Plateaus*? At first sight, the answers to these questions are probably going to be negative, though our 'no' will almost certainly have to be somewhat less emphatic where the second and third questions are concerned.

There are only a couple of references to Althusser in *A Thousand Plateaus*, but what is there indicates explicitly that Deleuze and Guattari consider Althusser's notion of the constitution of social individuals as subjects to be profoundly mistaken. To quote them:

> Neither is it a question of a movement characteristic of ideology, as Althusser says: subjectification as a regime of signs or a form of expression is tied to an assemblage, in other words, an organization of power that is already fully functioning in the economy, rather than superposing itself upon contents or relations between contents determined as real in the last instance. Capital is a point of subjectification par excellence. (Deleuze and Guattari 1987: 130)

Deleuze and Guattari's rejection of the concept of ideology clearly stems from their conviction that the Althusserian conception of ideology relies on the discredited base-superstructure distinction. As they see it, subjectification is constituted by an assemblage or organisation of power that already functions in the economic 'base', and so cannot be seen as the outcome or resultant of processes located purely at the 'superstructural' level, which of course for Althusser is determined 'in the last instance' by the economic 'base'. And yet, and yet . . . it is by no means obvious that Althusser is as wedded to the base-superstructure distinction in the way ostensibly presumed by Deleuze and Guattari. After all it could be argued that Althusser's treatment of ideology, resting as it does on the crucial proposition of an 'overdetermination' of all the apparatuses, is intended precisely to obviate any reliance on the unacceptable 'base-superstructure' distinction.[2] What if we accept, for the purposes of argument at any rate, that the notion of an interpellation can be detached from any unacceptable reliance on the 'base-superstructure' distinction (postponing for the time being judgement on Althusser's putative weddedness to this distinction), so that an interpellation could in principle be said to take place as long as some kind of apparatus or agency constituted by the appropriate disposition of power provides enabling conditions for its occurrence? If this much is acknowledged or conceded, then it may be possible to say that subjects could be interpellated by state assemblages of the kind identified and described by Deleuze and Guattari in *A Thousand Plateaus*. A great deal will hinge on the interpretation placed on the notion of such an interpellation, and how we specify the stakes that are at issue in retaining this Althusserian notion. At any rate, there is here the core of a hypothesis that is worth examining as a prolepsis to the question of the kind of political subject, with its allied account of political sovereignty, to be found in *A Thousand Plateaus* and other associated writings by Deleuze and Guattari, whether authored individually or conjointly (or with other authors in the case of Guattari).

What kind of political subject, if any, can continue to exist in the conjuncture of a 'post-political' politics, and has this subject to possess an intrinsic and defining connection to the political sovereignty that grounded the classical Citizen Subject of the philosophical tradition that extends from Hobbes to Hegel, via Rousseau and Kant, which took the representation of the will of the citizen to be the hallmark of the political?

Using the writings of Georges Dumézil as their initial template, Deleuze and Guattari provide a fascinating narrative when addressing the question of political sovereignty in the plateau titled 'Treatise on Nomadology'.[3] Invoking Dumézil's dualism of the shaman-king and the priest-jurist, Deleuze and Guattari go on to say:

> Undoubtedly, these two poles stand in opposition term by term, as the obscure and the clear, the violent and the calm, the quick and the weighty, the terrifying and the regulated, the 'bond' and the 'pact', etc. But their opposition is only relative; they function as a pair, in alternation, as though they expressed a division of the One or constituted in themselves a sovereign

unity. 'At once antithetical and complementary, necessary to one another and consequently without hostility, lacking a mythology of conflict: each specification at any one level automatically calls forth a homologous specification on another. The two together exhaust the field of the function'. They are the principal elements of a State apparatus that proceeds by a One-Two, distributes binary distinctions, and forms a milieu of interiority. It is a double articulation that makes the state apparatus into a *stratum*. (Deleuze and Guattari 1987: 351–2)[4]

Deleuze and Guattari take Dumézil's personifications, at once complementary and mutually reinforcing, of the magician-king and the jurist-priest to constitute the two-pronged function of the state. They also follow Dumézil in opposing to this state apparatus, and thus the figures of the magician-king and the jurist-priest, the counter-force represented by the war machine. The respective properties possessed by the state apparatus and the war machine can be tabulated in the following manner:[5]

| State Apparatus | War Machine |
| --- | --- |
| Sovereignty (*pouvoir)* | power (*puissance*) |
| Law | event |
| fixity of Being | ontological innovation |
| gravity | celerity |
| the public | secrecy |
| binary distributions | multiple becoming |
| permanence | evanescence |
| conservation | power of metamorphosis |
| milieu of interiority | milieu of exteriority |
| internal, biunivocal relations | external relations |
| *polis* | *nomos* |
| semiology | strategy, pragmatics |
| 'striated' space | 'smooth' space |
| coding/decoding | scrambling of the codes |
| territorialisation/ deterritorialisation | movement without possession of territory |
| king, jurist | warrior, prophet |
| concentration | dispersion |
| strategies of exclusion | resistance, openness |
| 'arborescent' | 'rhizomatic' |
| hierarchical | non-hierarchical |
| identity | transformation |
| individuality | singularity |
| false plenitude, empty repetition | facing the void |
| delimitation | immeasurability |
| Goethe, Hegel | Kleist, Artaud |

| | |
|---|---|
| organs of power | packs, bands |
| theorems | problematics |
| formal concentration of power | solidarity |
| religion | offences against gods and priests |
| harmony | rhythm |
| architecture, cooking | music, drugs |
| history | geography |
| measured time (*chronos*) | indefinite time of event (*Aeon*) |
| Egyptian state | Moses |
| Man | 'becoming-woman' |

Deleuze and Guattari caution against viewing the opposition between the state apparatus and the war machine in strict binary terms:

> The problem is that the exteriority of the war machine in relation to the State apparatus is everywhere apparent but remains difficult to conceptualize. It is not enough to affirm that the war machine is external to the apparatus . . . What complicates everything is that this extrinsic power of the war machine tends, under certain circumstances, to become confused with one of the two heads of the State apparatus. Sometimes it is confused with the magic violence of the State, at other times with the State's military institution . . . So there is a great danger of identifying the structural relation between the two poles of political sovereignty, and the dynamic interrelation of these two poles, with the power of war . . . [W]henever the irruption of war power is confused with the line of State domination, everything gets muddled; the war machine can then be understood only through the categories of the negative, since nothing is left that remains outside the State. But, returned to its milieu of exteriority, the war machine is seen to be of another species, of another nature, of another origin. (Deleuze and Guattari 1987: 354)

Turning to the question of Althusserian interpellation, it seems plausible, if not obvious, to say that any neo-Althusserian wishing to retain the notion of such an interpellation while adhering to Deleuze and Guattari's conception of political sovereignty, will have to accept that any such interpellation at the hands of the state apparatus will necessarily be according to 'theorems' derived from the twin poles of its political sovereignty, to wit, the shaman-king and the jurist-priest. For Deleuze and Guattari the law of the state is despotic and priestly in its most fundamental impulses, and anything like an interpellation (admittedly not a notion Deleuze and Guattari would want to use) is perforce conducted in congruence with those 'theorems' sanctioned by the state's despotic and sacerdotal orders, these sacred or quasi-sacred orders persisting even when the polity in question is a liberal democracy with an accompanying normativity ostensibly resting on entirely secular premises. Ethico-political subjects interpellated in this way will therefore be caught up in a transcendental validation of their subjectivities – legitimation at the hands of the state for Deleuze and Guattari always places the subject at the mercy of an *arché* or founding principle that requires the citizen to be created in the image of the state's figures of sovereignty, in this case the overarching despot and priest. The outcome will in any case be a thousand little despots, a thousand little priests, all defined as model citizen subjects.

The state, on this account, is the product of thought, a thinking which is inextricably linked to a desire that for Deleuze and Guattari is ubiquitous and endlessly productive:

> [E]verything is production: *production of productions*, of actions and of passions; *production of recording processes*, of distributions and of co-ordinates that serve as points of reference; *production of consumptions*, of sensual pleasures, of anxieties, and of pains. Everything is production, since the recording processes are immediately consumed, immediately consummated, and these consumptions directly reproduced. (Deleuze and Guattari 1983; 10)

The implications of this position are profound and radical, and they point, among other things, to a significant difference between a standard and almost normative reading of Foucault and the authors of *Capitalism and Schizophrenia*. Deleuze and Guattari clearly accord great importance to 'desiring-production' (as indicated by the above passage). But this undeniable saliency of 'desiring-production' does not translate into the primacy of the modes of production as such, which is what one would expect of a more conventional Marxist or *Marxisant* thinking. Instead Deleuze and Guattari bestow this primacy on the so-called machinic processes, that is, the modes of organisation that link all kinds of 'attractions and repulsions, sympathies and antipathies, alterations, amalgamations, penetrations, and expressions that affect bodies of all kinds in their relations to one another' (Deleuze and Guattari 1987: 90). The modes of production depend on these machinic processes for their constitution (Deleuze and Guattari 1987: 435). The upshot is that the modes of production are always themselves the product or derivation of a ceaselessly generative desire: what enables each mode to be constituted is an always specific, indeed aleatory, aggregation of desires, forces and powers. The organisation of productive desire gives the mode of production its enabling conditions, and not vice versa, as is the case in some of the more typical Marxisms. In arriving at this formulation, though, Deleuze and Guattari are very much in line with what Marx himself said about the necessity for society to exist before capitalism can emerge in anything like a fully-fledged form: a society-state with pre-existing surpluses must already exist if the (capitalist) extraction of surplus-value is to take place. To quote Deleuze and Guattari:

> Marx, the historian, and Childe, the archaeologist, are in agreement on the following point: the archaic imperial state, which steps in to overcode agricultural communities, presupposes at least a certain level of development of these communities' productive forces since there must be a potential surplus capable of constituting a State stock, of supporting a specialized handicrafts class (metallurgy), and of progressively giving rise to public functions. This is why Marx links the archaic State to a certain [precapitalist] 'mode of production'. (Deleuze and Guattari 1987: 428)

The state, in other words, gives capital its 'models of realization' (Deleuze and Guattari 1987: 434). But the state that provides capital with the models it needs in order to be effectuated is already functioning even before it manifests itself as a concretely visible apparatus. The state, in this case the palaeolithic state, destroys or neutralises the hunter-gatherer societies that it came to supersede, but before this happens there must be a necessary point of convergence between the state and the hunter-gatherer troupes. This point of convergence, which the troupes ward off and anticipate at the same time, designates a situation or space in which – 'simultaneously' – the existing hunter-gatherer formations are dismantled and their successor state-formations put in place. In the words of Deleuze and Guattari, the two sets of formations unfold 'simultaneously in an "archaeological", micropolitical, micrological, molecular field' (Deleuze and Guattari 1987: 431).[6]

The state, on this view, achieves its 'actuality' through a complex and uneven process that involves the arresting or caging of non-state formations, so that both state and non-state formations exist in a field of perpetual interaction. This interactive field, in the parlance of Deleuze and Guattari, is irreducibly 'micropolitical' or 'molecular', and so stateformations, which for them are of course quintessentially 'macropolitical' or 'molar', are not positioned in a field that has already been transformed by the state apparatuses or their prototypes into something that is (now) exclusively 'macropolitical' or 'molar'. It is virtually an axiom for Deleuze and Guattari that before and alongside the macropolitical there is always the micropolitical. The state has perforce to interact with the micropolitical. This is at odds with a certain interpretation of Foucault (here regarded as the exemplary philosopher of the micropolitical) which views micropolitics to be a relatively new 'development' arising more or less strictly in response to forms of power, pre-eminently 'biopower', that did not exist before the onset of the most recent phases of modernity. While it is not quite clear if Foucault himself should be saddled with this

view, it remains the case that for Deleuze and Guattari the state apparatuses always emerge in a molecularised field that the state never entirely
contains or neutralises. The appearance of the state cannot therefore be
the outcome of its own efficacy, of any inherent propensity on its part to
generate its own enabling conditions. Whatever its powers, autogeny is
beyond the power of the state to accomplish. Micropolitics has therefore
always been antique in its provenance, and the state came about as an
invention designed to arrest these micropolitical forces. Moreover, as an
invention, the state had necessarily to be 'thought' before it could begin
to be efficacious in any social and political field.[7]

But the state has to deny this irremovable factitiousness of its 'origins',
and present itself precisely as its 'opposite', that is, as an unthought (at any
rate where 'origins' are concerned): 'Only thought is capable of inventing
the fiction of a state that is universal by right, of elevating the state to the
level of de jure universality' (Deleuze and Guattari 1987: 375). Thought
confers on the state its character of a singular and universal form, the
fullest expression of the rational-reasonable (le rationnel-raisonnable).
The foremost exponent of this 'thought' behind the genesis of the state is
of course Hegel, who explicitly views the state as the embodiment of the
universal, as the realisation of reason, and thus as the spiritual community
that incorporates all individuals within itself. Against this view, which
derives the state from the rational-reasonable, Deleuze and Guattari hold
that it is the rational-reasonable itself that is derived from the state. The
state provides the formal conditions for the enactment of the rational-
reasonable and thought (as the primary instantiation of the rational-
reasonable) in turn necessarily confers on the state its 'reason' (lui donner,
necessairement 'raison'). Reason or thought becomes the province of the
state on this Hegelian (or quasi-Hegelian) view, and Deleuze and Guattari
therefore propose a wresting of thought from the state and a complementary returning of the state to thought, in the form of an acknowledgement
of the state's irreducible fictiveness.[8]

The archaic state that arose from a recoding of the primitive territorial codes of the hunter-gatherer troupes instituted an organised production associated with the creation of 'a particular kind of property, money,
public works . . .' (Deleuze and Guattari 1987: 448). But this archaic
State was not able to prevent a substantial quantity of 'decoded flows'
from escaping:

> The State does not create large-scale works without a flow of independent
> labor escaping its bureaucracy (notably in the mines and in metallurgy). It
> does not create the monetary form of the tax without flows of money escap-
> ing, and nourishing or bringing into being other powers (notably in commerce

and banking). And above all it does not create a system of public property without a flow of private appropriation growing up beside it, then beginning to pass beyond its grasp; this private property does not itself issue from the archaic system but is constituted on the margins, all the more necessarily and inevitably, slipping through the net of overcoding. (Deleuze and Guattari 1987: 449)

This epochal transformation confronted the succeeding state apparatuses with a new task. Where the previous state-form had to overcode the already coded flows of the hunter-gatherer groups, the new state apparatuses had to organise conjunctions of the decoded flows that had been escaping their archaic predecessor. These became the apparatuses of a polynucleated and more complex kind of state. But even here the state could not prevent decoded flows from escaping (yet again), and the most recent versions of these flows attained an 'abstract', 'generalized' conjunction which overturned their adjacent state apparatuses and created capitalism 'at a single stroke' (Deleuze and Guattari 1987: 452–3). Capital thus represents a new and decisive threshold for the proliferation of flows, and, in the words of Deleuze and Guattari, this 'force of deterritorialization infinitely [surpasses] the deterritorialization proper to the State' (Deleuze and Guattari 1987: 453). But capital's superiority in this regard does not spell the end of the state. Instead the state undergoes a further mutation, and the modern nation-state is born.

The relation between the state and capital is thus one of reciprocity. Capitalism is an 'independent, worldwide axiomatic that is like a single City, megalopolis, or "megamachine" of which the States are parts, or neighborhoods' (Deleuze and Guattari 1987: 453). The state-form is not totally displaced by the 'worldwide, ecumenical organisation' of capital, but it has, in its modern manifestation, become a 'model of realisation' for capital. As such, it is the function of each state today to '[group] together and [combine] several sectors, according to its resources, population, wealth, industrial capacity, etc' (Deleuze and Guattari 1987: 454). Under capitalism, the state serves 'to moderate the superior deterritorialization of capital and to provide the latter with compensatory reterritorializations' (Deleuze and Guattari 1987: 455). The state becomes a field for the effectuation of capital, and it does this by reharnessing and reorganising flows which capital brings together and decomposes. Capitalism will even organise and sustain states that are not viable, for its own purposes, primarily by crushing minorities through integration and extermination. The primacy of capital manifests itself at the highest level of abstraction: capital is an international organisation that can organise with a prodigious resourcefulness the various state formations in ways that ensure their fundamental 'isomorphy' (which is not to be confused with 'homogeneity' in Deleuze and Guattari's scheme).

International capitalism is capable of bringing about the 'isomorphy' of very diverse forms and their attendant forces. In his Leibniz book, Deleuze maintains that cultural and social formations are constituted on the basis of 'concerts' or 'accords' (Deleuze 1993: 130–7). These 'accords' are organising principles which make possible the grouping into particular configurations of whole ranges of events, personages, processes, institutions, movements and so forth, such that the resulting configurations become integrated formations. As a set of accords or axioms governing the accords that regulate the operations of the various components of an immensely powerful and comprehensive system of accumulation, capital is situated at the crossing-point of all kinds of formations, and thus has the capacity to integrate and recompose capitalist and non-capitalist sectors or modes of production.[9] Capital, the 'accord of accords' par excellence, can bring together heterogeneous phenomena, and make them express the same world, that of capitalist accumulation. Thus, in Malaysia, for example, the accord (or set of accords) the 'hi-tech' world of downtown Kuala Lumpur (which until recently was the location of the world's tallest skyscraper), and the accord (or set of accords) that constitutes the world of Stone Age production to be found among the tribespeople in the interiors of East Malaysia (Sabah and Sarawak) are not inter-translatable (or not directly or immediately so); but what the 'accord of accords' created by capitalism does, among a myriad other things, is to make it possible for the artifacts produced by the 'indigenous' peoples of these interior regions to appear on the tourist markets in downtown Kuala Lumpur, where they are sold alongside Microsoft software, Magnavox camcorders, Macintosh Power Books, and so on. The disparate and seemingly incompatible spheres of production and accumulation represented by downtown Kuala Lumpur and the interior regions of Sabah and Sarawak (which are only about 500 miles away from Kuala Lumpur) are rendered 'harmonious' by a higher-level accord or concert established by capital, even though the lower-level accords remain (qua lower-level accords) disconnected from each other. Each lower-level accord retains its own distinctive productive mode and its associated social relations of production, even as it is brought into relationship with other quite different modes and social relations of production (each of course with their own governing ground-level accords) by the meta- or mega-accord that is capitalism in its current world-integrated phase. The 'concerto grosso' brought about by this prodigiously expansive capitalist accord of accord enables the lower-level accords to remain dissociated from each other while still expressing the same world, the world of the current paradigm of accumulation. In a country like Malaysia, and indeed anywhere else in the world, every and any kind of production can thus be incorporated by the capitalist algorithm and made to yield a surplus-value. This development has effectively dismantled the intellectual terms of the age-old debate about 'pre-capitalist' modes of production and their relation to a successor capitalism. This debate was concerned, in the main, with the putative 'laws' that underlay the supersession of the 'pre-capitalist' modes by their capitalist successors, but the question of this supersession has become moot in the current phase of accumulation: as the case of Malaysia illustrates, the 'pre-capitalist' modes can continue to exist in precisely that form, but are inserted at the same time into a complex and dynamic network that includes, in the spirit of a vast and saturating ecumenism, all the various modes of production, 'pre-capitalist' and capitalist alike, so that they function in concert with each other, in this way promoting, of course, the realisation of even greater surplus-values.[10]

The systemic loss of accords here is significant for the constitution of a political subjectivity inasmuch as any such subjectivity and its accompanying ideology relies on a taxonomy governed by notions of 'inside' and 'outside', 'belonging' and 'non-belonging', and so on, and with the loss of such meta-accords, the subject becomes a never-ending work in progress.

Accords are constituted by selection criteria, which specify what is to be included or excluded by the terms of the accord in question. These criteria also determine with which other possible or actual accords a particular accord will be consonant (or dissonant). The criteria that constitute accords are usually defined and described by narratives governed by a certain normative vision of truth, goodness and beauty (reminiscent of the so-called mediaeval transcendentals, albeit translated where necessary into the appropriate contemporary vernacular). A less portentous way of making this point would be to say that accords are inherently axiological, value-laden. What seems to be happening today, and this is a generalisation that is tendentious, is that these superposed narratives and the selection criteria they sanction, criteria which may or may not be explicitly formulated or entertained, are being weakened or qualified in ways that deprive them of their force. Such selection criteria tend to function by assigning privileges of rank and order to the objects they subsume ('Le Pen is more French than Zidane', 'One cannot be a good American and a communist', 'Turks are not Europeans', and so on). The loss or attenuation of the customary force of such accords makes dissonances and contradictions difficult or even impossible to resolve, and, correlatively, makes divergences easier to affirm. Events, objects and personages can now be assigned to several divergent and even incompossible series, a phenomenon spectacularly demonstrated by Lautréamont's uncannily surrealistic definition of reality as 'the chance encounter between a sewing-machine and an umbrella on a dissecting-table'.[11]

Such a Lautréamontean, culturally-sanctioned disposition in the present-day, conducing as it does to a traffic in all kinds of incompossibilities and divergences, is becoming increasingly commonplace. As each of us takes the opportunity to negotiate for the fifteenth or hundredth or whatever time, the several historical avant-gardes, the writings of Borges, cyberpunk and so forth, we become familiarised with the propensities of a Lautréamontean consciousness in ways not available to a learned and cosmopolitan person living as recently as fifty years ago. Thus, for instance, we have a whole genre ('magical realism') predicated on the logic of incompossibility (something can be a bird and Simon Bolivar at the same time, and even more 'implausibly', at the same point in space); there is a new technological form based on the same logic (such as the morphing that Michael Jackson undergoes in his video *Thriller*); as well as entire schools of music which use tones in series that escape or block any kind of resolution by the diatonic scale (as in the work of John Cage or Toru Takemitsu or free improvisational jazz).[12] Such examples can be multiplied according to one's taste.

This pervasive weakening of the force of these 'transcendental' accords, and of the narratives and images which sustain them, may be associated with the collapse of a number of once widely entrenched distinctions: as was just noted, the boundaries between public and private, inside and outside, before and after, political left and political right and so on, have all become difficult, if not impossible, to uphold. In the process, however, accords thus detached from the narratives and other conditions capable of guaranteeing their stability likewise become 'impossible'. We may be living in worlds that are no longer predicated on any real need to secure and maintain accords, worlds characterised by sheer variation and multiplicity (but still functioning according to an axiomatics – for example capital – that ensures their fundamental isomorphism in the face of this uncontainable diversity), worlds that partake of a neo-Baroque perhaps more 'truly' Baroque than its predecessor, as Deleuze has maintained in his book on Leibniz. Or rather, these are worlds in which the work of accords is now done emblematically and allegorically, so that there is no real accord for what it is that, say, constitutes 'Englishness' (or perhaps more accurately, there is now the realisation that our accords determining what it is that constitutes 'Englishness' rest on an ineliminable fictiveness, so that these accords lack any kind of transcendental legitimation). In the absence of anything approximating to a transcendental back-stopping, 'being English' can only be designated ascriptively or emblematically, that is, non-absolutely, as when Queen Elizabeth II (who had as much claim to be regarded as German as English) is so easily allowed to 'count' as 'English', while supporters of the late Enoch Powell, an anglophone and intellectually upscale version of Jean-Marie Le Pen, were able nastily to cavil over whether a London-born son or daughter of a Jamaican immigrant could justifiably be regarded as 'English'.

The ascriptive or emblematic imputation of 'Englishness' would allow it to be placed into at least a couple of divergent series. There would be Enoch Powell's grimly robust and settled series, which would effectively confine 'Englishness' to him and his benighted ilk, but other more expansive series would include London-born children of Jamaican immigrants, the half-American Winston Churchill, the Canadian-born English tennis player Greg Rusedski, and so on. Crucial to this more ascriptive way of assigning or determining identities is the abandonment of the concept in favour of description (a move delineated by Deleuze in his Leibniz book). Typically, the specification of an identity requires that the identity under consideration be determinate in regard to a concept ('being a communist', 'being Irish', 'being an economist' or whatever), a concept whose range of applicability is regulated by certain criteria of belonging. These criteria are motivated and underpinned by accords of the kind described above, and the breakdown of these accords means that the concepts they support and organise can be replaced by descriptions. Hence, for example, in place of the concept 'being an English person' one could have the descriptions 'Queen Elizabeth II conducting herself as an English woman', 'Greg Rusedski is the Canadian-born tennis star who plays for England', 'the Japanese-born anglophone novelist Kazuo Ishiguro', and so forth. Such descriptions, as opposed to the concept 'being English', would allow 'Englishness' to be used ascriptively or emblematically, so that 'it' could be placed, depending on the particular instances involved, in two or more divergent series. This substitution in principle of the description for the concept would be a not inappropriate way of acknowledging the emergence of a new intellectual and cultural condition (we could call it the time after the end of the Empire, which is 'our time' undeniably) in which it has become more difficult than ever to claim that there really are 'transcendental' accords which subtend this or that way of designating 'Englishness'.

The worlds opened up by *Capitalism and Schizophrenia* are worlds whose accords are characterised in very decisive ways by the kinds allegorising and emblematising propensities just described. These are worlds marked by the 'systemic' loss of transcendental accords; they are worlds that are perhaps seeing the exponential growth of the capacity to accommodate what Deleuze and Guattari call 'the anomalous' (*l'anomal*). The anomalous, in their view:

> has nothing to do with the preferred, domestic, psychoanalytic individual. Nor is the anomalous the bearer of a species presenting specific or generic characteristics in their purest state; nor is it a model or unique specimen; nor is it the perfection of a type incarnate; nor is it the eminent term of a series; nor is it the basis of an absolutely harmonious correspondence. The anomalous is neither an individual nor a species; it only has affects, it has neither familiar nor subjectified feelings, nor specific or significant characteristics. (Deleuze and Guattari 1987: 244)

The realm of the anomalous, for Deleuze and Guattari, lies between the domain of 'substantial forms' and that of 'determined subjects'; it constitutes 'a natural play full of haecceities, degrees, intensities, events, and accidents that compose individuations totally different from those of the well-formed subjects that receive them' (Deleuze and Guattari 1987: 253).[13] The upshot is that each individual is a potentially infinite multiplicity, the product of a phantasmagoric movement between an inside and an outside.[14]

All this amounts to the lineaments of a new and interesting theory of the place of the 'subject' in the cultures of contemporary capitalism. *Capitalism and Schizophrenia* approaches this theory of the 'subject' via a theory of singularity – 'singularity' being the category that more than any other goes beyond the 'collective' versus 'individual' dichotomy that is essential to the Hobbes–Rousseau–Hegel tradition of reflection on the state or sovereign. This account of singularity, and here I have to be very brief and schematic, can in turn be connected up with the theory of simulation given in Deleuze's *Logic of Sense* and *Difference and Repetition*, since for Deleuze simulation (or the simulacrum) is the basis of singularity.[15]

In a universe of absolute singularities, production can only take the form of singularity: each singularity, in the course of production, can only repeat or proliferate itself. In production each simulacrum can only affirm its own difference, its distanciation from everything else. Production, on this account, is a ceaselessly proliferative distribution of all the various absolute singularities. Production, in Deleuze's nomenclature, is always repetition of difference, the difference of each thing from every other thing. Capitalism, though, also embodies a principle of repetition. The axiomatic system that is capitalism is one predicated on identity, equivalence and intersubstitutivity (this, of course, being the logic of the commodity-form as analysed by Marx). In which case, repetition in capitalism is always repetition of the non-different; or, rather, the different in capitalism is always only an apparent different, because it can be overcome and 'returned', through the process of abstract exchange, to that which is essentially the same, the always fungible. Capitalism, as *Capitalism and Schizophrenia* indicates, effects an immense series of transformations (deterritorialisations) only to make possible more powerful recuperations and retrenchments: it breaches limits only in order to impose its own limits, which it 'mistakenly' takes to be co-extensive with those of the universe.[16] The power of repetition in capitalism is therefore negative, wasteful and ultimately non-productive. Capitalistic repetition can therefore be said to be non-being in Spinoza's sense, a conclusion that Deleuze and Guattari, and Negri, do not hesitate to draw.

Capital, in the scheme of *Capitalism and Schizophrenia*, is constitutively unable to sustain a culture of genuine singularities, even though of course it creates the conditions for the emergence of a culture that could, with the requisite transformations, mutate into a culture – a culture that will however necessarily be 'post-capitalist' – which has the capacity to produce such singularities.[17] Intrinsic to the notion of a singularity is the principle that a common or shared property cannot serve as the basis of the individuation of X from all that is not-X: if I share the property of being over six feet tall with anyone else, then that property cannot, in and of itself, serve to individuate either me or that person. A singularity, the being-X of that X that makes X different from all that is not-X, cannot therefore unite X with anything else. Precisely the opposite: X is a singularity because it is not united to anything else by virtue of an essence or a common or shared nature. A singularity is a thing with all its properties, and although some commonality may pertain to this thing, that commonality is indifferent to it qua singularity. So, of course, Félix Guattari will have the property 'being French' in common with other people, many millions of them in fact. But a singularity is determined only through its relation to the totality of its possibilities, and the totality of possibilities that constitutes Guattari is the totality of an absolute singularity – if another being had each and every one of the possibilities whose totality constituted and thus individuated Guattari, then that being would perforce be indistinguishable from Guattari.

In a time when 'transcendental' accords can no longer really give us our worlds, we have to look for worlds that give us a different basis for the construction of solidarities, worlds in which a new kind of politics can find its *raison d'être*. This politics will start from the realisation that our criteria of belonging are always subject to a kind of chaotic motion, that our cultures have always told us an enabling lie when they denied this, and through this denial have made possible the invention of nation-states, tribes, clans, political parties, churches, perhaps everything done up to now in the name of community. The reader of Deleuze and Guattari may have the feeling, of both dread and exhilaration at the same time, that that time, the time up to 'now', has begun inexorably to pass. But we still need our solidarities, now more than ever. They are indispensable for any politics capable of taking us beyond capitalism. These solidarities, however, will be based not on the securing of 'transcendental' accords – capitalism, that most revolutionary of forces, has moved that possibility into desuetude. Our solidarities will be predicated instead on what the reader of Deleuze and Guattari will know as the power of singularity, a power still perhaps in search of its appropriate models of realisation.[18]

Since this politics still awaits its models of realisation, the power of singularity, which despite the absence of these models is still precisely that, a power, can only manifest itself as the undertaking of a certain risk, the 'playing of uncertain games', all the things that conduce to the 'revolutionary-becoming' of people who have not yet made the revolution their explicit agenda. What will be the relation of this 'revolutionary-becoming' to the project of the state? Can the solidarities associated with these singularities be regimented, and thus neutralised, by the state in ways that preempt insurmountably the prospects of any kind of revolutionary transformation?

The flows of power in the current social and political dispensation are fluid and relatively open, even as they are powerfully managed and contained by the élites who rule us. This development underlies the increasingly widespread perception that governments in the advanced industrial countries wield more and more control despite the simultaneous prevalence of ideologies of deregulation, privatisation, and 'getting the government off the backs of the people' (the mantra of Ronald Reagan among others). And so it looks increasingly as if the notion of representation, which made the previous kind of 'citizenship politics' possible has now been supplanted, even as the instruments which underpin it are treated as sacred objects. There is perhaps no better example of this than the American Constitution, traduced by an ever-expanding capitalist depredation even as its traducers profess their undying veneration for this old document.[19] The blocking of any passage through the philosophy and politics of representation underlying such developments will have significant effects not only on our conceptions of citizenship, but also on our related notions of ethnicity, race, patrimony, clan, nation and sovereignty. These notions have deeply ingrained personal resonances that will continue to be felt despite the criticisms directed by philosophers and theorists at the concept of representation. But if the philosophy of representation no longer works, and its limitations are impossible to conceal, what then should be put in its place? The invention of something different (such as the Deleuzian notion of a political desire or willing based on singularities not regulated by transcendental accords) to put in place of the system of representations that has governed thinking and practice about ethnicity, race, patrimony, clan, nation and sovereignty – these representations being the cornerstone of the *épistème* or *mentalité* that has prevailed since 1789 or 1492 (used here as emblematic markers) – will have to be an immense collective undertaking, perhaps spanning many generations. The core of this system of representation is its imperative that all are required to 'belong' in some way or other to the various collectivities superintended by this system's logic. An enabling political desire will free us from the need to continue to make this a world where all are required to belong to such collectivities.

State power is, of course, the most significant impediment to the realisation of this undertaking. The state identifies, counts and assigns to its various classificatory systems countless numbers of human beings, all as part of its administrative remit, and the pressing question for the Deleuzian account of political desire is its capacity to mobilise desire in ways that make possible an obviation of state power. The world is changing even as we reflect on it. The collapse of the Soviet Union has been largely instrumental in the emergence of a US hegemony. As a result, the antagonism between capitalism and bureaucratic socialism has been replaced by a range of struggles among competing brands of capitalism (German social market capitalism, the Blairite Third Way, American free-market capitalism, and so on). Here the outcome is still uncertain, as indicated by the continuing world economic stagnation and the wars being fought by the Bush administration and its allies. Despite this uncertainty, there are a number of trends in the international system that appear to be fairly consequential. Pre-eminent among these is a more active role in this system for regional as well as local states, and these are being accompanied by new structures of cultural identification that are tied to regions or subregions rather than nation-states (such as the various 'separatisms' associated with the Basques, Catalonians, Chechnyans, Kurds, Corsicans, Irian Jayanese, Sri Lankan Tamils, Punjabi Sikhs, Kashmiris, Eritreans, or the people of Aceh).[20] One outcome of this development is the increased coexistence of the transnational and the interlocal, with the nation-state having a transformed but still noteworthy function as the apparatus that manages the flows between them. Conceptions of sovereignty and citizenship are being modified in the process, especially since the state-system is de-emphasising govern*ment* in favour of govern*ance* and *meta-governance* as older and more expansive official state institutions are scaled down or sidelined, and administration increasingly becomes the process of organising flows between a range of agencies and networks of power and information (governance) and of devising the 'axioms' to link together and harmonise all these structures and movements (meta-governance).[21] Conceptions of citizenship, and their attendant forms of political desire and agency, become increasingly flexible and compartmentalised.

The state will only be replaced or restructured slowly. In failed states such as Somalia, for instance, a state-form of some kind will have to be introduced prior to the pursuit of its possible supersession, and this because no viable system for the allocation of resources exists in the Somalias of this world, and the possibility of revolutionary transformation in such countries presupposes the existence of such a system to serve as a conduit for decision-making. A counter-capitalist project of the kind delineated in *Capitalism and Schizophrenia* is not likely to succeed unless the social movements that are its vehicle are able to operate at the level of the nation-state (though they would, of course, certainly not be confined to working at this level).[22] Of course this counter-project has to be efficacious at other levels if it is to be successful, including the education, taxation and bureaucratic systems, and also show itself capable of sustaining 'a more general vision of the democratisation of societies and their political and economic management' (Amin 2000: 84). But the project is, for the less-developed countries at any rate, a project that involves the mobilisation of a new and different kind of popular national movement. Here an important distinction between the state apparatus and the nation is to be made, and Samir Amin has plausibly argued that the appropriation of the state apparatus is usually the object of a country's national bourgeoisie (who will reconcile themselves to recompradorisation by external capitals as long as it will leave the state apparatus in their hands), while the construction of the project of national liberation involves not only delinking (needed to avert recompradorisation) but also the formation of a 'popular hegemonic alliance' among the people (see Samir Amin 1990:136).

The construction of a comprehensive national popular alliance, functioning autonomously of the state system, will furnish the stimulus for adopting a different kind of allocation strategy, one premised on a (selective) delinking, and embarked upon with the purpose of transmuting the state apparatus (since the state is the institutional assemblage that has final control of the regime of growth, and indeed there can be no properly-constituted regime of growth without the involvement of the state). The first priority, therefore, is a 'destatised' collective national liberation project, the success of which will then lead to a reconstitution of the state itself. Most existing proposals for economic and political reform in the less-developed countries view the reform and reconstitution of the state as the principal objective whose attainment will then lead to a whole range of other benefits ('efficient' economic development, protection of human rights, the upholding of democracy, and so on). This is to put the proverbial cart before the horse, since in many less-developed countries the state is merely an instrument at the disposal of the ruling élite (who tend invariably to be the recipients of the substantial personal benefits to be derived from subservience to the Washington Consensus, and so on), and it will be necessary, therefore, to have an alternative and non-state oriented base within the less-developed countries from which the project of state reform can be initiated and sustained.

I have indicated that *Capitalism and Schizophrenia* is perhaps best viewed as a compendium of political knowledge, 'non-molar' and 'non-arborescent' in aspiration and putative scope, which furnishes 'axioms' for the pursuit of the revolutionary project of surmounting capitalism. Deleuze and Guattari insist that there are no pre-given laws to shape or entail this outcome: only struggle, and failures always accompany successes in struggle, can do this. The only other alternative is acceptance of the current finance-led, equity-based growth regime with its concomitant American hegemony and continuing worldwide economic polarisation.

## References

Agamben, G. (1993), *The Coming Community*, trans. M. Hardt, Minneapolis: University of Minnesota Press.

Althusser, L. (1969), 'Contradiction and Overdetermination', in L. Althusser *For Marx (1969)*, trans. B. Brewster, London: Penguin Books, Part III.

Althusser, L. (1971), 'Ideology and Ideological State Apparatuses', in L. Althusser (1971), *Lenin and Philosophy and Other Essays*, trans. B. Brewster, London: New Left Books, pp. 127–86.

Amin, S. (1990), *Delinking: Towards a Polycentric World*, trans. M. Wolfers, London: Zed Books.

Amin, S. (1999), 'For a Progressive and Democratic New World Order', in F. Adams, S. D. Gupta and K. Mengisteab (eds) (1999), *Globalization and the Dilemmas of the State in the South*, London: Macmillan, pp. 17–32.

Amin, Samir (2000), 'Conditions for Re-Launching Development', in K. McRobbie and K. Polanyi (eds) (2000), Karl Polanyi: *The Contemporary Significance of The Great Transformation*, New York: Black Rose Books, pp. 73–84.

Cage, John (1969), 'Diary: Emma Lake Music Workshop 1965', in J. Coge (1969), *A year from Monday: New Lecture and Writings*, Middletown: Wesleyan University Press, p. 22.

Deleuze, G. (1994), *Difference and Repetition*, trans. P. Patton, New York: Columbia University Press.

Deleuze, G. (1990), *The Logic of Sense*, trans. M. Lester with C. Stivale, New York: Columbia University Press.

Deleuze, G. (1993), *The Fold: Leibniz and the Baroque*, trans. T. Conley, Minneapolis: University of Minnesota Press.

Deleuze, G. (1995), *Negotiations, 1972–1990*, trans. M. Joughin, New York: Columbia University Press.

Deleuze, G. and Guattari, F. (1983), *Anti-Oedipus: Capitalism and Schizophrenia*, trans. R. Hurley, M. Seem and H. R. Lane, Minneapolis: University of Minnesota Press.

Deleuze, G. and Guattari, F. (1987), *A Thousand Plateaus: Capitalism and Schizophrenia*, trans. B. Massumi, Minneapolis: University of Minnesota Press.

Deleuze, G. and Parnet, C. (1987), *Dialogues*, trans. H. Tomlinson and B. Habberjam, New York: Columbia University Press.

Dumézil, G. (1948), *Mithra-Varuna*, Paris: Gallimard.

Gupta, D. and Mengisteab, K. (1999), *Globalization and the Dilemmas of the State in the South*, London: Macmillan.

Jessop, B. (1997), 'Capitalism and its Future: Remarks on Regulation, Government and Governance', *Review of International Political Economy* 4: 561–81.

Lazare, Daniel (1996), *The Frozen Republic: How the Constitution is Paralyzing Democracy*, New York: Harcourt Brace.

Lazare, D. (2001), *The Velvet Coup: The Constitution, the Supreme Court, and the Decline of American Democracy*, London: Verso.

Polanyi, K. and McRobbie, K. (eds) (forthcoming), *Karl Polanyi: The Contemporary Significance of The Great Transformation*, New York: Black Rose Books.

Surin, K. (1991), 'The Undecidable and the Fugitive: *Mille Plateaux* and the State-Form', *SubStance* #66: 102–13.

Surin, K. (1994), ' "Reinventing a Physiology of Collective Liberation": Going "Beyond Marx" in the Marxism(s) of Negri, Guattari, and Deleuze', *Rethinking Marxism* 7: 9–27.

Surin, K. (1995), 'On Producing the Concept of a Global Culture', *The South Atlantic Quarterly* 94: 1,179–99.

Surin, K. (1997), 'The Epochality of Deleuzean Thought', *Theory, Culture & Society* 14: 9–21.

Žižek, S. (1997), *A Plague of Fantasies*, London: Verso.

# Notes

1. For Althusser's account of interpellation, see his 'Ideology' (1971).
2. See Althusser (1969) where it is clearly stated that the 'superstructure' exercises a 'specific effectivity' on the base. It could certainly be argued on behalf of Deleuze and Guattari that the positing of such an 'effectivity' on the part of the 'superstructure' only compounds the original problem, since any significant 'effectivity' on the part of the 'superstructure' will only qualify or diminish the capacity of the 'base' to serve as a determinant 'in the last instance'. This is too complex an issue to be resolved here, but it needs to be noted that Althusser is perhaps not quite the naïve proponent of the 'base-superstructure' dichotomy that Deleuze and Guattari take him to be.

3. Like each of the plateaus in *A Thousand Plateaus*, the 'Treatise on Nomadology' has a date attached to it, in this case 1227, the year in which Genghis Khan died. Deleuze and Guattari give no explanations for their choice of such dates, and one can only surmise here that Genghis Khan's *Pax Mongolica* is for Deleuze and Guattari an emblematic instance of a counter-sovereignty to be posed against the sovereignty of the *polis* that he challenged from his moveable base in the steppes. This much can be gleaned from Deleuze and Guattari 1987: 417–19, 518–522.

4. Emphasis as in original. Translation slightly altered. The interior quotation is from Dumézil (1948: 118–24), which deals with the difference between the bond and the contract.

5. For these properties, see Deleuze and Guattari (1987: 352ff., 435–6).

6. It should be pointed out, though, that the state is understood by Deleuze and Guattari in two senses. In one sense it is to be identified with the formations and apparatuses that constitute it. In another, it is, pre-eminently, a metaphysical conception, a machine of transcoding that (unlike the assemblages which embody it and which have to be constructed and positioned at this or that point in social space) 'comes into the world fully formed and rises up at a single stroke, the unconditioned Urstaat' (see Deleuze and Guattari 1987: 427).

7. It follows from this that there is a sense in which consciousness (taken here to include all the ramified outreachings of desire), constitutes something like a domain of the virtual, and so precedes the 'actuality' of social apparatuses and formations. The 'thinking' of the state is a function of consciousness par excellence, and is therefore the product of this virtuality. Clearly this has significant implications for any simplistic claims about the primacy of the 'actually' material in a Marxist thought and practice: the virtual, as Deleuze and Guattari, following Bergson, have insisted, cuts across the division between the possible and the actual. 'Before Being there is politics (1987: 203), certainly, but inextricably bound up with politics is the thinking that is located in the realm of the virtual, and this thinking breaches the long-held distinctions between 'thought' and 'practice' and 'materialism' and 'idealism'.

8. Some of the ensuing formulations have been taken from my 'The Undecidable' (1991).

9. To quote Deleuze and Guattari: 'There is no universal capitalism, there is no capitalism in itself; capitalism is at the crossroads of all kinds of formations, it is neocapitalism by nature' (1987: 20). In *Anti-Oedipus*, Deleuze and Guattari indicate how capitalism is able to perform this integrative function:

> Capitalism is in fact born of the encounter of two sorts of flows: the decoded flows of production in the form of money-capital, and the decoded flows of labor in the form of the 'free worker'. Hence, unlike previous social machines, the capitalist machine is incapable of providing a code that will apply to the whole of the social field. By substituting money for the very notion of a code, it has created an axiomatic of abstract quantities that keeps moving further and further in the direction of the deterritorialization of the socius' (Deleuze and Guattari 1983: 33).

10. There have, of course, long been economic world-systems, as Andre Gunder Frank, Christopher Chase-Dunn, Janet Abu-Lughod and others have pointed out. My claim that capitalism in its current dispensation takes the form of a meta-accord is not about the world-system as such, but rather about its present manifestation, that is, the way or ways in which the meta-accord that is capital gets to establish a world-system with a fundamentally isomorphic structure, something that did not occur with previous world-systems.

11. Strictly speaking, this is Lautréamont's definition of beauty, but since Lautréamont is explicit in maintaining that all thought is premised on an ontology of 'objective chance', it is necessarily also his definition of reality.

12. Cage thus describes his work as 'music without measurements, sound passing through circumstances'. See Cage 1969: 22. Slavoj Žižek has, I believe, made a similar point about divergence and incompossibility when he says that many different sets can in principle be derived from the same collection. See Žižek 1997. Several sentences in this section are reproduced from my 'on Producing' (1995).

13. Elsewhere Deleuze says that: '[T]he Anomalous is always at the frontier, on the borders of a band or multiplicity; it is part of the latter, but is already making it pass into another multiplicity, it makes it become, it traces a line-between' (see Deleuze and Parnet 1987: 42).

14. In an interview on Foucault and his work, Deleuze refers to this movement between outside and inside as something which involves 'subjectless individuations' (see 'A Portrait of Foucault', in Deleuze 1995: 116). These 'subjectless individuations' are, of course, a defining characteristic of the anomalous. I am almost certainly going further than Deleuze and Guattari in my use of the anomalous. They take this category to be a defining feature of the 'line of flight', which is present wherever lines of flight are to be found. In the account given here, I take the anomalous to be pervasively present in the epoch of the breakdown or dissolution of 'transcendental' accords, that is, I view it as the operation of a currently regnant capitalist cultural logic. This, however, is entirely compatible with the positions set out in *Capitalism and Schizophrenia*. In Deleuze and Parnet, Deleuze says:

> The state can no longer . . . rely on the old forms like the police, armies, bureaucracies, collective installations, schools, families . . . It is not surprising that all kinds of minority questions – linguistic, ethnic, regional, about sex, or youth – resurge not only as archaisms, but in up-to-date revolutionary forms which call once more into question in an entirely immanent manner both the global economy of the machine and the assemblages of national States . . . Everything is played in uncertain games, 'front to front, back to back, back to front . . .' (Deleuze in Deleuze and Parnet 1987: 146–7)

15. For his account of simulation, see Deleuze (1968: 66ff.), and (1990: 253–79). Deleuze's theory of simulation is complex, but its gist can be stated thus: if, contrary to Plato and the tradition of philosophy derived from him, there can be no primacy of a putative original over its copy, of a model over its representations, so that there can be no basis for differentiating between 'good' original and 'bad' copy, then everything is itself a 'copy-original' – it is an 'original' of itself, or rather, its 'origin' is a copy or 'shadow' of itself. In the absence of any possibility of separating copies from ostensible originals, each thing, in simulation, is thus an absolute singularity. Everything is different from everything else, and this in turn is the basis of multiplicity. In this and the next few paragraphs I have taken several sentences from my 'Reinventing' (1994).

16. To quote Deleuze and Guattari:

> If Marx demonstrated the functioning of capitalism as an axiomatic, it was above all in the famous chapter on the tendency of the rate of profit to fall. Capitalism is indeed an axiomatic, because it has no laws but immanent ones. It would like for us to believe that it confronts the limits of the Universe, the extreme limit of resources and energy. But all it confronts are its own limits (the periodic depreciation of existing capital); all it repels or displaces are its own limits (the formation of new capital, in new industries with a high rate

of profit). This is the history of oil and nuclear power. And it does both at once: capitalism confronts its own limits and simultaneously displaces them, setting them down again farther along. (Deleuze and Guattari 1987: 463)

17. Capitalism, by removing the conditions that enable 'transcendental' accords to maintain themselves, in the process promotes a cultural logic that favours the description over the concept, and this cultural logic also contains within itself propensities that weaken or obviate the dichotomy between the individual and the collective, and thus creates the conditions for the emergence of a culture that, with the supersession of capitalist 'non-being', will allow singularity potentially to become generalised as a cultural principle.

18. The sketchy account of singularity given here is taken from the much more substantial treatment in Giorgio Agamben (1993). Several sentences in this section are reproduced from my 'The Epochality' (1997).

19. A point well-made in Daniel Lazare (1996) and (2001).

20. For discussion, see Bob Jessop (1997).

21. This formulation is owed to Jessop (1997: 574–5).

22. Samir Amin has argued that only in this way can the system of a globalised economic polarisation be neutralised and ultimately dismantled. See Amin (1990 and 2000).

# Chapter 4

# The Becoming-Minoritarian of Europe

*Rosi Braidotti*

No notion is more contested in European politics and social theory than the sociopolitical space of the European Union (EU). The EU is a molar political entity that has become an internationally significant economic player, but it also offers a critical political vision that universalises its own concept of 'civilisation'. As a progressive project, the EU constitutes an alternative to the aggressive neo-liberalism of the USA on a number of key issues (privacy; telecommunication; genetically modified food and the environment) and as an advocate of human rights and world peace. It is a project that is faced with a diverse set of contradictions.

On the one hand, Europe celebrates transnational spaces, but on the other hand, it is witness to the resurgence of hyper-nationalisms occurring at the micro-level. The cosmopolitan global city and paranoid Fortress Europe stand face-to-face as opposite sides of the same coin. In an attempt to bypass the binary of global versus local, and so as to destabilise the established definitions of European identity, I will narrate an alternative vision of Europe's 'becoming-minoritarian'. The decline of Eurocentrism will be taken as a premise that points to a qualitative shift in our collective sense of identity. Contained within the progressive project of the EU are the seeds for a post-nationalist sociopolitical space, which is to say, putting it in more Deleuzian terms, the possibility of a radical 'becoming-minoritarian' is immanent to the sociopolitical space of the EU.

As part of both the de-Nazification and the economic reconstruction of Europe following World War II, the common European space was created, but this move was not immune to resistance at the national level. In fact, the notion of a common Europe continues to encounter enormous resistance (Morin 1987; Spinelli 1992). Several progressive political movements today, ranging from the Green Party to the European Social Forum and the feminists, give top priority to a post-Eurocentric vision of the

European Union. Politically speaking, the nationalist and xenophobic tenets of the Right vehemently oppose the EU, producing a wave of paranoid fear that is both anti-European and racist to the core (Hall 1987 and 1990). In this way, the EU project is caught in the schizoid political economy of postmodernity, paradoxically positioned between an increasingly globalised perspective and an equally intense fragmentation (Appadurai 1994). Globalisation enacts both a profound cultural and economic homogenisation and an extreme concentration of power in very few hands. Thus, a new, allegedly post-nationalist identity coexists with the return of micro-nationalisms, xenophobia, racism and anti-Semitism (Benhabib 1999). Common European citizenship and currency coexist with increasing internal fragmentation and regionalism. The disintegration of the former Soviet empire simultaneously marks the triumph of the capitalist market economy and the return of ethnic wars of an only apparently archaic kind. The 'new' Europe is therefore trying to steer its course in the midst of complex and contradictory co-ordinates.

Yet strong opposition to the EU can also be heard from a largely nostalgic Left. The cosmopolitan tradition of socialism militates against the European dimension: solidarity with the third-world always carries a politically correct consensus, whereas an interest in European matters is dismissed as narcissistic and vain. Advocating a project concerned with strengthening international working-class solidarity, the European Left is slow to understand the non-dialectical, non-topological and non-teleological and hence schizophrenic nature of advanced capitalism (Deleuze and Guattari 1977 and 1987).[1]

## De-centring Europe

Historically, continental philosophy – prior to and including post-structuralism – is connected to the issue of European identity and 'civilisation'. Since the end of the nineteenth and the start of the twentieth century, the 'crisis' of European philosophy has both reflected and highlighted larger sociopolitical issues related to the geopolitical status of Europe, colonialism and a growing sense of crisis around European identity.[2] According to an entire generation of post-structuralists – Foucault, Deleuze, Derrida and Irigaray – especially after World War II the crisis of philosophical humanism historically coincides with the decline of Europe as an imperial world power. Recently, wise old men like Habermas and Derrida along with progressive spirits like Balibar have taken the lead, stressing the advantages of de-centring Europe as a socopolitical laboratory so as to develop a post-nationalist sense of citizenship.

As a world power Europe practised a form of universalism concomitantly excluding difference. According to a post-structuralist frame of reference these constitutive 'others' are the specular complement of the subject of modernity. They are the woman, the ethnic or racialised other, and the natural environment. Respectively, they constitute the second sex or sexual complement of Man; the coloured, racialised or marked 'other' that allows the Europeans to universalise their whiteness as the defining human trait; and the environment against which technology is pitched and developed. These 'others' are of crucial importance to the constitution of the identity of the universal called Europe. One cannot move without the other, therefore the redefinition of European identity intrinsically poses the question of the social and discursive status of 'difference', both in the sense of sexual difference and that of ethnic diversity.[3]

The project of European unification involves a shift in consciousness that in turn expresses the critique of the self-appointed missionary role of Europe as the alleged centre of the world. A post-nationalist vision of Europe entails a process of becoming-minoritarian, one that works to promote the deterritorialisation of the false universalism underpinning European identity, so as to propose a post-nationalist vision of Europe.[4] As a post-nationalist project, the EU will, ideally, undergo a change in consciousness, moving towards a more accountable eco-philosophy of European multiple belonging. The opposite of the grandiose and aggressive universalism of the past, being both a situated and accountable perspective, this image of a post-nationalist Europe turns our collective memory to the service of a new political and ethical project. It looks to the future confidently and to the past without nostalgia. As such it is a creative gesture, producing horizons of hope and, simultaneously, constructing the possibility of a future that is alive to difference and change.

One concrete example of this process is the rethinking of 'whiteness'. For people who inhabit the European region, the present is marked to an unprecedented degree by transculturality, migration and flows of people. We are perhaps witnessing the end of European cultural homogeneity. As Michael Walzer (1992) has argued, cultural homogeneity is the foundational political European myth in much the same way as multiculturalism is a prevailing American myth. Of course, European history at any point in time provides ample evidence to the contrary: waves of migrations from the east and the south make a mockery of claims to European ethnic or cultural homogeneity, while the persistent presence of Jewish and Muslim citizens in Europe challenges the traditional European identification with Christianity. Nonetheless, the myth of cultural homogeneity is crucial to the tale of European nationalism.

Today these myths are being exposed and exploded as questions concerning entitlement and agency seep to the surface. Thus, the EU is faced with the following issue: can one be European, Black and Muslim? One of the radical implications of the project of the EU is the possibility of giving a specific location, and consequently historical specificity to anti-racist whites. Now, the question itself can racialise our location. This is quite a feat because until recently only white supremacists, Nazi skinheads and other neo-fascist groups actually put forward a theory of biological and cultural essentialism on the inherent qualities of white people. Apart from this, whiteness was quite simply invisible, an unseen factor by whites. It took the work of black writers and thinkers to expose whiteness as a political issue. Located in the lily-white purity of our universalist fantasy, disembodied and disembedded, 'we' actually thought we had no colour.

In his analysis of the representation of whiteness as an ethnic category in mainstream films, Richard Dyer (1997) argues that, being the norm, whiteness is invisible, as if this is natural, inevitable or the ordinary way to do things. The source of the representational power of white lies in the propensity to be everything and nothing at the same time, whereas black, of course, is always marked off as *a* colour. The effect of this structured invisibility and the process of naturalising whiteness is that it masks itself as a 'colourless multicolouredness'. White contains all other colours. White is the void that lies at the heart of a system, defining the contours of both social and symbolic visibility in regimes of colonial domination. For Deleuze and Guattari (1977 and 1987) no dominant notion – such as masculinity or race – can have a positive definition, that is to say, the prerogative of being dominant is that a concept defined oppositionally produces the marks of oppression and/or marginalisation. The superiority of the dominant is registered in its ability to position the other as inferior, without seeming to do so. The dominant concept is always an 'invisible hand'. We tend to perceive it as a comparatively benign point of reference. Its function appears to be nothing other than as a term to index and patrol access and participation to entitlements and powers. Thus, the invisibility of dominant concepts is also the expression of their insubstantiality – which makes them all them more effective against the countless others on whose structural exclusion their power rests.

The immediate consequence of this invisibility is not just political, but methodological as well. Whiteness, like all molar categories, is hard to grasp critically; it tends to break down into ethnic and nationalist subcategories: Irishness, Italianness, Jewishness, and so on. It follows therefore, that non-whites have a much clearer perception of whiteness than whites. The reverse, however, is not the case: blacks and other ethnic minorities do not need this specular logic in order to have their own location. Cultural identity, as external and retrospective, tends to be defined by Europeans in the confrontation with other – usually black – peoples. This is similar to the experiences of Irish, Italian and Jewish immigrants in countries like the US, Canada and Australia. Their 'whiteness' emerged oppositionally, as a factor that concomitantly distanced them from natives and blacks. Feminist critics like Frankenberg (1994a and 1994b) and Brodkin Sacks (1994) have provided detailed analyses of this phenomenon of 'whitening' by which Euro-immigrants – especially Jews and Italians – were constructed as 'whitened' citizens in the US. The extent to which this kind of 'whitened' identity is illusory, as much as it is racist, can be seen in how divided the diasporic, Euro-immigrant communities actually are. But all are equally 'whitened' by the gaze of the coloniser who is bent on pitching them against the black population.

By learning to view their subject position as racialised, white people can work towards anti-racist forms of whiteness, or at least anti-racist strategies that deterritorialise whiteness. Interestingly, this strategy carries with it enormous benefit for people currently migrating from the east of Europe. Comparable dynamics are operating within the EU, which result in a new racialised hierarchy that polices access to full EU citizenship. Thus, peoples from the Balkans, or the south-western regions of Europe are considered to be not quite as 'white' as the rest of Europe. The whitening process expands with the new frontiers of the EU pushing outwards the 'illegal others'. But this process quite consciously needs an 'other', a people whose skin is still darker, less white, than the newly anointed. An oriental or eastern ethnic divide is operating which equates EU citizenship with whiteness and Christianity, casting shadows of suspicion on all 'others'. Locations are historicised and situated on contingent foundations that structure one's being-in-the-world, one's social modes of belonging and not belonging. In other words, being diasporic, nomadic, hybrid, or in-between are not equivalent. Sociologically these translate into different structural locations in respect to language, culture, class, labour, access and participation in power (in the broadest sense of the term). The task of the social critic is to make relevant distinctions among these different locations and map points of intersection in order to create a politically invested cartography, identifying a common ground that can be shared by multiply-located subjects committed to constructing new post-national subjectivities and not merely to deconstruction for its own sake. I call this the new materialism of post-humanist subjects. It refers to subjects who are embedded, embodied and accountable, but not territorialised, molarised and unified. It implies, too, a nomadic politics: a politics of affirmative or creative modality. In this way I share the thesis put forward by another Deleuzian philosopher Edouard Glissant (1997). He, too, develops an effective rhizomatic poetics and politics, taking as his point of reference the historical experience and the specific location of Africans and West Indians caught in the transatlantic slave trade. He argues that even an experience as devastating as slavery produces specific forms of knowledge and subjectivisation that transcend the burden of the negative.

There are several important features at stake in Glissant's remarkable position; the first is the primacy of the relation over any of its terms, including the negative ones. A relation functions through the middle, the 'milieu'. Peoples who are culturally and ethnically positioned in the middle – like the Caribbeans or West Indians – have a head start in understanding the crucial importance of the relation. However, they also have a historical legacy of destruction and violence that is hard to transcend insofar as it includes both the erasure of the original culture and the adoption of the colonising culture by force. In response to this ethical and political challenge, Glissant actively theorises the becoming-minoritarian (or rhizomatic) of blacks, Creoles, descendants of slaves and other colonised peoples. This is described as a spiritual and logistical shift in the structure of the subject, one that advances a sense of openness toward both self and other.

Glissant's position includes a sharp critique of Europe, which is based on the ontology of sameness or the rule of one. This includes a dualistic relationship to the rest of the humans. There exists a dominant mode of nomadism in Western culture – in the form of epic journeys of discovery all of which find their historical apogee in colonialism. The power of sameness in the West is best described in terms of monolinguism, or the illusion of a single cultural and linguistic root. In what appears to be a very Deleuzian stance, Glissant plays the rhizome against the root and calls for a global polylinguism. This includes the deconstruction of the hubris of European master cultures and the arrogance with which they consider their languages as the voice of humanity. This universalist pretence is one of the mechanisms supporting colonialism. It also entails the reappraisal of minor languages, dialects and hybrids in a phenomenon that Glissant describes as 'creolisation'.

Glissant offers a striking example of the poetics of relation in his analysis of how the French colonisers spoke their own, 'home grown' dialects – Norman or Breton – rather than the high and noble language of the French nation, in the Caribbean territories. This bastardised language mingles with the local languages creating a crossover between two distinct but analogous forms of linguistic non-purity. Creolisation, therefore, cuts both ways and it differs from the master language in its very structure. The thought of relation as a form of philosophical nomadism stresses the importance of the middle and this shifts our thinking away from concepts of purity, origins and oneness. Glissant defines this productive multiplicity as 'echoes of the world' – modalities that resonate with the vitality of human biodiversity on both a biological and cultural level. These modes reconnect us to the living chaos of the world as living matter in transformation: a dynamic resilient *bios-zoe* force of global creolisation. Glissant captures this vitality and honours it as a poetics, or ethics of rhizomatic interconnections.

Philosophical nomadism pursues the same critique of power as black and post-colonial theories, not in spite, but because of the fact that it is located somewhere else. It addresses in both a critical and creative manner the role of the former 'centre' in redefining power relations. Margins and centre shift and destabilise each other in parallel, albeit dissymmetrical, movements.

As the project for a post-nationalist European Union demonstrates, the challenge is to invoke rhizomatic interventions that destabilise dogmatic, hegemonic, exclusionary power structures lying at the heart of dominant subjectivities and identity formations underpinning these. If we are to move beyond the sociology of labour mobility and the breast-beating of critical thinkers squashed by white guilt, we need to enact a vision of the political subject that encompasses change in the way relations are territorialised along the cultural, linguistic, economic, political and social co-ordinates. The point is not merely to deconstruct identities or loudly proclaim counter-identities but to open up identity to different connections able to produce multiple belongings that in turn precipitate a non-unitary vision of a subject. Such a subject actively constructs itself in a complex and internally contradictory set of social relations. To achieve this, first we need to embrace intensive movements that activate processes of change rather than fixating on essences. This means sociological variables (gender, class, race and ethnicity, age, health) need to be supplemented with a theory of the subject that calls into question the inner fibres of self-production. This requires the desire, ability and courage to sustain multiple belongings in a context that predominantly celebrates and rewards unified identities.

So how does the sociopolitical space of becoming-minoritarian work? This question anticipates a notion of European space of mediation that is an open, multi-layered project, one that has no fixed essence. As

Balibar suggests (2001 and 2002) a space of mediation provides a space of critical resistance to hegemonic identities of all kinds. My own choice to rework whiteness in the era of postmodernity is firstly to situate it in the geohistorical space of Europe and the political project of the EU. This amounts to historicising it and demystifying its allegedly 'natural' location. The next step is to analyse and revisit it critically until it opens onto a new practice of flexible and multi-layered European subjectivity. The third step consists in trying to relocate European identity with the aim of undoing its hegemonic tendencies. I refer to this alternative conception of identity as 'nomadic'. Being a nomadic European subject means to be in transit within different identity-formations, but also to be sufficiently anchored to a historical position so that one can also accept responsibility for the position one takes. The key words here are: 'accountability' and the 'strategic relocation of whiteness'. The privilege that came with white invisibility that was conferred on Europeans and also positioned it as the alleged centre of the world is also dispelled by the 'becoming-minoritarian of Europe'. By assuming full responsibility for the partial perspective of its own location the concept of a minoritarian European space allows for an alternative political vision to surface, one that acknowledges the scattered hegemonies of a globalised world no longer dominated by European power alone.

## Complex Shifting Locations, Not Multitudes

Recently, the issue of Europe as an alternative political model has also become central to Antonio Negri (Friese, Negri and Wagner 2002). Although in many senses Negri's position differs from that of Deleuze, there are significant points of comparison between the two. Negri combines a monistic Spinozist political economy with a post-Marxian brand of materialist analysis of labour conditions under advanced capitalism. Like Deleuze, Negri searches for a productive space of becoming-revolutionary, yet he goes on to locate the motor of world resistance in his concept of the 'multitude'. He also singles out the new EU as the political arena where the – allegedly rhizomic – politics of the multitude confront the gravitational pull of a globalised empire.

The multitude is, in fact, the appointed alternative to global capitalism. I share Negri's normative injunction, namely that of creating social horizons of political hope, but I cannot fully share his zealous conviction that this is the only, or necessarily revolutionary option sanctioned by history and the will of the multitude. His analysis of the contemporary political situation relies on the becoming-woman of labour and the renewed emphasis on the materiality of corporeal bodies. This constitutes a 'micro-political' form of activism, one that resonates with Guattari's notion of transversal subjectivity. This notion is crucial to Negri's work with Michael Hardt and their critique of globalisation. Together they argue that in advanced capitalism, the priority of material labour over immaterial labour is steadily being eroded. And though they recognise that material forms of labour are statistically still in the majority, they argue that immaterial labour is rapidly assuming the position of cultural dominance. The 'information society' is based on immaterial labour: that is labour which prioritises the 'content' of our heads rather than the muscle-strength of our bodies or tactile skill of our hands. This position also gives weight to the production and reproduction of affects, like caring and the creation once more of fading community connections. Historically, though, the latter has been the province of women's work, yet now it constitutes a central piece of capitalist production. Caring and affective labour are both material and immaterial; they simultaneously produce communities and the regulatory effects of biopower.

Hardt and Negri stress the immaterial and affective nature of the labour force; this being one that trades in phonetic skills, linguistic ability and proper accents services, as well as requiring attention, concentration and great care. However, they neglect to consider the gendered political structures of advanced capitalism or the contradictions inherent to the process of becoming-woman of labour. To illustrate this shortcoming in their argument let us consider a new category in the political economy: the new digital proletariat. The most striking example of this is provided by the workers in call centres that process phone enquiries from locations miles away from the callers' homes. Denounced strongly by Arundhati Roy (2001), these 'call centres' or data outsourcing agencies are a multi-billion dollar industry that have attracted a great deal of critical attention both in mainstream and in alternative media.

Roy (2001) describes in detail the 'call centre College' on the outskirts of Delhi in a suburb called Gurgaon. Here, hundreds of Indian graduates are trained to perform the backroom operations of transnational companies. They answer queries on a wide range of subjects ranging from car rentals and credit card inquiries to plane tickets. The key is never to let the caller suspect that their call is being processed in Delhi. Thus, the students have to learn to speak English with the appropriate and expected accents – generally Australian, British or American – they need to read the local newspapers to be up to date on small items of news and, of course, they need to erase their own identity and change names in order to 'pass'. Whilst certainly reminiscent of those age-old problems of working-class exploitation, this kind of labour presents a whole new kind of labour exploitation.

In a series of visual installations, the Raqs Media Collective (Biemann 2003) presented an incisive critique of the specific forms of simulation embodied in these call centres, namely the erasure of their remoteness from the callers' homes. They cite the example of a woman called Sunita who is known on the phone as Sandra. Replying to phone enquiries Sunita simulates Sandra who is supposed to live in Minneapolis, US. This strategy of simulation is not mere impersonation as there is no visual or physical contact between the parties involved. Nor can it be seen as a form of identification, as the worker need not feel or experience herself as being from a different culture/nation in order to fulfil her contractual obligations. It is more of a logistical issue: working in a call-centre is a matter of carefully orchestrated simulation. As such, it requires a radical 'othering' of oneself, or a form of schizophrenia that entails the reification of the worker's own life-world. Not unlike characters in a chat room, the call-centre worker performs her labour market persona in such a way as to emerge from the process neither wiser, nor enriched (especially considering that wages in the developing world call centres are paid one tenth of their Western counterparts), but rather firmly located as: 'the emerging digital proletariat that underpins the new world economy' (Biemann 2003: 85).

The kind of cultural cross-dressing performed by call-centre digital proletarians is neither the creative mimesis of strategic repetitions, nor is it the destabilising effect of queer identity politics. It is simply today's variation on the theme of what Deleuze and Guattari have identified as capitalism's demand that the worker be pre-mutilated so as fit into the global marketing of both material commodities and of Western lifestyles, cultures and accents. This *tour de force* by the digital workers of the new global economy rests on an acute and explicit awareness of one's location in space and time. It is a territorial issue and as such it raises serious questions about border-crossings, nomadic shifts and paths of deterritorialisation. It is quite clear that the allegedly ethereal nature of cyberspace and the flow of mobility it sustains is fashioned by the material labour of women and men from areas of the world thought to be peripheral. This space of fluctuation is highly racialised and sexualised. A new 'feminisation' and 'racialisation' of the virtual workforce has taken place, which amounts to the deterioration of rights and conditions.

Although Hardt and Negri theorise the schizophrenic dimension of capitalism, they fail to practise what they preach. Their vision of the allegedly ongoing revolutionary process, which they express in a euphoric and at times hyperbolic language, contradicts the conceptual premises of their thought. Theirs remains a highly abstract project, one that fails to ground itself in the embedded and embodied brands of materialism that feminist theory has developed. The process of becoming-revolutionary is a rather ascetic and humble process: an art or a practice. There is no over-arching meta-narrative of one global multitude in either feminist notions of situated knowledges (Haraway 1988) or in Deleuze's philosophy of radical immanence.

## Becoming Ethical

What is the ethical import of the process of multiple belongings and a becoming-nomadic whereby affects take centre stage? Let us begin by moving this question away from Negri's metaphysics of labour towards Deleuze's philosophy of radical immanence. Becoming-political involves a radical repositioning or intensive transformation on the part of subjects who want to become-minoritarian in a productive and affirmative manner. It is clear that this shift requires changes that are neither simple, nor self-evident. These changes mobilise the affect of the subjects involved and can be seen as a process of transforming negative passions into affirmative ones. Fear, anxiety and nostalgia are clear examples of the negative emotions involved in the project of detaching ourselves from familiar forms of identity. Achieving a post-nationalist sense of European identity requires the disidentification from established, nation-bound points of reference. Such an enterprise inevitably entails a sense of loss as cherished habits of thought and representation are relinquished.

The beneficial side effects of this process are unquestionable (as I have already enumerated above) and in some way they compensate for the pain loss produces. Thus, the critical relocation of whiteness can produce an affirmative, situated anti-racist European subject-position. In a more Spinozist vein, it also produces a more adequate cartography of our real-life conditions, free from delusions of grandeur. This mature and sober-ing experience is, however, also an enriching and positive one. Migrants, exiles and refugees all have first-hand experience of the pain and loss felt as a result of being uprooted and forced into dis-identifying with familiar identities. Diasporic subjects of all kinds express the same sense of wounding. Multi-locality is the affirmative translation of this negative sense of loss. Following Glissant, the becoming-nomadic points to a process of positive transformation of pain of loss, turning it into the active production of multiple forms of belonging and complex allegiances. What is lost in the sense of fixed origins is gained in an increased desire to belong, in a multiple rhizomic manner that overcomes the bilateralism of binary identity formations.

The qualitative leap through pain, across mourning landscapes of nostalgia, is a gesture of active creation, one that affirms new ways of belonging. It is a fundamental reconfiguration of our way of being in the world that acknowledges the pain of loss whilst moving beyond this pain. This is the defining moment of becoming-ethical: the movement across and beyond pain, loss and negative passions. The real aim of the process is to overcome the stultifying effects of passivity that pain can produce. In this way, the internal disarray, fracture and pain provide the ethical conditions for transformation. Clearly, this is an antithesis of the Kantian moral imperative to avoid pain, or to view pain as the obstacle to moral behaviour. Nomadic ethics is not about avoiding pain, rather it is concerned with transcending the resignation and passivity that ensue from being hurt, lost and dispossessed. One has to become ethical as opposed to just applying moral rules and protocols as a form of self-protection. Transformations express the affirmative power of life as the vitality of *bios-zoe*, the very opposite of morality.

Edgar Morin also acknowledges the importance of pain in stirring forth ethical and political consciousness (Morin 1987). He describes his 'becoming-European' as a double affect: the first concerns a disappointment with the unfulfilled promises of Marxism. The second is compassion for the uneasy, struggling and marginal position of post-war Europe squashed between the US and the USSR. The pain of this awareness that Europe was ill-loved and a castaway: *'une pauvre vieille petite chose'* ('a poor old little thing') (Morin 1987: 23) results in a new kind of bonding and a renewed sense of care and accountability. The sobering experience – the humble and productive recognition of loss – has to do with self-representation. Established mental habits, images and terminology railroad us backwards toward established ways of thinking about ourselves. Traditional modes of representation are legal forms of addiction. To change them is not unlike undertaking a detoxification cure. A great deal of courage and creativity is needed to develop forms of representation that do justice to the complexities of a subject. We already live and inhabit social reality in ways that surpass tradition: we move about in the flow of current social transformations, in hybrid, multicultural, polyglot, post-identity spaces of becoming (Braidotti 2002). We fail, however, to bring them into adequate representation. There is a shortage on the part of our social imaginary, a deficit of representational power that underscores the political timidity of the European unification process. Some of this difficulty is contingent and may be linked to the lack of a European public space, as Habermas suggests (1992); or the lack of visionary leadership among politicians, as Mény put it (2000). In any case, European issues fail to trigger our imagination.

The real issue, however, is conceptual: how do we develop a new post-nationalist European social imaginary through the pain of dis-identification and loss? Given that identifications constitute an inner scaffolding that supports one's sense of identity, how do changes of this magnitude take place? Shifting an imaginary is not like casting away a used garment; it is more akin to shedding an old skin. Whilst it may happen more frequently at a molecular level, when it occurs in the social arena it tends to be a painful experience. This is a collective activity, a group project that connects active conscious and desiring citizens. It points towards a virtual, but no less real, destination – a post-nationalist Europe – without being utopian. As a project it is historically grounded, socially embedded and already partly actualised in the joint endeavours of those who are currently working towards it. If this is in any way utopian, it is only in the sense of the positive affects that are mobilised in the process: the necessary dose of imagination, dreamlike vision and bonding, all of which a social project needs in order to advance.

Feminism is a significant example of this kind of transformative political project: feminists take a critical distance from the dominant social institutions of femininity and masculinity, and choose instead to relate these to other variables, such as ethnicity, race and class. Feminist theory has addressed the issue of the reconstruction of the social imaginary through the emphasis it has placed both on identification (as a factor in identity formation) and dis-identification (strategically using this to raise consciousness). However, it has mostly achieved this within a psychoanalytic framework, choosing to emphasise the imaginary as the process of linguistic mediation. This refers to a system of representation by which a subject gets captured by ruling social and cultural formations: legal attachments to particular identities, images and terminologies. For Althusser and Lacan, these are governed by a symbolic system as it is represented in the Law of the Phallus. The interaction or mediation between the self and these imaginary institutions provides the motor for the process of becoming-subject. Needless to say, for Lacan this process labours under the burden of negativity, as lack, mourning and melancholia. This is also a legacy from Hegel, reducing the subject to a process of being-subjected-to, for instance in the negative sense of power as *potestas*.

The post-structuralist generation, starting with Foucault, challenged both the negativity and the static nature of the Lacanian master code on which all forms of mediation are supposed to hinge. The binary opposition of self versus society is too narrow to account for the complex workings of powering our culture. A thick and highly dynamic web of power effects is the factor through which self and society are mutually shaped by one another. The choreography of constraints and entitlements, controls and desire is the hard core of power. This core is devoid of any substantial essence and is a force, or activity – a verb that is, not a noun. Power as positive or *potentia* is crucial in forming the subject as an entity enmeshed in a network of inter-related social and discursive effects; here biopower, or the power over living matter, is one good example of this. For Deleuze and Guattari, as for Foucault, the system of mediation is not merely linguistic, it is also material.

What might be termed Deleuze's 'social imaginary' (setting aside for the moment the fact that he rejects the Lacanian concept of the imaginary, as well as its Althusserian inflection) would not be postulated along linguistic lines at all – it would be like a prism, or a fractal that disintegrates the unity of vision into bundles of multi-directional perceptive tools. Deleuze relies on Spinoza's idea of 'collective imaginings' (Gatens and Lloyd 1999) to elucidate the following important idea: 'social imaginary' is ultimately an image of thought. That is to say, it is a habit that captures and blocks alternative ways of thinking about ourselves and the environment. Collectively, we can empower some of these alternative becomings. This being is a collective and affective process. European post-nationalist identity is such a project: political at heart, it has a strong ethical pull made up of conviction, vision and desire. As a project it requires active participation and a striving toward what we are capable of becoming more than defining who we are. This liberatory potential is directly proportional to the desire and collective affects it mobilises. The becoming-minoritarian of Europe actively experiments with different ways of inhabiting social space.

Far from being the prelude to a neo-universal stance, or its dialectical pluralist counterpart, or even the relativistic acceptance of all and any locations, the project of the-becoming-minoritarian of Europe is an ethical transformation by a former centre that chooses the path of immanent change. Through the pain of loss and disenchantment, just like 'post-Woman women' have moved towards a redefinition of their 'being-gendered-in-the-world', 'post-nationalist Europeans' may be able to find enough self-respect to become the subjects of multiple ecologies of belonging.

# References

Appadurai, A. (1994), 'Disjuncture and Difference in the Global Cultural Economy', in P. Williams and L. Chrisman (eds) (1994), *Colonial Discourse and Post-Colonial Theory*, New York: Columbia University Press, pp. 324–39.

Balibar, E. (2001), *Nous, citoyens d'Europe? Les frontiers, l'état, le peuple*, Paris: Editions de la Découverte.

Balibar, E. (2002), *Politics and the Other Scene*, London: Verso.

Benhabib, S. (1999), 'Citizen, Resident and Alien in a Changing World: Political Membership in a Global Era', *Social Research* 66 (3): 709–44.

Benhabib, S. (2002), *The Claims of Culture*, Princeton: Princeton University Press.

Bhabha, H. (1994), *The Location of Culture*, London and New York: Routledge.

Biemann, U. (ed.) (2003), *Geography and the Politics of Mobility*, Vienna: General Foundation.

Brah, A. (1993), 'Re-Framing Europe: En-Gendered Racisms, Ethnicities and Nationalisms in Contemporary Western Europe', *Feminist Review* 45 (autumn): 9–28.

Brah, A. (1996), *Cartographies of the Diaspora*, London and New York: Routledge.

Braidotti, R. (1994), *Nomadic Subjects*, New York: Columbia University Press.

Braidotti, R. (2002), *Metamorphoses*, Cambridge: Polity Press.

Braidotti, R. (2003a), 'L"Europe peut-elle nous faire rêver", interview with A. Corsani, *Multitudes Europe Constituante?*' 14: 97–109.

Braidotti, R. (2003b). 'La penseé féministe nomade', *Multitudes 12, féminismes, queer, multitudes*: 27–47.

Brodkin Sacks, K. (1994), 'How did Jews Become White Folks?', in S. Gregory and R. Sanjek (eds) (1994), *Race*, New Brunswick: Rutgers University Press, pp. 78–102.

Deleuze, G. and Guattari, F. (1977), *Anti-Oedipus. Capitalism and Schizophrenia*, trans. R. Hurley, M. Seem and H. R. Lane, New York: Viking Press/ Richard Seaver.

Deleuze, G. and Guattari, F. (1987), *A Thousand Plateaus: Capitalism and Schizophrenia*, trans. B. Massumi, Minneapolis: University of Minnesota Press.

Dyer, R. (1997), *White*, London and New York: Routledge.

Foucault, M. (1977), *Surveiller et Punir*, Paris: Minuit.

Frankenberg, R. (1994a), 'Introduction: Points of Origin, Points of Departure', in R. Frankenberg (1994a), *White Women, Race Matters*, Minneapolis: University of Minnesota Press, pp. 1–22.

Frankenberg, R (1994b), 'Questions of Culture and Belonging', in R. Frankenberg (1994b), *White Women, Race Matters*, Minneapolis: University of Minnesota Press, pp. 191–235.

Friese, H., Negri, A. and Wagner, P. (2002), *Europa Politica. Ragioni di una Necessita*, Roma: Manifestolibri.

Gatens, M. and Lloyd, G. (1999), *Collective Imaginings: Spinoza, Past and Present*, London and New York: Routledge.

Glissant, E. (1997), *Poetics of Relation*, trans. B. Wing, Ann Arbor: University of Michigan Press.

Habermas, J. (1992), 'Citizenship and National Identity: Some Reflections on the Future of Europe', *Praxis International*, (April) 12 (1): 1–34.

Hall, S. (1987), 'Minimal Selves', in S. Hall (1987), *Identity: The Real Me*, ICA Documents, London, pp. 44–6.

Hall, S. (1990), 'Cultural Identity and Diaspora', in J. Rutherford (ed.) (1990), *Identity: Community, Culture, Difference*, London: Lawrence and Wishart, pp. 222–37.

Hall, S. (1992), 'What is this "Black" in Black Popular Culture?', in Gina Dent (ed.) (1992), *Black Popular Culture*, Seattle: Boy Press.

Haraway, D. (1988), 'Situated Knowledges: The Science Question in Feminism as a Site of Discourse on the Privilege of Partial Perspective', *Feminist Studies* 14 (3): 575–99.

Harding, S. (1993), *The 'Racial' Economy of Science*, Bloomington: Indiana University Press.

Hardt, M. and Negri, A. (2000), *Empire*, Cambridge: Harvard University Press.

Lutz, H., Yuval-Davis, N. and Phoenix, A. (eds) (1996), *Crossfires. Nationalism, Racism and Gender in Europe*, London: Pluto Press.

Mény, Y. (2000), '*Tra Utopia e realta*'. *Una Costituzione per l 'Europa*, Firenze: Possigli Editore.

Morin, E. (1987), *Penser l'Europe*, Paris: Gallimard.

Morrison, T. (1992), *Playing in the Dark. Whiteness and the Literary Imagination*, Cambridge: Harvard University Press.

Regulska, J. (1998), 'The New "Other" European woman', in V. Ferreira, T. Tavares and S. Portugal (eds) (1988), *Shifting Bonds, Shifting Bounds. Women, Mobility and Citizenship in Europe*, Oeiras: Celta Editora, pp. 41–58.

Roy, A. (2001), *Power Politics*, Cambridge: South End Press.

Spinelli, A. (1992), *Diario europeo*, Bologna: Il Mulino.

Spivak, G. C. (1987), *In Other Worlds: Essays in Cultural Politics*, London: Methuen.

Walzer, M (1992), *What it means to be an American*, New York: Marsilio.

Yuval-Davis, N. and Anthias F. (eds) (1989), *Woman–Nation–State*, London: Macmillan.

## Notes

1. More recently, however, the issue of European politics has begun to receive a new lease on life, through political movements like the European Social Forum and the anti-Iraq war movement along with intellectual interventions from the likes of Balibar, Meny, Negri, Passerini and others.
2. Nietzsche and Freud, then Husserl and Fanon and later Adorno and the Frankfurt school are evidence of this trend.
3. I have analysed the political status of otherness in *Transpositions. On Nomadic Ethics* (Cambridge: Polity Press, forthcoming in February 2006).
4. The work of post-colonial and anti-racist feminist thinkers on power, difference and the politics of location, all of whom are familiar with the European situation, helps illuminate these paradoxes in contemporary Europe (Spivak 1987; Hall 1990 and 1992; Brah 1993 and 1996; Harding 1993; Lutz et al. 1996; Yuval-Davis and Anthias 1989).

# Chapter 5
# Borderlines

## Verena Andermatt Conley

In their dialogues and collaborations, Gilles Deleuze and Félix Guattari enquire of the nature of borders. They summon principles of inclusion and exclusion associated with borderlines. They eschew expressions built on the polarities of 'either . . . or' and in their own diction replace binary constructions with the conjunctive 'and'. Furthermore, in 'Rhizome,' the introduction to *A Thousand Plateaus*, they argue for rhizomatic connections – fostered in language by 'and . . . and . . . and' – to replace what they call the arborescent model of the ubiquitous Western tree (Deleuze and Guattari 1987). In constant movement, the tissues and tendrils of rhizomes call attention to the horizontal surfaces of the world in which they proliferate. They bring to their observer a new sense of space that is seen not as a background but a shape that, with the rhizome, moves and forever changes. In the field of play Deleuze and Guattari often produce hybrid, even viral connections and downplay the presence of genealogies conveyed in the figure of the tree bearing a stock-like trunk. Rhizomatic connections form open territories that are not constricted by the enclosing frame of a rigid borderline.

In the same breath the two philosophers argue for 'smooth' spaces of circulation. They take a critical view of 'striated' spaces, replete with barriers and borders that are part of an 'arborescent' mentality. Striated spaces cross-hatched by psychic or real borderlines drawn by the state (social class, race, ethnicities) or by institutions (family, school), prevent the emergence of new ways of thinking. Crucial, Deleuze and Guattari declare, is the mental and social construction of new territories and the undoing of inherited barriers. Institutional, familial and even psychoanalytical striations that impede a person's mobility in mental and physical spheres need to be erased or, at least, drawn with broken lines. When guilt is at the basis of the unconscious, productivity and creativity are diminished. Movement is also arrested wherever the state erects barriers between social classes, races and sexes.

To facilitate connections and erase mental or physical borders, Deleuze and Guattari want to do away with the state as well as its institutions. It is as anarchists of sorts and with an insistence on aesthetic paradigms that Deleuze and Guattari argue for making connections and for an ongoing smoothing of striated spaces. In the pages to follow, I will argue that today the problem of borders and barriers is as acute as ever. I will probe how Deleuze and Guattari's findings on rhizomes and smooth spaces elaborated in a post-1968, European, context might work today in a changed world-space. Is the struggle still between a paternal, bourgeois state and its subjects? Are the state and its institutions still targeted in the same way? Is the undoing of the subject – often through aesthetics – still valid, or is there a need for a more situated subject? We will first rehash the Deleuzian concepts of rhizome and smooth space before investigating whether and how these concepts are operative in the contemporary world.

Since 1968, the world has undergone many changes. Over the last few decades, decolonisation, transportation and electronic revolutions have transformed the world. They have led to financial and population flows. Financial flows seem to be part of a borderless world. Today, human migrations occur on all continents. They are producing multiple crossings of external borders that in many places have resulted in local resistance and, in reaction, to the erection of more internal borders that inflect new striated spaces in the form of racism and immigration policy. The ultimate goal for the utopian thinker espousing the cause of rhizomatic thinking is smooth space that would entail the erasure of all borders and the advent of a global citizenry living in ease and without the slightest conflict over religion or ideology. In the transitional moment in which we find ourselves arguing for smooth space can easily lead to a non-distinction between alternative spaces in which goods and currencies circulate to the detriment of the world at large.

To account for the transformation specifically of the state and its subjects in a global world, I will argue by way of recent writings by Etienne Balibar for the continued importance of rhizomatic connectivity and also for a qualified notion of smooth space. Striated spaces will have to be continually smoothed so that national borders would not simply encircle a territory. Borders would have to be made more porous and nationality disconnected from citizenship so as to undo striated space inside the state by inventing new ways of being in common. Such a rethinking of borders would lead to further transformations by decoupling the nation from the state. It would open the possibility of – rhizomatic – connections and new spaces. It would produce new hybrids everywhere without simply a 'withering away of the state' as advocated by Deleuze and Guattari. Currently, subjects (defined as humans who are *assuettis* [subjected] to paternal state power) also want to be citizens (who can individually and collectively define the qualities of their *habitus* or environment). Yet, the latter are still part of the state. They are not yet entirely global, transnational citizens or cyber-citizens. While information networks seem to operate like rhizomes, it is of continued importantance to retain the notion of state but to define it with more porous, connective borderlines so as ultimately to disconnect citizens from nationality.

Deleuze and Guattari figure with other philosophers, anthropologists or sociologists who, following 1968, pay renewed attention to space. Their focus on space reappears at the very time Cartesian philosophies undergo radical changes due to the acceleration of new technologies and rapid globalisation.[1] Many thinkers – Henri Lefebvre, Michel de Certeau, Jean Baudrillard, Paul Virilio – condemn what they perceive as the increasing encroachment of technologies that quickly replace more traditional ways of being in the world. People who find themselves out of synch with their environment urge recourse to the body and new ways of using language. Deleuze and Guattari insert themselves into that line of thinking. Their criticism of the static order is twofold. They criticise an inherited spatial model defined by vertical orderings that has dominated the West. In that model, space was considered to be pre-existing. It became a simple décor for human action. Deleuze and Guattari propose not only a criticism of the static model but also invent an entirely new way of thinking space. They propose a more horizontal – and, paradoxically, if seemingly two-dimensional, even more spatial – thinking of the world in terms of rhizomatic lines and networks. In accordance with Deleuze and Guattari's way of thinking through connections, the two regimes always coexist in an asymmetrical relation. They can never be entirely separated or opposed.

In 'Rhizome', first published in French in 1976 and translated into English as 'On the Line', Deleuze and Guattari claim that for several hundred years it was believed that the world was developing vertically in the shape of a tree (Deleuze and Guattari 1983). The choice of a tree limits possibilities. The mature tree is already contained in the seed. There is some leeway as to form and size, but the seed will become nothing more than the tree that it is destined to be. In lieu of the tree, Deleuze and Guattari propose an adventitious network, a mobile structure that can be likened to underground filaments of grass or the mycelia of fungi. A rhizome moves horizontally and produces offshoots from multiple bifurcations at its meristems. It changes its form by connecting and reconnecting. It does not have a finite or ultimate shape. Space does not pre-exist the rhizome; rather, it is created through and between the proliferating lines. Rhizomes connect and open spaces in-between which, in the rooted world of the tree, an inside (the earth) is separated from an outside (the atmosphere).

Unlike the tree, the rhizome can never be fixed or reduced to a single point or radical core. Its movement is contrasted with the stasis of the arborescent model. In 'Rhizome' the vertical, arborescent model contributes to the creation of striated spaces. In the ebullient imagination of the two authors it appears that the latter slow down and even prevent movement of the kind they associate with emancipation and creativity. Instead of imitating a tree, Deleuze and Guattari exhort their readers to make connections by following multiple itineraries of investigation, much as a rhizome moves about the surfaces it creates as it goes. Rhizomes form a territory that is neither fixed nor bears any clearly delimited borders.

In addition to this novel way of thinking rhizomatically, the philosophers make further distinctions between smooth and striated spaces. Smooth spaces allow optimal circulation and favour connections. Over time, however, smooth spaces tend to become striated. They lose their flexibility. Nodes and barriers appear that slow down circulation and reduce the number of possible connections. Writing *Anti-Oedipus* in a post-1968 climate, Deleuze and Guattari propose rhizomatic connections that continually rearticulate smooth space in order not only to criticise bourgeois capitalism with its institutions – the family, school, church, the medical establishment (especially psychiatry) – but also to avoid what they see as a deadened or zombified state of things.[2] They criticise the state for erecting mental and social barriers and for creating oppositions instead of furthering connections. Institutions and the state are seen as the villains that control and immobilise people from the top down. They argue that when the family, the church or the 'psy' instil guilt in a child, mental barriers and borders are erected. The child's creativity, indeed its mental and physical mobility are diminished in the process. Such a condition cripples many adults who have trees growing in their heads. Deleuze and Guattari cite the example of Little Hans, a child analysed by Freud and whose creativity, they declare, was blocked by adults who wrongly interpreted his attempts to trace lines of flight within and through the structure of the family into which he had been born (Deleuze and Guattari 1987: 14). The state, too, functions by ordering, organising and arresting movement, by creating relations of inclusion and exclusion.

The state facilitates the creation of rigid and often ossified institutions. It enacts laws of inclusion and exclusion that order the family and the social in general. It tries to immobilise and dominate the social world.

Yet the social cannot be entirely dominated. The organising régime of the order-word is never stable. It is constantly being transformed. Lines detach themselves from fuzzy borders and introduce variations in the constant of the dominant order. These variations can lead to a break and produce lines of flight that bring about entirely new configurations. Of importance in the late 1960s and 1970s is the doing away with institutions and the state that repress subjects. In *Anti-Oedipus*, the philosophers show how institutions like the family and psychiatry repress sexuality and desire in order to maximise their revenue. They argue for the creation of smooth spaces where desire can circulate freely.

In *A Thousand Plateaus*, the bourgeois state ordered by the rules of capitalism is criticised. Deleuze and Guattari rarely contextualise the 'state' in any specific historical or political terms. Constructing a universal history of sorts, the philosophers note that the state apparatus appears at different times and in different places. This apparatus is always one of capture. It appropriates what they call a 'nomadic war machine' that never entirely disappears. The nomadic war machine eludes capture and traces its own lines of flight. It makes its own smooth spaces. Here Deleuze and Guattari have faith in 'subjects' who undermine control by creating new lines of flight. These subjects deviate from the dominant order that uses 'order-words' to obtain control. Order-words produce repetitions and reduce differences. They produce molar structures and aggregates that make it more difficult for new lines to take flight. Yet something stirs, something affects a person enough to make her or him deviate from the prescriptive meanings of these words. Deleuze and Guattari would say that the subject molecularises the molar structures imposed by the state. People continually trace new maps and invent lines of flight that open smooth spaces. Deleuze and Guattari call it a 'becoming-revolutionary' of the people.

In 1980, the philosophers also claim that humans inaugurate an age of becoming-minoritarian. The majority, symbolised by the 35-year-old, white, working male, they declare, no longer prevails. A new world is opening, a world of becoming-minoritarian in which women, Afro-American, post-colonial and queer subjects of all kinds put the dominant order into variation. Changes of this nature occur at the limit of mental and social territories, from unstable borders without any clearly defined division between inside and outside. They occur in and through affects, desire and language. For Deleuze and Guattari, becoming-minoritarian must be accompanied by a withering of the state and its institutions without which any generalised transformation would be impossible. Though they make clear in 'Rhizome' that the connections they advocate are different from those of computers that function according to binary oppositions, the philosophers keep open the possibilities of transformations of subjectivities by means of technologies (Deleuze and Guattari 1987: 475).

Deleuze and Guattari are keenly aware both of the ways that technologies transform subjectivities *and* of writing in a postcolonial, geopolitical context. Nonetheless, they write about the state in a rather general and even monolithic way without specifically addressing a given 'nation-state'. It is as if the real villain were a general European concept of state inherited from the romantic age. The institutional apparatus of the state dominates and orders its subjects, preventing them from being creative or pursuing their desires. It keeps them from making revolutionary connections (Deleuze and Guattari 1987: 473). To construct rhizomes and create smooth spaces for an optimal circulation of desire, the state, armed with its 'order-words', has to be fought until, finally, it withers away and, in accord with any and every utopian scenario, all identity is undone.

In some of his recent essays, Balibar meditates, at a distance of several decades from the pronouncements of Deleuze and Guattari, on political space and borders (Balibar 1998, 2003 and 2004). Writing on institutions, nation-states and global space at the beginning of the twenty-first century, he repeatedly criticises the Deleuzian concept of space for being too close to that of a 'capitalist hyperspace'. He does not accuse Deleuze (and indirectly Guattari) of being on the side of a corporate régime; rather, he argues that the philosophers' concept of space lends itself to being appropriated by both the Left and the Right. Balibar's criticism reminds us that Deleuze and Guattari affirm that a concept can carry both positive and negative valences at the same time. Balibar never elaborates on his criticism. He criticises Deleuze for constructing mental territories that are not sufficiently tied into context and action. For our purposes here it is important to note that Balibar writes at a time that is very different from the post-1968 spirit in which both volumes of *Capitalism and Schizophrenia* – that Balibar presumably has in mind – were written. That year was indeed an opening – Deleuze and Guattari considered it to be an *event* of the kind that Paul Patton discusses in chapter 6 of this volume – and the impact of economic globalisation was not felt until a decade or so later. In the context of 1968, intellectuals of Deleuze and Guattari's stripe dealt with the opposition between subjects and the state with its bureaucratic nightmare, its paternalism and the stifling of creativity this resulted in. It is as anarchists but hardly as globalists that Deleuze and Guattari call for the withering away of the state.

Since the publication of the two volumes on capitalism and schizophrenia, the world has undergone many changes. More recently and in response to these changes Balibar and others have discussed the state in terms of the 'nation-state' in an effort to rethink the very relation between the two terms. At stake is less the generic state, as bureaucratic machine that oppresses its own subjects, than a specific nation-state that equates the two terms with one another in order to erect barriers, close borders and produce both social and mental inclusions and exclusions. To account for these transformations that are the effect of decolonisation and especially economic globalisation, the subject that was reinvented post-1968 has recently been supplemented, as in the writings of Balibar, with the notion of the citizen.[3]

Decolonisation has helped accelerate a generalised becoming-minoritarian. It has contributed to global migration and it has also led to a reconfiguration of the very notion of minority in less romanticised ways. In an entirely economically globalised world, the idea of revolution is rather ineffable. The concept of the state, too, has evolved and may no longer be the same enemy that it was once perceived to be. Migration, global trade and dramatic increases in the world's population have shifted the emphasis on the state away from the vision of a bureaucratic system that controls subjects. Of importance today is a different kind of state, decoupled from the 'nation', a 'community of fate' in which people, linked by an imperfect citizenship, are actively engaged in a continual remapping of inner and outer borders. As Balibar shows, in today's world there are financial and populations flows (Balibar 1998: 123). While financial flows circulate quite freely, population flows are controlled by borders. The state, weakened by financial globalisation, often uses its remaining power to regulate population flows. At the same time, the state helps enforce citizens' rights.

Before discussing how Deleuze and Guattari's notions of rhizomatic connections and smooth space might work in today's changed world in view of the criticisms waged by Balibar, it may be fruitful to glance at some of Guattari's later writings. In one of his last essays, *The Three Ecologies*, Guattari points to the post-communist world in which he finds himself (Guattari 2000). Like Balibar, he notes an intensification of capitalism with its money flows that are paralleled by human flows. Guattari claims that the impact of the media impedes connections. The media have contributed to the impoverishment of the world in terms of familial – a surprise to the reader of *Anti-Oedipus* – and social relations, and generally human solidarity has gone along with it. The subject completely disappears with the media's efforts to infantilise public opinion. The same uniform thinking and the same emotions grip the entire world. In his epigraph borrowed from Gregory Bateson, Guattari notes that: '[T]here is an ecology of bad ideas, just as there is an ecology of weeds' (Guattari 2000: 27). We could add that media discourse produces the kind of conservative 'hyperspace' noted by Balibar.

Writing at the time of the fall of the Iron Curtain, Guattari welcomes the disappearance of the artificially erected barriers between East and West as having at least a double benefit. It will now be possible to do away with a simplistic and artificial binary model of Cold War capitalism in favour of a more global, multipolar world where a false binary logic of inclusion and exclusion no longer holds. Henceforth, new connections will be made across the globe. A multipolar world is in ongoing negotiation. Guattari sees the opportunity to address more concretely the imbalances between North and South, that is, often between the ex-colonisers and the former colonies. To the undoing of these geopolitical imbalances, he again adds the rise of women's rights in spite of setbacks at the hands of various fundamentalisms.

Guattari clearly separates political militantism from aesthetic paradigms. It is by way of the latter that he continues to argue for the production of connections and the smoothing of space. He insists on the necessity of undoing borders and of creating an optimal circulation of ideas. Borrowing again from Bateson, Guattari underlines the distinction between a mental, a social and a natural ecology. Mental ecology deals with the circulation of ideas; social ecology, with social construction; natural ecology, with the relation with and treatment of nature irrespective of technology. Though he deals with contemporary geopolitics, Guattari continues to uphold the importance of mental ecology. Ideas do not necessarily coincide with the limits of the subject or the borders of a nation-state. They emerge in a context and form a territory. Territories are produced through connections that are forever remade and refashioned. Still critical of the state and its institutions, Guattari notes the emergence of a worldwide desire to create new territories that do not coincide with those organised by global capitalism.

While suggesting the possibilities of new connections and of smoothing spaces, Guattari witnesses a progressive abstraction of signs. Existential territories are threatened when all efforts converge toward a production of signs. The new capitalism is based on semiotic regimes: economic, juridical, techno-scientific and others producing subjectification (Guattari 2000: 48). Different régimes are no longer ordered hierarchically. They coexist and can be endlessly manipulated by the media. In face of this threat, Guattari welcomes the makers of a resistance who ask for territorial autonomy in all of its forms. Territories do not have to be real; they can be mental. Their inventors always trace new maps and new lines of flight that break away from heavily striated spaces that are controlled by the media. In 1989, Guattari hopes to see the early signs of a post-media age. He does not, however, advocate a return to a pre-technological age. On the contrary, computers will be part of the creation of new subjectivities without which no changes can take place at a geopolitical level.

Contrary to earlier pronouncements, in *The Three Ecologies*, Guattari argues for the subject but qualifies its construction. The subject, as he puts it, 'is not a straightforward matter' (Guattari 2000: 35). The subject, prevented from thinking by media discourse, has to be reinvented in a multipolar world. The construction of non-Oedipal, creative subjects, both singular and collective, is of continued importance for the creation of new territories that, far from coinciding with, undermine the borders of the self, the state and its institutions. Guattari warns his readers repeatedly that unless new lines of flight can be drawn, the world will succumb to the order that globalism in collusion with the media imposes. This order reduces diversity and produces sameness. Everything is under the sign of profit. The circulation of ideas is blocked, social exchanges are ossified and nature is sullied. The subject is infantilised. Strong borders cross both inside and between states. Guattari reaffirms the importance of utopian thinking. He argues for the continued possibility of inventing smooth spaces and of an optimal circulation of ideas in a new geopolitical context. He emphasises the importance of contemporary geopolitics and of militantism. He separates, however, political action from mental ecologies, that is from rhizomatic thinking and from the accelerated smoothing of striated spaces the necessity of which he continues to advocate.

Unlike Guattari, Deleuze attests to a progressive loss of inventions. In 'Post-Scriptum to a Society of Control,' Deleuze updates his earlier pronouncements on the state of the world (Deleuze 1995). His voice is less hopeful when he sees a world even more bound by the shackles of global capitalism. He elaborates in detail on economic changes and on the evolution of a capitalism of accumulation to one of finance. He, too, shows how the new financial flows affect humans all over the world. He is keenly aware of the loss of creative movement, of the increased striation of world-space and also of the structural absence in a networked world of a division between inside and outside. Many institutions that he previously criticised he now declares are the leftovers of a disciplinary society on the verge of disappearance (Deleuze 1995: 179). They have lost their usefulness. Their disappearance does not produce more smooth spaces. Deleuze shows how in this different world people no longer actively search for openings. Aesthetics are under the sign of profit. Learning processes have changed. People acquire skills. When humans enter what, in the wake of the poet William Burroughs, Deleuze calls the new 'society of control', the distinction between an inside and an outside as in the Foucauldian 'disciplinary society' no longer has currency. In a global, networked society, people are in competition with one another. Solidarity becomes more difficult. A new global capitalism sharply reduces the possibilities of becoming by striating space in a way different – but no less lethal – than an earlier one. We may begin to wonder if Deleuze's last note, apparently written just before he took his life in 1995, refers to a feeling of the philosopher's impotence in a global world.

Let us return here to Balibar and to his criticism of Deleuze (and Guattari) for their use of smooth space as 'hyperspace'. Balibar, too, argues for the undoing of borders and the opening of spaces. He writes of the necessity of connections and the importance of becomings but finds that Deleuze and Guattari's notion of smooth space has little practical value in the twenty-first century. It is too decontextualised and not sufficiently tied to action. We can only speculate that had Balibar read the philosophers' later texts rather than their earlier writings of the 1970s, he might have qualified his pronouncements. With Balibar we can say, however, that the rise of a global capitalism based on capital flows and accompanied by demographic upheavals that give a false impression of smooth space, has led to renewed attention to the very notion of the subject, the state and its institutions.

The generic state that since the aftermath of the French Revolution was said to oppress the subject by striating space and that was the target both of *Anti-Oedipus* and *A Thousand Plateaus*, is, indeed, in need of reassessment. Threatened by economic globalism, the state is awash in financial flows and transactions that go beyond national borders. It has lost some of its importance. At the same time, it is being transformed. It has the task of controlling its borders and of 'defending' its space from the onslaught of immigrant populations. More importantly for our purposes, it has to redefine itself as an entity in an era where nationality can no longer be equated with citizenship. The struggle now appears to be less between the state and its subjects as it had been in the aftermath of the 1960s than, as I have tried to show in this chapter, around the very notion of the nation-state, citizenship and its borders. With the weakening of the state, people fear losing their rights as citizens. The dissolution of the subject was the answer to a repressive, patriarchal state. In an era of transnational financial and human flows, there is a pressing need to reassess both the notion of the subject and of the state. In today's novel situation, the question of the state and of its borders – must be asked anew.

Given the large numbers of immigrants, how are borderlines to be redefined? What kind of ways of being in common can be invented? What kinds of 'imperfect' citizenship? Is it possible, with Balibar, to have faith in institutions though the latter, as Deleuze points out, are also part of a disciplinary era that is now coming to a close? What kind of connections can be made and what kind of smooth spaces invented that would not simply join those of global capitalism against which, according to Balibar, there is no organised resistance? Is it productive in today's climate to continue advocating a global becoming-revolutionary of the people or a subject in constant metamorphosis? Guattari addresses the importance of geopolitics and of the construction of a 'subject' (Guattari 2000). Toni Negri notes that Deleuze appears to give renewed attention to subjectification in his later writings (Deleuze 1995: 175–6). In their later writings, both Deleuze and Guattari seem to give more importance to some kind of subject. Does the subject today have to be complemented again by the citizen? And, most importantly, is it productive to continue separating thinking from action, or does thought need to be translated directly into action? In a world that appears increasingly decontextualised under the impact of technologies and migrations, paradoxically, there seems to be a pressing need for context, a desire for situating the 'subject' and for reinventing the citizen.

The invention of new spaces always carries a component of fiction. Smooth space is one of them. Yet, as Balibar argues, a fiction that opposes all institutions rejoins that of economic globalism which promotes the circulation of goods while remaining silent about the non-circulation of populations. At this juncture it is easy to see how Balibar assumes Deleuze and Guattari's smooth space resembles capitalist hyperspace. While borders often exist neither for goods, nor even less for financial transactions, they indeed do for people who attempt to assail and cross them. The struggle today then is not so much between the individual oppressed by the state, as for the citizen's right to both *move* and *be*. Of importance is the creation of a space from which one can speak as citizen. Social relations, Balibar argues with Deleuze and Guattari, are based on conventions. The notion of citizenship too has to be continually reinvented just

as, in this global age of accelerated transition, the state is being transformed. If the tautology of a 'global world' has currency, the notion of
state as an entity defined by closed space and borders needs to be
rethought in a different context from the one that prevailed several
decades ago.

It is on the notion of the state, institutions and borders that Balibar
takes issue with Deleuze and Guattari. He questions the philosophers'
insistence on doing away with the state and all institutions and on espousing smooth spaces that are too abstract and not sufficiently tied into
action. Balibar wants to open new spaces by transforming existing borderlines. The latter have to be made more porous before they can be
erased. He wants to reinvent institutions rather than harbour revolutionary zeal that would do away with them entirely. Both institutions and the
state have to be renegotiated. New connections have to be made. Today,
citizens and non-citizens often turn to the state when they find themselves
without rights or protection of any kind. A weakened state is called upon
to protect citizens' rights and rethink the very notion of its territories and
limits, that is, of its borderlines. In a multipolar world, what Deleuze and
Guattari called 'becoming-minoritarian' has to be questioned anew. The
nagging dilemma continues to be one of opening new spaces and of
becomings. More important than simply being done with the state, are
ways of reflecting on its relation to inclusion and exclusion, that is, to its
policies of citizenship and those concerning myriad types of borders. For
both the state and the citizen the stake is indeed one of connecting, nego-
tiating and accepting the existence of other models and of other spaces.

Deleuze and Guattari rightfully claim, as Heraclitus once did, that the
world is in constant change and that these changes seem to have accelerated. In a multipolar world that is continually reconfiguring itself, it is
imperative for philosophers to adapt their thinking to changing contexts.
In a world that is increasingly the site of conflicting universalities – and
no longer simply that of Western universalism – is it possible to dream
of smoothing space so as to do away with all borders, or do we have to
deal with real cases in given geopolitical contexts? We have already noted
that Deleuze and Guattari's insistence on connections, on the 'and' rather
than the 'either – or' is more important than ever. So is their ongoing
smoothing of striated spaces as long as the utopian, as Balibar argues,
does not exclude concrete action. The utopian view with its counterpart
based in action is, however, not entirely incompatible with Deleuze and
Guattari's vision. Action, no matter how messy and exasperating it may
be, requires that we constantly return to the utopianism. At a time when
strongly marked borders have to be redrawn to improve the world,

concrete cases of 'striation' bring forward the condition of possibility in which smooth spaces serve the ends of practical action. It is not an easy task, yet the idea of smooth space prompts both awareness and engagement. Thus, it is of continued importance to make connections, to open spaces and undo fixed mental and physical borders and barriers; to travel in space, between identities, not so much to undo them but rather to question the subject, the citizen and the state. Only then can we make dashed and dotted lines out of borderlines.

# References

Balibar, E. (1998), *Droit de cité*, Paris: L'Aube.
Balibar, E. (2003), *L'Europe, l'Amérique, la guerre*, Paris: La Découverte.
Balibar, E. (2004), *We, The People of Europe?* trans. J. Swenson, Princeton: Princeton University Press.
Bhabha, Homi K. (2004), 'Statement for the *Critical Inquiry* Board Symposium', *Critical Inquiry* 30 (2) (Winter): 342–9.
Deleuze, G. and Guattari, F. (1977), *Anti-Oedipus: Capitalism and Schizophrenia*, trans. R. Hurley, M. Seem and H. R. Lane, New York: Viking Press.
Deleuze, G. and Guattari, F. (1987), *A Thousand Plateaus: Capitalism and Schizophrenia*, trans. B. Massumi, Minneapolis: University of Minnesota Press.
Deleuze, G. and Guattari, F. (1983), 'On the Line', trans. J. Johnston, New York: Semiotext(e).
Deleuze, G. (1995), *Negotiations*, trans. M. Joughin, New York: Columbia University Press.
Guattari, F (2000), *The Three Ecologies*, trans. I. Pindar and P. Sutton, London: Athlone.

# Notes

1. Cartesian philosophies equate space with immobility or the stasis of *res extensa*.
2. See Deleuze and Guattari (1977, vol. 1). In an interview with C. Clément, Guattari declares: 'May 68 came as a shock [*ébranlement*] to Gilles and me, as to so many others: we did not know each other, but this book, now, is nevertheless a result of May' (Deleuze 1995: 15).
3. Among those who make use of Balibar's notion of citizen, we can cite Homi K. Bhabha, 2004.

## Chapter 6

# The Event of Colonisation

## Paul Patton

Colonisation was not a topic that figured largely in Deleuze's work. He made only occasional passing remarks about it, such as those in a 1982 interview with Elias Sanbar.[1] Here, in discussing an analogy drawn between the Palestinians and Native Americans, he contrasts the position of colonised peoples who are retained on their territory in order to be exploited with the position of those who are driven out of their territory altogether. The Palestinian people, like the indigenous inhabitants of North America, are a people driven out (Deleuze 1998: 26). This analogy is limited in a number of respects. First, as Deleuze himself notes, the Palestinians, unlike the Native Americans, do have an Arab world outside of Israel from which they can draw support. Second, like indigenous peoples in many parts of the world, neither the Native Americans nor the Palestinians are completely in the situation of refugees. Rather they are peoples who are often displaced from their traditional homelands but who, whether displaced or not, remain captives of the colonial state established on their territories. In this sense, they are subject to 'internal' colonisation of the kind practised in North America, Australia and parts of Africa rather than the 'external' colonisation practised by European powers in other parts of Africa, Asia and the South Pacific.

I have argued elsewhere that, despite their relative lack of concern with colonial issues, Deleuze and Guattari do provide conceptual resources for thinking about the problems of internal colonisation and decolonisation (Patton 2000: 120–31). Their theory of the state as apparatus of capture is especially helpful in understanding the mechanisms by which new territories and peoples are subsumed under the sovereignty of existing states. Their concepts of deterritorialisation and the resultant metamorphosis of assemblages are suggestive in relation to the challenge to existing legal forms of capture of land posed by the jurisprudence of Aboriginal or Native title. As with any such process of deterritorialisation, the outcome will depend on the kinds of deterritorialisation and reterritorialisation in play within a given context. In this chapter I propose to pursue this topic with particular regard to Deleuze's way of thinking about events.

In a conversation with Raymond Bellour and François Ewald published in 1988, Deleuze suggested that his work had always been concerned with the nature of events: 'I've tried in all my books to discover the nature of events: it's a philosophical concept, the only one capable of ousting the verb "to be" and its attributes' (Deleuze 1995: 141). While this concern with the event is clearly more pronounced in some of his books than in others, it remains a prominent theme from *The Logic of Sense* (Deleuze 1990) until *What is Philosophy?* (Deleuze and Guattari 1994). However, we should not rush to conclude that Deleuze produced a coherent metaphysical theory or concept of the event. His claim in the interview with Bellour and Ewald is more modest, namely that he has repeatedly tried to discover the nature of events. These efforts involved him in a series of engagements with earlier metaphysical theories of events, especially those of the Stoics, Leibniz and Whitehead. They result in a number of theses on the nature of events in general, including both everyday trivial events, such as cutting something with a knife, and large-scale historical events, such as wars and revolutions.

My aim here is not to examine all of these engagements in order to expound or to criticise Deleuze's successive views on the nature of events. Instead, I propose to outline some of the principle recurrent theses put forward from *The Logic of Sense* onwards, and to apply these to the historical event of colonisation, especially the legal dimensions of this event as it occurs in common law countries such as Australia. My interest in bringing the jurisprudence of colonisation together with Deleuzian theses about the nature of events is twofold: first, to ask whether, and if so in what ways, these theses can help us to understand the historical phenomena associated with such large-scale historical events; and second, in keeping with the methodological counsel Deleuze offers to Jean-Clet Martin, to ask whether the colonial example helps us to appreciate some of the more puzzling aspects of Deleuze's thinking about events. [2]

In testing Deleuzian theses on the nature of events in this manner, I assume the underlying pragmatism of his conception of philosophy according to which the concepts that it invents are assessed not for their truth or falsity but for the degree to which they are 'Interesting, Remarkable, or Important' (Deleuze and Guattari 1994: 82). Concepts are interesting, remarkable or important when they give expression to new problems or to solutions to problems already posed. However, the conditions of the problems addressed by philosophy are not found in the empirical reality of things, as they are for the sciences, but in the 'intensional conditions of consistency' of the concepts themselves. In other words: 'If the concept is a solution, the conditions of the philosophical problem are found on the plane of immanence presupposed by the concept' (Deleuze and Guattari 1994: 80–1). In these terms, we can ask what is the problem to which colonisation offers a solution and what are the conditions of this problem?

According to Deleuze and Guattari, philosophy creates concepts on a plane of immanence and these concepts express or 'bring forth' pure events (Deleuze and Guattari 1994: 199). Events are actualised in states of affairs, bodies and the lived experience of people, but as philosophers we 'counter-actualise' events when we step back from states of affairs, bodies and experiences in order to isolate or extract a concept. It follows that philosophy creates many of the events in terms of which we understand and react to the processes and states of affairs which condition our lives: concepts of fairness, equality and justice; concepts of social contract, revolution, democracy to come; or, to take an example from Rawls, the concept of a well-ordered society governed in accordance with principles of justice. It is apparent that the question of the usefulness of Deleuzian theses about events is intimately bound up with his conception of the purpose and function of philosophy. The value of 'counter-actualising' events through the invention of concepts will depend in part on how we understand the nature of those events. After setting out the key elements of Deleuze's concept of events, I will ask how, in Deleuzian terms, we should understand the event of colonisation.

## Events and Language

Deleuze's thinking about the nature of events has always relied heavily upon the Stoics who, he suggests, were the first to create a philosophical concept of the event (Deleuze 1993: 53). They drew a fundamental distinction between a material or physical realm of bodies and states of affairs and a non-physical realm of incorporeal entities that included time, place and the sense of, or 'what is expressed' in, statements (*Lekta*). They took the sense of a statement to be identical with the event expressed in it: '[S]ense, *the expressed of the proposition*, is an incorporeal, complex and irreducible entity, at the surface of things, a pure event which inheres or subsists in the proposition' (Deleuze 1990: 19). This Stoic metaphysics implies that events stand in an essential relationship both to bodies and states of affairs on the one hand, and to language on the other: 'The event subsists in language, but it happens to things'

(Deleuze 1990: 24). As a result, it implies a number of further theses, firstly about the relationship between incorporeal events and language, and secondly about the relationship between incorporeal events and physical configurations of bodies. I begin with the relationship between events and language since this has implications for our understanding of the functions of language.

Deleuze's thesis about the intimate relationship between events and the forms of their linguistic expression forms the basis for the pragmatics outlined in 'November 20, 1923: Postulates of Linguistics' (Deleuze and Guattari 1987: 75–110). The argument of this plateau extends J. L. Austin's concept of the illocutionary force which accompanies all linguistic utterances to suggest that language use involves the attribution or effectuation of the 'incorporeal transformations' current in a given society at a given time. Such incorporeal transformations are events. They typically involve changes in the properties of the body concerned, such as changes of status or changes in relations to other bodies. For example, at the conclusion of a criminal trial:

> [T]he transformation of the accused into a convict is a pure instantaneous act or incorporeal attribute . . . The order-words or assemblages of enunciation in a given society (in short, the illocutionary) designate this instantaneous relation between statements and the incorporeal transformations or noncorporeal attributes they express. (Deleuze and Guattari 1987: 80–1)

All such incorporeal transformations are identifiable by reference to the date and time of utterance, hence the title of this plateau: 'November 20, 1923' refers to the day on which, in response to runaway inflation, the old German reichsmark was declared no longer valid and replaced by a new currency. Understood in these terms, language is not simply the representation of states of affairs but the attribution of certain events to them. Its primary function is not to communicate information but to act upon the world. Everyday life is punctuated by interpersonal linguistic events such as promises, warnings and declarations of love or of enmity. History is also marked by linguistic events such as declarations of independence, of war, or the assertion of sovereignty over vast areas of land previously unclaimed by European powers.

Like many world historical events, colonisation is a complex process involving different kinds of incorporeal transformation such as the naming of prominent geographical features along a newly discovered coast, or flag-raising ceremonies accompanied by proclamations of possession in the name of the colonial sovereign. The latter appear to be modern equivalents of the 'magical capture' that Dumézil describes as one of the two poles of sovereignty in Indo-European mythology (Deleuze and Guattari 1987: 424–5). Stating, claiming or naming something is never sufficient to actualise a particular event, but these purely linguistic acts of declaration or attribution are often important and sometimes necessary conditions of actualisation. The pragmatic dimension of language outlined by Deleuze and Guattari explains why politics frequently takes the form of struggle over appropriate terminology with which to describe events. Disagreements over what happened often take the form of disputes over the appropriate event attribution. Was the colony 'settled' by brave pioneers or was it 'invaded' without regard for the lives or property of the indigenous inhabitants? Did the ensuing destruction of peoples and cultures amount to 'genocide' or were they simply 'swept away by the tide of history'?

## Events and Bodies

The Stoic conception of events implies a distinction between events proper, pure events, and their actualisation or, as Deleuze and Guattari later say, their 'incarnation' in particular bodies and states of affairs. Deleuze insists on the irreducibility of events to bodies and states of affairs, just as he does on the irreducibility of sense to the proposition in which it is expressed: sense is only identical to the event '*on the condition that the event is not confused with its spatio-temporal realization in a state of affairs*' (Deleuze 1990: 22). Elsewhere, he insists that this is not a distinction between two kinds of events but a distinction between 'the event, which is ideal by nature, and its spatio-temporal realization in a state of affairs' (Deleuze 1990: 53). Events are not ideal forms abstracted from the specific features of any one occasion. They are not universals but singular incorporeal entities. As such, they are entities of a different kind from physical bodies. They may be expressed in particular configurations and movements of bodies, in the way that a particular battle is made up of the movements of certain bodies and pieces of equipment, but the event of battle is not confined to these particular elements since it can recur on other occasions when it would be expressed in entirely different elements.

This distinction raises further questions about the nature of pure events and the nature of their relationship to particular occurrences or instantiations of those events. As both singular and recurrent entities, events must be supposed to be identifiable as the same event even as they vary from one occasion to the next. In this sense, they are open-ended and indeterminate idealities, characterised by their 'iterability' in Derrida's sense of the term. In this manner, for example, in 'Signature Event Context' he speaks of the 'pure event' of a signature, reproducible and recognisable on different occasions but at the same time irreducible to any determinate number of such occasions (Derrida 1988: 20). Derrida's distinction between particular occurrences and the 'pure reproducibility of the pure event' mirrors Deleuze and Guattari's distinction between historical events as these are incarnated in bodies and states of affairs and the pure events that are only imperfectly actualised in the linear time of history: '[W]hat History grasps of the event is its effectuation in states of affairs or in lived experience, but the event in its becoming, in its specific consistency, in its self-positing concept, escapes History' (Deleuze and Guattari 1994: 110).

Deleuze understands the one-many relation between such pure events and their actualisations along the lines of the relation between a problem and its solutions: events are 'problematic and problematizing' (Deleuze 1990: 54).[3] By 'problem', he means a virtual structure whose nature is never entirely captured in any given specification or determination of its conditions. In this sense, he aligns the distinction between an ideal event and its spatio-temporal realisation with the distinction between a problem as such and its determination in a manner that permits a solution. In these terms, he can speak of the 'problem' of language as such, prior to any determinate language, the 'problem' of society prior to any determinate set of relations of production and exchange or, we might add, the 'problem' of political community prior to any determinate form of political organisation (Deleuze 1994: 186, 203–6). Specification is necessary for the production of particular solutions, but the pure problem-event is not thereby dissolved or exhausted since there always remains the possibility of other specifications and other solutions. We must distinguish between the empirical event, which is a particular determination of the problem, and the problem-event that, in its pure form, remains 'immaterial, incorporeal, unlivable: pure reserve' (Deleuze and Guattari 1994: 156).

## The Problem of Colonisation

Consider colonisation as a pure event in these terms. As a preliminary characterisation, we can say that it is a recurrent, asymmetrical encounter predominantly between European nations and Aboriginal societies in various parts of the world. Historically, it has tended to involve the incorporation or at least the subordination of a territory along with its peoples and resources by another, more powerful people organised as a sovereign state. Deleuze and Guattari define sovereign statehood by reference to the event of capture. Nation-states were formed in Europe by the capture of local territories and the transformation of these into more or less uniform lands and peoples. The essential elements of capture as they define it are the constitution of a general space of comparison and the establishment of a centre of appropriation. The uniformity of land, labour and people are essential conditions for the extraction of rent, profit and taxes that provide the financial basis for the development of modern nation-states. Like those at home, newly colonised territories outside of Europe were usually encumbered by indigenous populations with their own distinctive social organisation and relations to the earth and its products. These typically involved particular varieties of what Deleuze and Guattari called 'territorial' social machines, in contrast to the despotic and axiomatic machines that give rise to European capitalism (Deleuze and Guattari 1977: 145–53). As such, they needed to be 'deterritorialised' in order to be reterritorialised as dependent colonies of the relevant European state.

The simultaneous deterritorialisation and reterritorialisation of newly 'discovered' territories took a variety of forms: economic, technological, affective and pathogenic as well as political transformations followed one upon the other in the early stages of contact. However, in the case of European colonisation by states that saw themselves as subject to an impersonal rule of law, one of the most important transformations was juridical. The sovereign asserted a legal claim to the territory in question, and reserved the sovereign right to allocate property in land, thereby transforming the territory into a uniformly appropriable and exploitable resource. It follows that a fundamental problem of colonisation is the jurisprudential one of imposing sovereign control over foreign territories and indigenous peoples. The state is sovereignty, Deleuze and Guattari assert, but 'sovereignty only reigns over what it is capable of internalizing' (Deleuze and Guattari 1987: 360).

Different solutions to this problem have been adopted in different parts of the world. These amount to different legal mechanisms for transferring sovereignty from the indigenous inhabitants to the colonial sovereign. They include treaties and purchase of tracts of land, along with simple appropriation of the land in those cases where it was considered empty of inhabitants with any legitimate claim (*terra nullius*). A common feature of all such instruments was the 'right of preemption' that reserved the right to acquire land from the Natives for the sovereign. Along with the power of the sovereign to allocate titles to land, this ensured the constitution of a uniform smooth space of potential real property where before there had been only foreign territories and foreign peoples with their own customs and laws. The sale of land often provided a means to finance the establishment of colonial governments and the settlement that followed.

None of this precludes the possibility of resistance to such régimes of colonial capture. On the contrary, the fact that the violence of colonisation is institutionalised in the form of law means that the colonial institutions themselves are open to reinvestment by other forces. Which of the various solutions to the jurisprudential problem is adopted determines the basis of the colonial sovereignty, the legal form of the settlements with indigenous peoples that follow, and the possibilities for reinterpretation of these legal settlements to accommodate greater freedom for the colonised. In these terms, contemporary efforts to undo the legal and political institutions of internal colonisation in countries with captive indigenous populations may be understood as attempts to return to the original conditions of the problem. They seek to 'problematise' existing solutions to the problem of colonial society in order to arrive at new ones.

Consider the jurisprudential transformations that have occurred with regard to the legal recognition of Aboriginal entitlements to land in Australia and Canada in recent years. In those territories acquired under the 'extended' version of the *terra nullius* principle in international law, which allowed territory to be considered empty for legal purposes even when it was inhabited, it had long been assumed that indigenous peoples never had any rights to the land since upon colonisation it became the property of the British Crown. Part of the justification for this view was the so-called 'barbarian hypothesis' according to which at the time of colonisation there were no recognisable legal owners of the land since the indigenous occupants were considered too low in the scale of civilisation to be considered as having any legal rights. Canadian courts began to dismantle this particular form of legal capture with the *Calder* case in 1973.[4] In Australia, it was not until the *Mabo* case in 1992 that the High Court decided that this was mistaken in law as well as in fact and that the indigenous inhabitants of the continent had retained some entitlements to land in accordance with their traditional laws and customs.[5] Australian law henceforth recognised a form of Aboriginal or Native title to land, although this remained a lesser form of entitlement than property ownership under the common law. The possibility of claiming Native title was subject to a range of further restrictive conditions, including the existence of an ongoing connection with the land on the part of the claimants and the absence of any acts by the Crown that might have extinguished Native title over the land in question. Despite these limitations, this landmark decision represented a break with nineteenth-century assumptions about the nature of Aboriginal societies and with the longstanding non-recognition of indigenous law and custom.

For reasons internal to the relationship between sovereign power and domestic courts, the *Mabo* decision did nothing to undermine the legal basis of the initial claim to sovereignty. However, in terms of the broader historico-political event of colonisation, it was widely regarded as having discredited the principle of *terra nullius* that had underpinned the imposition of British sovereignty. This principle was now considered to be the product of particular racist assumptions embedded in earlier decisions from colonial courts all the way up to the Privy Council. The historico-political significance of the *Mabo* case was greatly enhanced by the fact that it was decided in the context of an existing national debate over reconciliation between indigenous and non-indigenous peoples. The decision had the effect of broadening the public debate beyond questions of property and land to include fundamental questions about the rule of law and the requirements of justice in the aftermath of extensive historical injustice. It unleashed a judicial and legislative process which effectively rewrote the legal terms upon which colonisation had taken place in Australia. Subsequent cases involved the revisiting of the terms of nineteenth-century pastoral leases and a reconsideration of the ongoing relationship that many Aboriginal peoples had maintained with their traditional lands.[6] While the outcome of these cases was not always favourable to the indigenous claimants involved, they nevertheless amounted to a renegotiation of the terms in which the jurisprudential problem of colonisation was originally solved.

This unexpected legal event might be said to have returned the nation to the problem of colonisation from which it emerged, not only to renegotiate the terms under which Aboriginal lands and Aboriginal people were subordinated to the authority of the British Crown but eventually to question whether the colonial encounter need have taken the form of the imposition of sovereignty at all. This is the import of the widespread demands in Australia for a treaty or some other document of reconciliation that would recognise the right of Aboriginal peoples to self-determination and self-government. It is also the import of the argument of Canadian political theorist James Tully that history provides us with other principles in terms of which the encounter between European nation-states and indigenous peoples might have taken place. These include the principles of recognition, consent and continuity that had long formed the basis of European as well as Native American inter-state or inter-national relations (Tully 1994: 169–80; 1995: 116–39).[7]

Tully's principles of a fair and just constitutional association and the demand of indigenous peoples for a treaty relationship point to the possibility that the problem to which colonisation provided a solution is not in its purest form a problem of capture but one of encounter. For European colonists throughout the modern period, the problem was posed on the basis of the belief that non-European peoples ranked lower on the scale of civilisation. The obligation to improve the condition of those lower on the scale went hand in glove with the right to annex their territory. However, if this axiom is abandoned, the problem appears in its pure state as that of the conditions of coexistence of different peoples. There are many inequalities on both sides of the divide between state-governed European societies and territorially governed indigenous societies, but the encounter between them need not have taken the forms of legal incorporation which it so often did. The event of colonisation might have unfolded on the basis of mutual respect and co-operation between equals. It might have been an encounter that was also an event of reconciliation between peoples and cultures largely unknown to one another.

## Time and Becoming

Deleuze's distinction between the pure event and its actualisation in particular circumstances is further reinforced by his suggestion that two distinct orders of time are involved. In *The Logic of Sense*, he proposes a division within time itself between a historical time within which events occur (*Chronos*) and a 'time of the event' (*Aion*) that cannot be reduced to the former time. This distinction provides the basis for the view that events proper in some sense 'escape History'. From the point of view of a materialist approach to history, however, this remains one of the most puzzling aspects of his concept of the event. Why draw this distinction in the first place and, having done so, how does the resultant 'aternal' concept of the event shed light on the historical events that determine our present and future possibilities? In order to see how the event of colonisation helps to illuminate Deleuze's concept of the 'aternality' of events, consider his reasons for distinguishing historical time and event time.

A first reason advanced in the opening paragraph of *The Logic of Sense* has to do with the paradoxical character, from the perspective of ordinary time, of pure events or incorporeal transformations. Deleuze takes an example from Lewis Carroll to show that events imply contradictory properties of a thing in a manner inconceivable within linear time. When we say that Alice grew (she became taller) this implies that she became taller than she was before. By the same token, however, she also became shorter than she is now (assuming that she continued to grow). Although she is not taller and shorter at the same time, she becomes taller and shorter at the same time, thereby exhibiting 'the simultaneity of a becoming whose characteristic is to elude the present' (Deleuze 1990: 1). It follows that, for Deleuze, events are co-extensive with becomings and that becomings exhibit contradictory properties in the absence of further specification of the temporal perspective from which we examine them: considered from the point of view of her smaller self engaged in growing, Alice becomes larger. Considered from the point of view of her larger self, Alice continues to become smaller than she is, although progressively less so. To take another example, consider what happens to $H_2O$ at zero degrees Celsius: water becomes ice or ice becomes water, depending on whether temperature is increasing or decreasing. In other words, whether we witness the freezing of water or the melting of ice depends on the temporal direction of the becoming involved.[8]

The paradoxical nature and 'impossibility' of pure events is a prominent theme in Derrida's recent work, but it is also implied in Deleuze's understanding of events, becomings and problems. For example, in *Difference and Repetition*, he describes the pure event of society as a paradoxical event that cannot be lived within actual societies, but 'must be and can only be lived in the element of social upheaval (in other words, freedom, which is always hidden among the remains of the old order and the first fruits of a new)' (Deleuze 1994: 193). The freedom expressed in such moments of revolutionary social upheaval may be described from the point of view of the old order as the descent into chaos, or from the point of view of the new as the necessary chaos from which new forms of order may emerge.

The situation of indigenous peoples who become colonised provides many examples of such contradictory properties. For example, with regard to their status as people subject to a rule of law, they pass from a law-governed state to one of complete lawlessness and at the same time from a state of complete lawlessness to a law-governed state, depending on whether we view the event from the point of view of indigenous law and custom or from that of the law of the coloniser.[9] In cases such as Australia, where colonisation took place on the legal basis that there were only primitive peoples living in accordance with customs that could not properly be considered laws but rather 'only such as are consistent with a state of greatest darkness and irrational superstition', this implied considerable ambivalence even with regard to the legal status of indigenous people within the newly founded colony.[10] On the one hand, they were subjects of the colonial sovereign and thus protected in the sense that crimes against them were not supposed to go unpunished. On the other hand, since they were not considered capable of swearing oaths, courts were not bound to take into account evidence they might have offered. This anomalous status was resolved by the implementation of statutory regimes for the 'protection' of Aboriginal peoples that assigned them to a special status deprived of most of the ordinary rights and duties of subjects (Chesterman and Galligan 1997: 11–57).

Similarly paradoxical transformations occurred with regard to the property rights of the indigenous inhabitants. If we consider the consequences of colonisation as these are now defined in terms of the doctrine of Aboriginal or Native title, this involved at once both the loss of entitlements as they existed under indigenous law and the acquisition of entitlements under common law. The paradox inherent in becoming dispossessed while simultaneously becoming bearers of common law Native title is reflected in some of the legal formulations offered by the courts. For example, one of the judges in the Australian *Mabo* case expressed the peculiar nature of Native title as a concept that straddles indigenous and common law in suggesting that: 'Native title, though recognised by the common law, is not an institution of the common law' (Bartlett 1993: 42). The 1997 *Delgamuukw* case, in which the Canadian Supreme Court finally settled some of the questions relating to the nature and limits of Aboriginal title, also took the view that Aboriginal title arose from the relationship between common law and pre-existing systems of Aboriginal law.[11] The court sought to resolve the paradox of simultaneously becoming dispossessed and becoming possessed by suggesting that Aboriginal title 'crystallized' at the time sovereignty was asserted (Persky 1998: 101).

A second reason for drawing a distinction between 'event time' and 'linear time' emerges when we consider the paradoxes involved in identifying, in historical time, the precise moment at which events occur. Suppose we take a time before the event and a time after: the infinite divisibility of the series of moments implies that there are two converging series on either side of the event, but no point at which these series meet. Thus, from the perspective of historical time, there is no present moment at which the event takes place:

> It rather retreats and advances in two directions at once, being the perpetual object of a double question: What is going to happen? What has just happened? The agonizing aspect of the pure event is that it is always and at the same time something which has just happened and something about to happen; never something which is happening. (Deleuze 1990: 63)

Colonial acquisition of new territory is elusive in precisely this manner. When did the colonisation of Australia occur? Was it the moment in 1770 when Captain Cook raised the British flag on a tiny island off the northern tip of Cape York and claimed sovereignty over half the continent in the name of King George III? Afterwards, as if to reinforce the claim, he named this rocky outcrop 'Possession Island' (Day 1996: 27). If Cook had effectively imposed British sovereignty, why did Governor Phillip repeat the ceremony after the arrival of the first fleet of convicts, not once but twice, on the shores of Sydney Cove on 26 January 1788? (Day 1996: 38). Taken in isolation, such singular events are insufficient to effect even the legal event of colonisation. Like declarations of war or independence, they only make sense in anticipation of the process and the institution that follows. At the moment of Cook's or even Phillip's flag ceremonies it is too soon to say that colonisation has taken place. At any moment thereafter it can be said that colonisation has already taken place.

Colonisation is a complex event that exhibits the kind of differential contamination between acts of institution and acts of preservation described by Derrida in 'Force of Law' (Derrida 1992: 38–44). The initial acts of proclamation and arrival anticipate the subsequent acts of invasion, dispossession and settlement while, at the same time, the subsequent policies and actions of colonial governors, magistrates, police and the settlers under their protection reproduce and reinforce the initial act of foundation. The imposition of a new law, new culture and new forms of government on the territory and its indigenous inhabitants continues the work of colonisation that was only nominally carried out by the initial assertion of sovereignty. The colonial example thus illustrates the manner in which events possess an inner complexity that is often imperceptible from the point of view of ordinary time. By the same token, this example points towards a third reason for regarding event time as another kind of time or another dimension within time, namely that this enables us to make sense of the internal structure and complexity of events. Their relations to other events structure them externally while, as Deleuze often comments, events can involve long periods when it appears that nothing is happening, then suddenly everything changes and nothing is the same as before. In *Difference and Repetition* and in *The Logic of Sense*, he cites the following passage from Péguy's *Clio* in support of the idea that events are always structured by their own singularities:

> Suddenly, we felt that we were no longer the same convicts. Nothing had happened. Yet a problem in which a whole world collided, a problem without issue, in which no end could be seen, suddenly ceased to exist and we asked ourselves what we had been talking about. Instead of an ordinary solution,

a found solution, this problem, this difficulty, this impossibility had just passed what seemed like a physical point of resolution. A crisis point. At the same time, the whole world had passed what seemed like a physical crisis point. There are critical points of the event just as there are critical points of temperature: points of fusion, freezing and boiling points, points of coagulation and crystallisation. There are even in the case of events states of superfusion which are precipitated, crystallised or determined only by the introduction of a fragment of some future event (Deleuze 1990: 53; 1994: 189).

Deleuze often draws a distinction between two kinds of occurrence that he characterises in terms of the mathematical distinction between ordinary and singular or remarkable points on a line. In historical terms, this corresponds to the difference between 'normal' events as defined within an established frame of reference and set of rules and 'extraordinary' events as involving the shift from one frame to another, or the replacement of one set of rules by another. Variants of this kind of distinction may be found, for example, in Thomas Kuhn's contrast between normal and revolutionary science or in Walter Benjamin's contrast between violence of foundation and violence of conservation. From the perspective of the realm of becoming in which events unfold their inner complexity, this distinction is not so much between conservation and creation as between two kinds of deterritorialisation or transformation of an existing assemblage. On the one hand, there are processes of 'continual variation' or deterritorialisation in which novelty emerges in the course of the repetition of established acts and events under different circumstances or in different contexts (this is what enables institutions such as the law to be transformed even as they are maintained and reproduced). On the other hand, there are sudden transitions to a different structural frame and with this the possibility of actualising a new kind of event. It is a matter of perspective whether we describe this as a distinction between two kinds of event or as a distinction internal to a given pure event.

Deleuze and Guattari identify two kinds of assemblage or process, for example when they distinguish between 'relative' and 'absolute' lines of flight or deterritorialisation. In conjunction with the thesis that societies are defined by their lines of flight or deterritorialisation, this distinction implies that fundamental social change happens in one of two ways. Sometimes it happens by degrees, as with the steady erosion of myths and prejudices about sexual difference and its implications for social and political institutions under the impact of feminism throughout the twentieth century. Sometimes fundamental social change occurs through the sudden eruption of events that inaugurate a new field of social, political or legal possibilities. These are turning points in history after which some things will never be the same as before, but they are not necessarily violent or bloody events. They are examples of 'a becoming breaking through into history' (Deleuze 1995: 153). Deleuze suggests that May 1968 was an event of this kind: a momentary instance of a pure event that French society proved unable to assimilate. The people showed themselves to be incapable of undertaking the collective self-transformation required to give historical reality to the new possibilities for life glimpsed in the events that unfolded (Deleuze 2003: 215–17). Despite the historical failure, the potential for radically different forms of social relation remains. Such moments of becoming breaking through into history testify to the manner in which pure events persist alongside the historical sequence of states of affairs.

Colonisation is an event of this kind: one that haunts the societies established on the territory of others who remain caught in a form of internal exile. As we saw earlier in relation to the problematic character of this event and contemporary efforts to renegotiate through legal and political means the terms of the original solution to the jurisprudential problem of colonisation, the event of colonisation may re-emerge into history in unexpected ways. This is what occurred in Australia with the 1992 *Mabo* decision and the sudden emergence of Native title jurisprudence within Australian law. A decision by the High Court reactivated an event that had never entirely passed but continued to hover over the history of relations between indigenous and non-indigenous Australians like mist over breaking waves. The historical moment in which this decision took place involved a return to earlier events of colonisation, collapsing elements of the colonial past into the present and making these parts of the ongoing elaboration of the future. At such moments, we glimpse the possibility of an altogether different relationship between indigenous and settler communities, premised on mutual recognition and equality rather than incorporation and subordination. In Deleuzian terms, the philosophical challenge is to extract a new concept from the colonial encounter and its aftermath, to counter-actualise this event in a manner that might open up the possibility of post-colonial society.

# References

Bartlett, Richard, H. (ed.) (1993), *The Mabo Decision*, Sydney: Butterworths.
Borrows, J. (2001), 'Questioning Canada's Title to Land: The Rule of Law, Aboriginal Peoples and Colonialism', in J. Borrows (2001), *Speaking Truth to Power: A Treaty Forum*, Ottawa: Law Commission of Canada; Vancouver: British Columbia Treaty Commission, pp. 35–72.

Chesterman, J. and Galligan, B. (1997), *Citizens without Rights: Aborigines and Australian Citizenship*, Melbourne: Cambridge University Press.

Day, D. (1996), *Claiming a Continent: A History of Australia*, Sydney: Angus and Robertson.

Deleuze, G. (1990), *The Logic of Sense*, trans. M. Lester and C. Stivale, with Boundas, C. (ed.), New York: Columbia University Press.

Deleuze, G. (1993), *The Fold: Leibniz and the Baroque*, trans. T. Conley, Minneapolis and London: University of Minnesota Press.

Deleuze, G. (1994), *Difference and Repetition*, trans. P. Patton, New York: Columbia University Press.

Deleuze, G. (1995), *Negotiations 1972–1990*, trans. M. Joughin, Columbia: University of Columbia Press.

Deleuze, G. (1998), 'The Indians of Palestine', trans. T. S. Murphy, *Discourse* 20 (3): 25–4.

Deleuze, G. (2003), *Deux régimes de fous: textes et entretiens 1975–1995*, ed. D. Lapoujade, Paris: Minuit.

Deleuze, G. and Guattari, F. (1977), *Anti-Oedipus: Capitalism and Schizophrenia*, trans. R. Hurley, M. Seem and H. R. Lane, New York: Viking Press.

Deleuze, G. and Guattari, F. (1987), *A Thousand Plateaus: Capitalism and Schizophrenia*, trans. B. Massumi, Minneapolis: University of Minnesota Press.

Deleuze, G. and Guattari, F. (1994), *What is Philosophy?*, trans. H. Tomlinson and G. Burchell, New York: Columbia University Press.

Derrida, J. (1988), *Limited Inc*, Evanston: Northwestern University Press.

Derrida, J. (1992), 'Force of Law: The "Mystical Foundation of Authority" ', in D. Cornell et al. (eds) (1922), *Deconstruction and the Possibility of Justice*, London and New York: Routledge, pp. 3–67.

Patton, P. (2000), *Deleuze and the Political*, London and New York: Routledge.

Persky, S. (ed.) (1998), *The Supreme Court Decision on Aboriginal Title: Delgamuukw*, Vancouver and Toronto: Greystone Books.

Reynolds, H. (1996), *Aboriginal Sovereignty*, Sydney: Allen and Unwin.

Tully, J. (1994), 'Aboriginal Property and Western Theory: Recovering a Middle Ground', *Social Philosophy and Policy*, 11 (2): 153–80.

Tully, J. (1995), *Strange Multiplicity: Constitutionalism in an Age of Diversity*, Cambridge: Cambridge University Press.

Tully, J. (1998), 'A Fair and Just Relationship', *Meanjin* 57 (1): 146–67.

# Notes

1. This interview originally appeared in *Libération*, May 8–9, 1982. It is reprinted in Deleuze 2003: 179–84.
2. In a letter originally published as a preface to Jean-Clet Martin's *Variations: la Philosophie de Gilles Deleuze* (1993, Paris: Editions Payot), Deleuze suggests that: '[I]t is always worthwhile in analysing concepts to begin with very simple, very concrete situations, rather than with philosophical antecedents or even with the problems as such . . .' (Deleuze 2003: 339).
3. Similarly, in *Difference and Repetition* Deleuze writes that 'problems are of the order of events' (Deleuze 1994: 188).
4. *Calder et al. v. Attorney-General of British Columbia* (1973), SCR 313.
5. *Mabo v. Queensland* (1992), 175 CLR 1; 66 ALJR 408; 107 ALR 1. Future references are to Bartlett 1993.
6. *Wik Peoples v. Queensland* (1996), 187 CLR 1; *Yorta Yorta Aboriginal Community v. Victoria* (2002), 194 ALR 538.

7. See also Tully (1998).
8. I owe this example to Eugene Holland.
9. John Borrows points out that, from the point of view of Aboriginal peoples, the Crown's assertion of sovereignty is an exercise of arbitrary power. It is carried out without consultation or consent. In consequence, taking seriously the principle that the rule of law stands as a bulwark against arbitrariness and oppression would invalidate the Crown's claims to sovereignty and support the continued sovereignty of the Aboriginal peoples: 'Canada's laws should be declared invalid, though enforceable, by the application of the rule of law until the parties resolve this situation through negotiation' (Borrows 2001: 54).
10. These are the terms in which Justice Burton described Aboriginal law in the 1836 New South Wales case of *R v. Murrell* (Reynolds 1996: 62).
11. *Delgamuukw v. British Columbia* (1997), 3 SCR 1010. Future references are to Persky 1998.

# Chapter 7

# Deterritorialising the Holocaust

*Adrian Parr*

> Remember what Amalek did to you on your journey after you left Egypt . . .
> you shall blot out the memory of Amalek from under the heaven. Do not
> forget! (Deuteronomy 25: 17–19)

> Holocaust survivor Jehuda Elkana publicly announced in 1988 that there
> is . . . no more important political and pedagogical task for the leaders of
> [Israel] than to side with life, dedicate themselves to the future, and not
> deal constantly with the symbols, ceremonies and lessons of the Holocaust.
> They must eradicate the domination of this historical memory over our life.
> (Cole 1999: 135)

Interestingly, the words of Elkana hauntingly echo those in Deuteronomy,
the selfsame phrase underpinning the activities in restless synagogues
worldwide during the festival of Purim.[1] When the name of Amalek's
descendant – Haman – is sounded everyone boos, hisses, makes noise
with a *greggar* (noisemaker) and stamps their feet (many have the name
of Haman written on the soles of their shoes so that when they stamp his
name is simultaneously erased).[2] Asserting the complexity of history, both
Elkana and Purim festivities position history between two irreducible differences: forgetting and remembrance. During Purim, memory is kept *in*
circulation as a problem taken up anew by each generation; the problem
is not one that can be reduced to either the blotting out of Amalek's name,
nor the call 'Do not forget'. Simply put, each generation probes history
with the question: how can we be inspired not crippled by memory? And
this question is largely a problem of how to deterritorialise the monu-
mentality of history, concomitantly invoking the double becoming of
'singular memory'.

  This chapter aims to explore the connection between history and
memory. I will propose there are two kinds of memory: singular and reterritorialising. The reterritorialising function of memory is developed by
Gilles Deleuze and Félix Guattari in *A Thousand Plateaus*. On this

account memory is a majoritarian system or molar formation. In true Deleuzian fashion, though, the majority is not held in opposition to the minority. Deleuze and Guattari maintain that minoritarian elements or forces subsist throughout the majoritarian system and it is here, along these minoritarian lines of becoming, that the very notion of what I will call a 'singular memory' appears.[3] In key respects the concept of singular memory is close to Deleuze's examination of 'a' memory in *Cinema 2* (1989) and it is even implied in the contrast he and Guattari form between blocks of memory and one's own specific memories in *A Thousand Plateaus* (1987). Singular memory then, enervates the majoritarian system of history. This is not to suggest that history is without value, rather, it is important we recognise that history is one way of studying the past and it certainly makes the past more comprehensible and accessible, but history cannot be equated with the past. The past on the whole is beyond history. What I find most interesting about memory is its pre-personal dimension, the way in which memory can overwhelm historical organisation and affirm a level of unconscious affect. What I therefore seek in the problem of memory is the question of desiring-production; how memory is social and engenders particular investments of desire.

## What does History Grasp?

In *What is Philosophy?* Deleuze and Guattari explain: 'What History grasps of the event is its effectuation in states of affairs or in lived experience, but the event in its becoming, in its specific consistency, in its self-positing as concept escapes History' (Deleuze and Guattari 1994: 110). In *A Thousand Plateaus* they insist history can be conceptualised in terms of past and future and they liken it to macropolitics, explaining this is because history is concerned with 'knowing how to win or obtain a majority' (Deleuze and Guattari 1987: 292). And here we need to keep in mind that 'majority', in the way that they intend it, does not refer to numbers or quantities but states of domination, and in this way it is the opposite of becoming, which is always minoritarian. A minority, they explain, is a molecular entity, a deterritorialising movement, a non-localisable relation or a zone of indiscernibility. On the other hand, the becoming of the minority can decompose the standard measure of the majority. Yet the problem of the majority and minority is not one of their opposition, rather it is one of becoming (Deleuze and Guattari 1994: 104). Proposing the concept of becoming here as the relation between minority and majority overturns the dualism at the heart of being. That is to say, it is not 'a being' that becomes but instead there exists a vibrant system of mutation and difference that inheres throughout life as a whole. In the context of his other work, the concept of becoming allows Deleuze to develop a dynamic account of time whereby he affirms the creative force of life and interrogates the limits of history. He shows that the time I myself may perceive and experience is really only one time. What he is more interested in are the lines of becoming defining times other than my own independent time, the time that marks different yet coexisting histories.

Together Deleuze and Guattari argue history is distinct from experimentation and the process of becoming. History, they insist, is best understood as a 'set of negative conditions' that enable experimentation (Deleuze and Guattari 1994: 111). We cannot understand the present by referring back to a past event, nor can we predict what the future will be based on what has happened to date; there simply is no unified historical sequence. This is because nothing ever remains the same, the present is always becoming what it is not and in the process there are always new variables or forces being introduced into the equation that complicate any teleological conception of historical time as an ordered series of events. Becoming cannot be defined as history, in fact they go so far as to announce that becoming is ahistorical, although in the absence of history the experimental flavour of becoming would simply remain unconditioned and undefined.

Ultimately what 'history grasps in an event is the way it's actualised in particular circumstances; the event's becoming is beyond the scope of history' (Deleuze 1995: 170). As such history is a negative precondition that facilitates experimentation with something that lies beyond history itself. This is not to say that history solves the problems lurking behind a pre-existing solution or even that it is only events that matter. Emphasising the problematic nature of events may at a brief glance seem to suggest that solutions are irrelevant to Deleuze. On the contrary, in *Bergsonism* Deleuze is quick to point out that: '[I]t is the solution that counts, but the problem always has the solution it deserves, in terms of the way in which it is stated . . . and of the means and terms at our disposal for stating it' (Deleuze 1991: 16). In this way, our problem here becomes one of how history can experiment with time and events without monumentalising the past, for instance, in the way that Freud tended to do when he privileged Oedipalised remembrance in his analysis of the unconscious.

What Deleuze and Guattari find useful in Freud is his discovery of libidinal desire, yet they fiercely contest the manner in which Freud personifies desire reducing it to a domestic representation of the Oedipus complex, denying the productive dimension of the unconscious along with it. They do not, however, reject outright the Oedipus complex, only the way in which it is mistakenly used as *representative* of an unconscious past. Actually, as will be discussed later in this chapter, if we don't consider the unconscious as an extension of 'my' own repression but take the alternative tack and say that 'I am the effect of unconscious investment', then Oedipus becomes most useful for understanding sociopolitical repression: 'Oedipus is a requirement or a consequence of social reproduction, insofar as this latter aims at domesticating a genealogical form and content that are in every way intractable' (Deleuze and Guattari 1977: 13). The genealogical form they speak of here prefers to consider, for instance, how the concept of 'the father' is produced not what the father figure is representative of, as Freud preferred. In practical terms this might be the history of sociopolitical investment in the father figure and the sorts of power relations such a history exposes.

What about memory though? Memory, for Deleuze, can be either a reterritorialising movement or the double becoming of history. For instance the memory that collects the memories of minorities is described as a 'majoritarian agency' that colonises minoritarian memory (Deleuze and Guattari 1987: 293).[4] Or, finding investment in the form of history memory enters into circulation with exchange and commodity value at which point it once again turns into a powerful reterritorialising movement. So when Deleuze and Guattari describe becoming as 'antimemory' what they are referring to is the reterritorialising function of memory that integrates the molecular memories of children, women and blacks into a majoritarian system of history. Prior to integration, though, memory remains outside circulation as pure production, a positive deterritorialising force of change, or a 'double becoming' as Deleuze describes it in *Cinema 2* (Deleuze 1989: 221).

I would like to propose that it is through the absolute unconditional and experimental force of singular memory that history is conditioned. This would seem to suggest that singular memory is the creative condition of history, its untimely aspect. Hence, the creativity of memory necessarily refers to the creativity *inherent* to memory itself – the production of memory as that whose power is non-existent, nonetheless the force of which persists. The alternative thesis that states memory has an inherent not created value, as the Freudian theory of the unconscious poses, means we inevitably end up monumentalising the past, or, as Ian Buchanan so convincingly demonstrates in his discussion of Daniel Libeskind's 'Freedom Tower', memorialisation turns the past into 'tokens that "stand for" the lost territory' (Buchanan in Buchanan and Lambert 2005: 31).

## Singular Memory

Whilst Deleuze and Guattari certainly criticise memory in *A Thousand Plateaus* as always having a reterritorialising function (Deleuze and Guattari 1987: 294), there is also scope within the broader corpus of Deleuze's theory of time for another kind of memory; what might be called 'singular memory'. The first synthesis and foundation of time is habit; memory depends upon habit to ground time (Deleuze 1994: 78). There are two mnemonic syntheses: active and passive. The active synthesis is representational: a material representation. The passive synthesis is a spiritual repetition that involves a pure past: a productive unconscious that exceeds habit and the present. Deleuze writes that the material repetition of memory is a 'repetition of successive independent elements or instants', in other words the calculated time of chronology or *chronos* as the Ancient Greeks called it. Conversely, the spiritual repetition of memory is a 'repetition of the Whole on diverse coexisting levels' (Deleuze 1994: 84). As the ground of time memory is the antithesis of becoming, but as the passive synthesis of time the repetition and difference of singular memory is connected to the empty form of time in all its becoming. Deleuze clarifies that spiritual:

> repetition unfolds in the being in itself of the past, whereas representation concerns and reaches only those presents which result from active synthesis, thereby subordinating all repetition, to the identity of the present present in reflection, or to the resemblance of the former present in reproduction. (Deleuze 1994: 84)

This brings us to the pressing question of how history and memory converge. Deleuze and Guattari say:

> History may try to break its ties to memory; it may make the schemas of memory more elaborate, superpose and shift co-ordinates, emphasize connections, or deepen breaks. The dividing line, however, is not there. The dividing line passes not between history and memory but between punctual 'history-memory' systems and diagonal or multilinear assemblages, which are in no way eternal: they are to do with becoming: they are a bit of becoming in the pure state; they are transhistorical. (Deleuze and Guattari 1987: 296).

If history does not merge with the event of 'singular memory', as I am calling it, then singular memory is where deterritorialisation and reterritorialisation meet (Deleuze and Guattari 1994: 110). This is the memory of double becoming; it 'is not a psychological memory as faculty for summoning recollections, or even a collective memory as that of an existing people . . . [it is] the strange faculty that puts into immediate contact the outside and the inside . . .' (Deleuze 1989: 221).

Not only is the value of singular memory a potential value, its actual value does not surface until the moment when remembrance takes place. As a whole, the past is virtual; it is independent of the actualisations produced through remembrance. Deleuze points out in *Bergsonism* each and every actualisation is a creation and condensation of all the possibilities stored within the whole of memory.[5] This invites us to approach memory as populated by pre-personal singularities, a singular memory that resists ownership by the self and cannot be inhabited by the thinking subject. The event that history tries to grasp, but which also persists beyond the scope of history, is the Deleuzian pre-personal singularity. What is grasped or brought into actualisation is one thing but then there still continues a virtual reality that has not yet been actualised. The limit of transcendental philosophy and metaphysics lies here in the way singularities are thought, that being within the confines of the subject or thinking self (Descartes' *cogito*). By contrast, for Deleuze what is needed is a conception of the pre-personal singularities that endure beyond the actualisations of self or a specific body. Here he brings to our attention the expressive horizon that traverses human beings, a field that is immanent to the thinking subject. Hence when we combine singularity with memory, memory is liberated from psychological consciousness. As the expressive, but not yet actualised field of time, singular memory is affective and productive.

How singular memory is implicated in and complicates history is what materialist psychiatry addresses:

> A materialist psychiatry is one that brings production into desire on the one hand and desire into production on the other. *Délire* turns not on the father; nor even 'the name of the father,' but on names in History. (Guattari in Deleuze 1995: 17–18)[6]

For example, the theory and practice of Freudian psychoanalysis advocates a return to a past time (a repressed Oedipal experience), hence Freud's whole idea of memory is reduced to a psychological function involving a return of the same time. On the other hand, Deleuze and Guattari prefer to think about the productive dimension of desire as the experience of repetition in terms of difference, an idea that contains within it the seed for a creative dimension to memory, insofar as it presupposes a future orientated perspective: a return that repeats to produce difference.[7] And it is this connection between memory, history and desire that will be the driving problem underpinning my discussion of the Holocaust further on in this chapter.

Deleuze and Guattari have an innovative and, maybe for some, idio-syncractic understanding of desire. Rather than consider the question of a body in terms of 'part objects' they prefer to think of it in terms of 'dif-ferential speeds' (Deleuze and Guattari 1987: 172). On the one hand they celebrate Melanie Klein's discovery of partial objects, and on the other they criticise her for not fully understanding the logic of partial objects because she considers these from the viewpoint of consumption, all the while failing to address their productive potential. For Klein, they explain, partial objects are 'destined to play a role in totalities aimed at integrating the ego, the object, and drives in later life, but they also con-stitute the original type of object relation between the ego, the mother and the father' (Deleuze and Guattari 1977: 44). Hence, Klein's under-standing of desire incarcerates desiring-production in the unified whole of complete objects. For example, the initial focus on the part object (the breast as a source of security, nourishment and satisfaction) comes at the expense of the whole. Eventually, Klein argues that the child at around three or four months of age starts to unify these parts into a whole object (mother) and subsequently desire in all its affective and productive potential is reduced to parental images and familial relations. In effect, what Klein does is simply 'water Oedipus down'; she miniaturises Oedipus, finding Oedipus everywhere, extending him to the 'very earli-est years of life' (Deleuze and Guattari 1977: 45).

What Deleuze and Guattari propose is that partial objects are prior to the figure of Oedipus, they are related to desiring-production and can therefore have 'sufficient charge in and of themselves to blow up all of Oedipus and totally demolish its ridiculous claim to represent the uncon-scious, to triangulate the unconscious, to encompass the entire produc-tion of desire' (Deleuze and Guattari 1977: 44). Furthermore they insist:

[S]ocial production and relations of production are an institution of desire, and affects or drives form part of the infrastructure itself. For *they are part of it, they are present there in every way* while creating within the economic forms their own repression, as well as the means for breaking this repres-sion. (Deleuze and Guattari 1977: 63)

Desire is productive and social, it is not instinctual as Freud posits, nor is it a 'drive' that sets out to integrate partial objects into a whole. In fact, unlike Klein, Deleuze and Guattari insist partial objects are not unified into the whole object of the mother or integrated into the 'self'; rather they are virtual. As virtual entities, partial objects can never be fully realised in reality as a single object, they are 'explosions, rotations, vibrations' (Deleuze and Guattari 1977: 44). Accordingly, desire is not contained within the body, instead it is the movement producing bodies and it also moves beyond individual bodies, it is in excess of a body. A social body that is understood as desiring-production then, may be reproducing itself but it is also deterritorialising, meaning that on another level it is undergoing change.

In *A Thousand Plateaus: Capitalism and Schizophrenia*, Deleuze and Guattari insist deterritorialisation is a movement. They liken it to a 'line of flight' insofar as it connects with other deterritorialising elements (as opposed to conjugating these), concomitantly changing something in its nature. What defines a deterritorialisation is not its speed (increases or decreases in acceleration) but rather its nature. Absolute deterritorialisations happen within the molecularity of the social, but they can occur only through relative deterritorialisations that take place on the molarity of collective and individual life (actuality). As such there is a 'perpetual immanence of absolute deterritorialisation within relative deterritorialisation' (Deleuze and Guattari 1987: 56).[8]

In light of my discussion here, I will be examining deterritorialisation in the context of singular memory, forming a distinction between the absolute unconditioned whole of memory and the conditioned form of history as that which is abstracted from desiring-production. This allows us to avoid reducing the memory of the Holocaust to a therapeutic function and to think about it in terms of an affective connection, a connection that in turn produces the Holocaust. This means that the Holocaust cannot be understood as a ground that is interpreted or that the history of the Holocaust represents the reality of the Holocaust, but that the Holocaust is an effect of how the Holocaust is in fact produced. Whilst I may have no personal memory of the Holocaust I am needless to say affected by it, but in a way that is completely different from a Holocaust survivor.[9] In this sense, memory is not just a conscious recollection but also an affective material consciousness. Deleuze and Guattari's discussion of Little Hans' horse underscores this point: in this instance the traumatic circulation of memory throughout the body is not representative but affective. Consequently memory is not necessarily the result of a subject recalling a trauma, instead memory produces relations of movement, the effect of which is trauma (Deleuze and Guattari 1987: 257).

## How can we Deterritorialise the Holocaust?

Architect Daniel Libeskind once wrote: '[H]istory is not the statistics of the six million Jews, but a unique Jewish individual multiplied six million times' (Libeskind 2001: 28). He points to the challenge that the memory of the Holocaust poses: history must somehow confront both the absolute dimension of six million Jews being systematically murdered and the specificity of individual lives lost. Strikingly, Libeskind is proposing that although the loss of life is experienced by individuals, the overall trauma of the Holocaust is felt collectively. Rising to confront the singular dimension of the whole of trauma head on entails a complex system of negative movements: absolute and relative. Even though this opposition may appear unsustainable it is via their tenuous connection that the ethical challenge of memory is culturally met: the moment when history becomes other than what it once was, that moment when singular memory breaks through the colonising and reterritorialising movement of memory and those historical lines that go from the 'present to the past, or to the representation of the old present' (Deleuze and Guattari 1987: 295). Remember, to cite Deleuze and Guattari, history is 'made only by those who oppose history (not by those who insert themselves into it, or even reshape it)' (Deleuze and Guattari 1987: 295). Perhaps then singular memory moves like a deterritorialising variable of the majoritarian dimension of history? For, as Deleuze and Guattari succinctly say: '[T]here is no medium of becoming except as a deterritorialised variable of a minority' and there is 'no history but of the majority, or of minorities as defined in relation to the majority' (Deleuze and Guattari 1987: 292). The proposition to 'deterritorialise the Holocaust' occurs when culture operates as both act and frame through which the excess of singular memory is pragmatically expressed not repressed, organised, and/or signified; examples of which we will now explore.

In 1988 German-born artist Hans Haacke constructed an obelisk that brought back to life the memory of Austria's participation in Nazi war crimes.[10] The work was titled *Und Ihr Habt Doch Gesiegt* (1988), meaning 'And You Were Victorious After All'. In South Herrengasse, in the middle of Graz, Haacke's obelisk was rebuilt at the selfsame site as the original (covering the Virgin Mary), directly referencing the memorial rally of 1938 that had been held for those National Socialists killed during the July 1934 Nazi putsch. Facing the obelisk was a large billboard of posters consisting of documents from 1938 whose content clearly expressed the fascistic investment of Austrian society. In this case the announcements included one on the celebration of the burning of a Jewish synagogue, one that outlined that the university would be instructing its students in 'racial laws' and so forth. But why repeat the past in the context of the present? Putting remembrance and forgetting to work, Haacke effectively threatened history with the double becoming of singular memory, simultaneously exposing the fascistic investment of the Austrian social sphere.

Briefly, the Moscow Declaration delivered by the Allies on 1 November 1943 announced that Austria was a victim of the Third Reich. But 'victim' was certainly the wrong word in the context of Austrian history. Occupied on 13 March 1938 by Hitler, Austria actively aided and participated in Nazism. What really happened as a result of the Moscow Declaration was that Austria found satisfaction in its victim status. For instance, in 1938 the Jewish population of Austria was approximately 210,000, of these nearly 65,000 were murdered whilst another 110,000 were forced to emigrate. The overall value of the property listed in the 'Committee Report' of the Austrian Reconciliation Fund Law that was confiscated during 1938 was valued at 2,041,828,000 Reichsmark, which is equivalent to approximately US $1.01 billion (www.austria.it/vers2.htm). I mean let's be honest, who in their right mind would proudly and comfortably acknowledge complicity with the Nazis! It wasn't until the 1990s that Austria began publicly to recognise the darker underbelly of its past and rethink its proactive role in facilitating fascism.[11] Conceived in reply to the uncontested historical narrative defining post-World War II Austria, Haacke's obelisk vigorously rubbed salt in old wounds. Allowing the reservoir of possible pasts to seep into the context of contemporary Austria, Haacke provisionally synthesised the social relations producing Austria's dominant history with singular memory. Confounding where memory ended and history began, his choice of Nazi emblems and themes within the context of Graz straddled the line of both forgetting and remembering, the combination of which *exceeded* historical actualisation. What became obvious was that the repressive nature of Austrian history was not the result of forgetting (a lack of memory), rather repression was exposed by Haacke as an excess of memory. At 3 a.m. on 3 November 1988, the final form of *Und Ihr Habt Doch Gesiegt* was shaped by the charged reactions of a neo-Nazi vandal who sabotaged the work.[12]

Haacke effectively summoned forth the fictional nature of Austria's institutionalised appropriation of memory; shedding light on an important problem to do with desire. Partially repeating the past through the idealised representation of it, he exacerbated the fascistic investment producing these representations. Austria may not have been a victim of Nazism then, but the comfort found in repressing its own complicity was in itself fascistic. This invites us to consider the idealised representation of history in a different light, not as ideology but as the product of social desire, meaning the ideal representation was produced through the pleasure gained in submitting to it, or as Deleuze and Guattari might put it: 'the repressed representative, on which the representation actually comes to bear; the displaced represented, which gives a falsified apparent image that it is meant to trap desire' (Deleuze and Guattari 1977: 115).

In particular, Deleuze and Guattari's idea of social desire, taken here from Wilhelm Reich, is especially useful when analysing the social relations underpinning representations of the Holocaust and Holocaust remembrance in general. They propose that desiring-production and social production are synonymous with one another. Desire, in and of itself, is without interest, it is simply a pre-personal neutral force of unconscious affect and affirmation that either takes on a schizoid (revolutionary, disruptive) or fascistic flavour. As such: '[U]nconscious investments are made according to positions of desire and uses of synthesis, very different from the interests of the subject, individual or collective, who desires' (Deleuze and Guattari 1977: 104). Desire, that is when it does not lean towards its own repression, can dismantle or deterritorialise the social order. Only by activating the absolute deterritorialising force of singular memory, as it exists immanently in the present, in the way that Haacke did with his obelisk, could memory be considered as a pre-personal ahistorical force, one that is related but different from history. This is because Haacke's piece was more concerned with the history of desiring-production and making affective connections not simply representing reality.

Our discussion now returns to Oedipus, the all-encompassing psychoanalytic figure that captures desire within the familial triangle of incest: Mummy, Daddy and me. Deleuze and Guattari rightly insist that Oedipus is a fiction; the lack that Oedipus invokes is itself a 'product of psychic repression' (Deleuze and Guattari 1977: 115). What this means then, is that Oedipus 'is only the represented, insofar as it is induced by repression' (Deleuze and Guattari 1977: 115). Meanwhile, desiring-production is the 'limit of social production' (Deleuze and Guattari 1977: 101). Oedipus simply displaces and internalises this limit so that it is made inoffensive. This is why Oedipus derives out of a reactionary unconscious investment of desire, an investment that conforms to the 'interests of the dominant class, but operates on its own account' (Deleuze and Guattari 1977: 105). What singular memory does is cut 'across the interest of the dominated, exploited classes' and Oedipalised remembrance, causing 'flows to move that are capable of breaking apart both the segregations and their Oedipal applications'; otherwise put: create flows that are capable of what Deleuze and Guattari call 'hallucinating history' (Deleuze and Guattari 1977: 105).

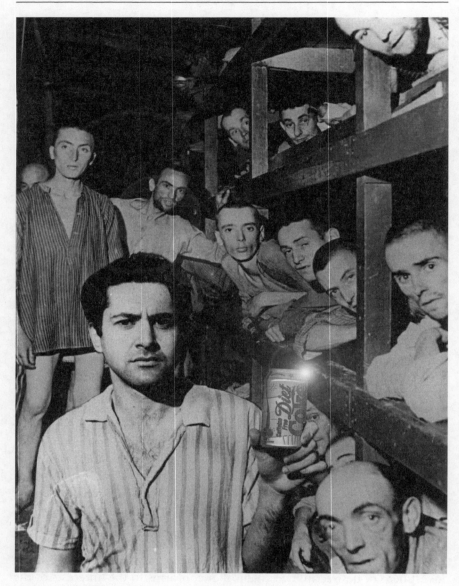

Alan Schechner, *Self-Portrait at Buchenwald: It's the Real Thing*, 1993

As expanding capital, the Holocaust is inherently meaningless; meaning only occurs at the level of the axiomatic: Hollywood, art, Holocaust education, museums, publishing, advertising, historical revisionism and the Israeli/Palestinian conflict. But how do we deterritorialise these meanings?

One answer lies in experimental culture, culture that deterritorialises standardised values and representations. Operating out of the specific context of consumerism, contemporary culture in its most radical form engages history as much as it does desiring-production and capital. Take the work of Alan Schechner for example, who explores the deeper problem of how Holocaust imagery is put to work.

In *Self-Portrait at Buchenwald: It's the Real Thing* (1993) Schechner inserts himself into a photo originally taken by Margaret Bourke-White in 1945 of the emaciated concentration camp detainees at Buchenwald. Looking the viewer firmly in the eye his posture seems to say: 'Come on, just try and consume this! I dare you!' In effect he decodes the way memory has been produced via a mechanism of co-ordination and control that codes the flow of singular memory. Proposing that there is no outside to the Holocaust image, he concomitantly opens up a space between the production and exchange/commodity value of Holocaust imagery. Surely, you cannot stand outside the image to articulate a unified theory or representation of the Holocaust without also posing the inherent value of the Holocaust image. But what is the problem with Holocaust imagery having an inherent value? As both the irony of the title and the triumphalism of Schechner's own self-portrait holding a can of Coke can invite us to consider, plainly the problem is that you end up codifying the image, making the history it is expressive of more susceptible to being turned into a commodity. Here he makes the representation function as part of the capitalist machinery, suggesting that without this, the image would no longer be productive.

The question is: how does this commodity enter the market? Is its value socially useful? Is it financially useful? The answer to these questions is 'yes'. Why? Because under these circumstances the Holocaust ends up being reified (it is regarded as having special value, a value that is in turn standardised because of its commodity status). Schechner dares to challenge the reification process by identifying a specific context – consumer culture – for the image. What this does is dismantle the whole idea that the image has an inherent value; rather the image is merely a simulacrum stimulating desiring-production.

Once again, in *Barcode to Concentration Camp Morph* (1994), Schechner sets out to break open the clarity of the image as a representation with a basis in fact; one that also has a special inherent value. Here the specificity of a group of concentration camp detainees is rendered completely abstract as he manufactures their image out of an abstract value: a barcode. The point is that Holocaust value does not originate in how much money is made from memory, but in the appropriation of how

memory is circulated; circulation is what enhances the abstract commodity value of memory whilst concomitantly expanding the value
produced from this sovereign process at the same time: abstract labour.
The documentary photograph in the hands of Schechner is a desiring-
production, the effect of which is history, a history that does not necessarily 'represent' reality but in all its affectivity certainly participates in
the production of Holocaust commodities. But how does history circulate? Schechner's answer is: as a cliché. What he does is present the cliché
to us, but in a manner that makes us uncomfortable, leaving us with
the question: how have we really survived the Holocaust? Tellingly,
Deleuze sorrowfully notes how we have all been tainted by Nazism:
'[E]ven survivors of the camps had to make compromises with it, if only
to survive' (Deleuze 1995: 172).

The former Israeli prime minister, Menachim Begin, himself a survivor
of the Holocaust, bluntly announced on 5 June 1982:

> Believe me, the alternative to fighting is Treblinka, and we have resolved that
> there would be no more Treblinkas. This is the moment in which a coura-
> geous choice has to be made. The criminal terrorists and the world must
> know that the Jewish people have a right to self-defense, just like any other
> people. (Shlaim 2001: 404–5)

In a similar vein, poet Tom Paulin was quoted in *The Guardian* vehemently proclaiming the Israeli Jews are 'Nazis and racists' who 'should be
shot dead . . . I feel nothing but hatred for them' (Foden and Mullan,
Saturday, 27 April 2002). More recently, when fourteen Orthodox teenage
girls were placed under arrest after protesting violently against Israel's
pull-out from Gaza, it was widely noted in the press that they had compared the prime minister, Ariel Sharon, to Adolf Hitler; whilst many Israeli
soldiers involved in the withdrawal expressed distress after they were
accused of being Nazis by fellow Jews (http://www.msnbc.msn. com/id/
8464410/). Strikingly, Begin uses the Holocaust as a crutch to justify
war against the infrastructure of the Palestinian Liberation Organisation
(PLO) in Lebanon; whilst the symbolic power of the Holocaust is used
by Paulin to reinforce ideologically Palestinian agency and the validity of a
Palestinian nation through the inscription of the Jewish body as absolutely
Other. Amazingly, in all these examples, visions for a future that is different, yet all the while related to the present and past, are compromised by
fascism, as the past is understood as determining the future.

Viewed from another angle, what we are dealing with here is largely
a problem of how decoded flows of mnemonic labour are turned into a
command to obedience. Singular memory is subjected to a process of

continual management that aims to prevent new social organisations from forming, this being the very reterritorialising function of memory that Deleuze and Guattari spoke of in *A Thousand Plateaus*. Put simply, Holocaust memory narrates a fixed national consciousness through historical consciousness. In his 'Postscript on Control Societies', Deleuze suggests the command to obedience, indicative of a control society, shapes and establishes the selfsame subjectivity of those using the command. What we end up with is servitude, and in this case the servitude comes from compromising with fascism, suggesting that in this instance Holocaust capital is given meaning through the axiomatic of fascism. More troubling for Israelis and Palestinians is that what they both end up with is the current situation of paranoid repression. Art, though, 'often takes advantage of this property of desiring-machines' explain Deleuze and Guattari, 'by creating veritable group fantasies in which desiring-production is used to short-circuit social production, and to interfere with the reproductive function of technical machines by introducing an element of dysfunction' (Deleuze and Guattari 1977: 31).

In *The Legacy of Abused Children* (2003), Schechner tackles the debilitating structure of repression clogging Israeli/Palestinian relations. Using images from the mass media he interrogates how memory and creativity, collectively, produce subjectivity. If desire is part of the infrastructure, as Deleuze and Guattari insist, then the infrastructure in the case of Palestinians and Israelis is violence. Repeating the image of a Jewish boy held at gunpoint by Nazi soldiers with an image of a frightened Palestinian, as the camera zooms in on the Jewish child who holds a photograph in his raised hands the shifting images concomitantly dominate and repress one another. We see the photograph of a young Palestinian who has wet himself as Israeli soldiers drag him away, and the camera continues its journey inwards so that the Jewish boy in the ghetto appears once again. What we are left with is a colonising play of moving images. Regardless of whether or not the violence is necessary for reasons of security, Schechner, much like Haacke did, introduces desire into the structure of this work exploring how it is socially organised: the repressive organisation underpinning Schechner's piece is both a productive and a reproductive force. As desire, singular memory is also a differential power, but through Holocaust investment, the Intifada and Israeli retaliation only end up repressing the radical potential this differential poses. What is really happening here is that 'a' Holocaust memory is being created; the memory itself does not belong to any one individual or group of individuals specifically. This is

Alan Schechner, The *Legacy of Abused Children*, 2003

the only way we can possibly understand the deterritorialising movement of singular memory, that 'block of becoming' that carries the
memory of the Holocaust off, creating the Holocaust not by the faculty
of memory but the desiring-production of singular memory in all its
affectivity. What both Haacke and Schechner do is fabricate the didac-
tic elements of Holocaust representation so as to oppose the linearity
of Holocaust memory, invoking forgetting so as to call forth the
Untimely.[13]

   A Deleuzian might say that the stalemate between the two bounded
national identities has emerged socially out of desire. For Jews to
acknowledge somehow that they are more than the Holocaust subject

negatively defined against the Palestinian, may in fact release the repressive investment of desire. Similarly, the Palestinians need to move beyond equating the Israeli Jews with Nazis. As Guattari proposed: '[T]he way interests are invested can be truly revolutionary, while at the same time leaving in place unconscious investments of desire that aren't revolutionary, that may even be fascistic' (Deleuze 1995: 18–19). Layering experiences of violence, Schechner produces a new collective subjectivity where the memories of both Jew and Palestinian intensify one another, one that no longer facilitates privatisation and segmentarity in contradistinction to the experiences of the other.

As Deleuze and Guattari would argue, repression is a fascistic organisation of desire, and I would like to add in the case of the Israeli/ Palestinian conflict, repression regulates mnemonic excess. In order to be the creative differential that challenges history, singular memory necessarily exceeds history. Hence, singular memory poses the possibility of deterritorialising the fascistic investment of history, because in its unconditional form it has the capacity to disrupt, and create divergences and new historical beginnings. The moment this movement is reterritorialised through the repressive investment of desire, the future ends up turning into some kind of casualty of the past. Maybe, then, the only way to move to singular memory is through what Slavoj Žižek has described in the context of communication and meaning in language, as *a leap of faith*. This, he says, is 'necessary and productive enabling communication precisely insofar as it is a counterfactual fiction' (Žižek 2004: 127). That said, the subjectivity of both Palestinians and Israeli Jews is cast out of the violence. In this light the unremitting subject-oriented perspective of both sides certainly needs to be deterritorialised. To become other than exclusively Palestinian or Jewish will certainly take a *leap of faith* allowing a more negative movement to emerge, one that is necessary if there is to be any kind of future for both sides.

In view of the continuing Palestinian/Israeli conflict and regardless of the recent withdrawal from Gaza, we are left wondering how the Holocaust and the possibility of non-existence determines the subjectivity of both Palestinian and Jewish subjects. Does it enter as the displaced limit, taking the form of universal control? Or is the possibility of non-existence the displaced limit of Jewish and Palestinian social organisation? The former is the over-coded function of an internal limit, preserving the past in determinate form, making memory conform to history. The latter is the free flow, yet differentiated force of memory that vivaciously conjures up familiar histories in unfamiliar ways.

The point here is not to 'not' remember the Holocaust, but to stimulate memory in a way that signals new ways of remembering and writing history: to forget in order to release and put to work the singular memory that coexists with history as a block of double becoming. Schechner invites us to consider that it is the role of culture to remember, not institutionalised politics, the dangers of which Haacke contentiously exposed. As for history, as long as it circulates between forgetting and remembrance, a little bit of singular memory will always escape and herein an ethical potential emerges. Indeed, only the open form of circulation can create a variety of alternatives for how the future might be. The ethical importance of culture appears full-throttle when it turns the unconditional impossibility of memory to political effect. For this precise reason, recognising the ethical possibilities of singular memory is to equip culture with the tools of forgetting and remembrance whilst simultaneously releasing it from the dereliction of historicity. As Guattari once said: '[I]t's not a matter of escaping "personally", from oneself but of allowing something to escape, like bursting a pipe or a boil' (Deleuze 1995: 19).

## References

Bauer, Y. (1982), *A History of the Holocaust*, New York: Franklin Watts.
Buchanan, I. and Lambert, G. (2005), *Deleuze and Space*, Edinburgh: Edinburgh University Press.
Cole, T. (1999), *Selling the Holocaust: From Auschwitz to Schindler*, New York: Routledge.
Committee Report. *Reconciliation Fund Law*, www.austria.it/vers2.html
Deleuze, G. (1989), *Cinema 2: The Time Image*, trans. H. Tomlinson and R. Galeta, Minneapolis: University of Minnesota Press.
Deleuze, G. (1991), *Bergsonism*, trans. H. Tomlinson and B. Habberjam, New York: Zone Books.
Deleuze, G. (1994), *Difference and Repetition*, trans. P. Patton, New York: Columbia University Press.
Deleuze, G. (1995), *Negotiations: 1972–1990*, trans. M. Joughin, New York: Columbia University Press.
Deleuze, G. and Guattari, F. (1977), *Anti-Oedipus: Capitalism and Schizophrenia*, trans. R. Hurley, M. Seem and H. R. Lane, Minneapolis: University of Minnesota Press.
Deleuze, G. and Guattari, F. (1987), *A Thousand Plateaus: Capitalism and Schizophrenia*, trans. B. Massumi, London: Athlone.
Deleuze, G. and Guattari, F. (1994), *What is Philosophy?*, trans. G. Burchell and H. Tomlinson, London: Verso.
Finkelstein, N. G. (2001), *The Holocaust Industry*, New York: Verso.
Foden, G. and Mullan, J. (2002),'When Authors Take Sides', *Guardian Unlimited*, Saturday, 27 April.
Libeskind, D. (2001), *The Space of Encounter*, New York: Universe.
Press Release (1988), 'Restitution of the Victims of the Nazi Regime', Austria, 16 December, www.austria.org/press/103.html.
Shlaim, A. (2001), *The Iron Wall: Israel and the Arab World*, New York: Norton.
Silberstein, L. (1999), *The Postzionism Debates: Knowledge and Power in Israeli Culture*, New York: Routledge.
Žižek, S. (2004), 'Iron and Gold', *New Left Review* (Jan./Feb.).

## Notes

1. Purim festivities begin at sundown on 14 March, according to the Gregorian Calendar, and during the month of Adar in the Hebrew Calendar, which is based on a lunar not a solar year.
2. According to Judaic teaching, Amalek was the first nation to have assailed the Jews during their exodus from Egypt. The Purim story is commonly associated with, or likened to the Holocaust.
3. I would like to thank Ian Buchanan for his critical input here in the development of this concept.

4. It is interesting to note Deleuze and Guattari distinguish between these two forms of memory by using a capital 'M' for the reterritorialising or colonising Memory and a lower case 'm' for minoritarian memories.

5. Deleuze explains that there are:

> four aspects of actualization: translation and rotation, which form the properly psychic moments; dynamic movement, the attitude of the body that is necessary to the stable equilibrium of the two preceding determinations; and finally, mechanical movement, the motor scheme that represents the final stage of actualization. All this involves the adaptation of the past to the present, the utilization of the past in terms of the present – what Bergson calls 'attention to life'. (Deleuze 1991: 70)

6. Martin Joughin offers a helpful explanation of Deleuze and Guattari's use of *délire* here. He says:

> Etymologically, *délirer* is to leave the furrow, go 'off the rails,' and wander in imagination and thought: meanings, images, and so on float in a dream logic rather than calmly following one another along the familiar lines or tracks of cold reason. But for Deleuze and Guattari solid 'reason' and free-floating *délire* are simply converse articulations of a single transformational 'logic of sense' that is no more anchored in a central fixed signifier – Lacan's 'name of the father' or *nom du père* (with its 'scriptural' resonance) – than in any supposedly fixed system of reference (of signifiers to ideas and things, including biological fathers) that Lacan's logic of signifiers supposedly supersedes. (Deleuze 1995: 186–7 fn.3)

7. A good example can be found in Chapter 10 of *A Thousand Plateaus*, where they positively engage with philosophers of the past announcing each investigation in the following way: 'Memories of a Bergsonian', 'Memories of a Spinozist' and so on.

8. It is also pertinent to note here that Deleuze and Guattari propose two kinds of relative deterritorialisation. A relative deterritorialisation, they explain, can be either negative, when lines of flight are subjected to reterritorialisation, or positive, such as when deterritorialising lines of flight continue to exist regardless of secondary reterritorialisation.

9. I would like to thank Ian Buchanan for bringing this distinction between personal and collective past/memory to my attention.

10. When the Nazis marched in Austria in 1938, the Austrian population, especially the Viennese, rallied to them with great enthusiasm. The arrest of political opponents was accompanied by massive action against the Jews. The process of degradation, terror, and expropriation that had taken five years in Germany was completed – indeed surpassed – in a few months in Austria. Men and women were forced to scrub streets on their knees, while crowds of Viennese stood by and cheered; shops were invaded, robbed, and their owners beaten; arbitrary arrests deprived families of fathers who were never seen again. (Bauer 1982: 106)

11. On 15 November 1994 Federal President Klestil announced:

> Today, we Austrians recognize that an acknowledgement of the full truth was long overdue. We know full well that all too often we have spoken of Austria as the first state to have lost its freedom and independence to National Socialism – and far too seldom of the fact that many of the worst henchmen in the Nazi dictatorship were Austrians. And no word of apology can ever expunge the agony of the Holocaust. In the name of the Republic of

Austria, I bow my head before the victims of that time. (Committee Report, Reconciliation Fund Law. www.austria.it/vers2.htm)

12. There is no post-fascist Austria if we take a minute to recall the public pro-Nazi affiliation of the democratically elected prime minister, Hans Gaider.
13. There are some really useful passages in *A Thousand Plateaus* that philosophically engage these ideas in detail (See Deleuze and Guattari 1987: 294–8).

# Chapter 8

# Becoming Israeli/Israeli Becomings

*Laurence J. Silberstein*

Although in previous writings on postzionism (Silberstein 1999), I drew my primary critical tools of analysis from Foucault, I had already begun to sense the importance of Deleuze and Guattari to my project. Applying such concepts as discourse, power relations, regimes of truth and power/knowledge, I analysed both Zionism and postzionism in terms of discourse and the debates between zionists and postzionists as a conflict of discourses. Over the years, however, I have increasingly sensed the inadequacy of that representation. Through a continued reading of Deleuze and Guattari, I have come to see ways in which their concepts move the discussion beyond the place enabled by my application of Foucault. Some of my own reservations have been cogently stated by Deleuze:

> If I speak, with Felix, of the agencement (assemblage) of desire, it is because I am not sure that micro-dispotifs can be described in terms of power. For myself, an agencement of desire is never either a 'natural' or a 'spontaneous' determination . . . Desire circulates in this agencement of heterogeneous elements, in this type of 'symbiosi' . . . In short, it is not the dispotifs of power that assemble (agenceraient) nor would they be constitutive; it is rather the agencements of desire that would spread throughout the formations of power following one of their dimensions. (Deleuze 1997: 185–6)

As Deleuze suggests, concepts such as apparatus and power relations are still useful. However, if the goal is to uncover and render visible the dynamic, complex productive forces that drive a national movement such as Zionism or a state like Israel, concepts such as desire and assemblage provide far more effective tools.[1] Whether the subject of analysis is assemblages such as Zionism/nationalism or Israel/nation, Deleuze helps us to move beyond unities, subjects and centralised authority and seek out the processes by means of which they are produced.

All processes take place on the plane of immanence, and within a given multi-plicity: unifications, subjectifications, rationalizations, centralizations have no special status: they often amount to an impasse or closing off that pre-vents the multiplicity's growth, the extension and unfolding of its lines, the production of something new. (Deleuze 1995: 146)

In Deleuze's terms, Zionism is perceived as an abstract machine, driven by the force of desire, producing new connections so as to make it possible for Jews to come together as a national assemblage. Such a representation of Zionism, differing significantly from dominant social scientific and historical representations, opens the way to a very differ-ent mode of analysis and critique. Instead of beginning with order and stability, with organisations, institutions and structures, I begin with the processes by means of which these are produced. Instead of thinking in terms of national (or any other kind of) identities, I look first at the mul-tiple lines and energies that produce them. In this chapter, I shall discuss various ways in which Deleuze enables a rethinking of Zionism and the Israeli state that it helped to produce; provide examples from recent Israeli scholarship, commonly labelled as postzionist, that provide support for a Deleuzian analysis of Zionism and Israel; and describe the ways in which my reading of Deleuze led me to rethink my interpret-ation of postzionism.

Concepts such as problematisation, deterritorialisation and reterritori-alisation help me to render visible the creative dynamics/processes that produce such subjectivities as the Hebrew/Jewish nation, the new Hebrew, and the sabra.[2] In zionist writings, Zionism was represented as the solution to 'the Jewish problem'. However, an analysis of these writ-ings reveals multiple and sometimes conflicting representations of the problem and, consequently, of its solution.[3] Thus, rather than begin with these different representations of the problem, Deleuze and Guattari would have us explore the processes by means of which particular prob-lematisations were produced. This then leads me to enquire into those processes that produced multiple representations of the Jewish problem in terms of anti-Semitism, economic competition, cultural decline, phys-ical deterioration, loss of connection with the land, lack of capacity for physical labour, or spiritual and artistic atrophy. This, in turn, helps to make clear that Jews, living in diverse spaces and in multiple national, political, social and cultural contexts, like any other groups, confronted multiple problems. The result is a loosening of both the problematising process whereby differing, often competing representations of the Jewish problem were produced and also the dispotifs by means of which they were produced and disseminated.

Moreover, whereas most analyses of Zionism take as given terms such as 'Jewish people' or 'Jewish nation', Deleuze and Guattari would insist that it is the processes of subjectification that demand our attention, not the molarised identities that they produce.[4] Thus, rather than take for granted a unified national identity, I am drawn to focus on the multiple lines by means of which Jewishness (later Israeliness) is mapped. Instead of thinking in terms of a single, unified zionist or Jewish subjectivity, Deleuze and Guattari place the emphasis on the complex processes whereby multiple subjectivities are produced and rendered commonsensical. In this way, Deleuzian concepts help to render visible the complex power-ridden processes through which Jews are represented as a nation and Israel as the nation's natural habitat. Although accepted in the majority representation as unproblematic, these doxa, when analysed through the concepts of Deleuze and Guattari, are shown to be the products of a dispotif, a machine that produces such subjects/objects as the Jewish people, homeland and exile. Whereas those who are effectively subjectified by these machinic processes take these to be commonsensical, Deleuze, like Foucault, urges us explore the underlying processes of subjectification.

Similarly, the critique of transcendentalising processes alerts us to the processes by means of which particular meanings, spaces, groups, practices or projects are imbued with transcendent meaning. In Zionism, as in most nationalisms, the nation, beyond being subjectified, is also rendered transcendent. This encourages an enquiry into those processes, theological and historiographic, whereby the national interpretation of Jewish life is elevated above all others.

As I have previously argued (Silberstein 1999), Deleuze and Guattari's concept of order words (*mots d'ordre*) provides an important tool for understanding such processes. Conventional studies tend to take basic zionist concepts such as *galut* (exile), *moledet* (homeland), *aliyah* (ascent to the land), *yeridah* (descent from the land), and *kibbush haaretz* (conquest of the land) as givens, paying little, if any attention to the processes whereby the spaces of the homeland are imbued with transcendent meanings. In Deleuze's terms, I am led to view these concepts, and others like them, as part of a linguistic network that codifies, directs, orders and limits. They also function to transcendentalise and privilege/deprivilege particular spaces and practices, enabling, in the process, the inscribing of molarising lines, molecular lines and lines of flight.

Insofar as the concept of homeland is, in Zionism, transcendentalised, the conquest of the land, whether through settlement practices or military action, is represented as a moral obligation. Moreover, an elaborate system of practices, including hikes, marches and classes, all function to imbue within the national subject an emotional attachment that motivates and reinforces this obligation.[5] Consequently, to leave the land and establish residence in another country is, in zionist terms, an act of betrayal, while emigrating from another country to the land of Israel is regarded as part of a redemptive process.[6] A Deleuzian analysis thus helps to render visible the production and enforcement of the dominant zionist binary of homeland/exile.[7]

From its beginnings, Zionism, in opposition to other dominant representations of Judaism, advocated the deterritorialisation of Jews from diaspora spaces as essential to solving 'the Jewish problem'. According to Zionism's nationalist logic, only when Jews are liberated, for example when they are deterritorialised from the destructive material, cultural and/or economic spaces of exile and securely established, or reterritorialised in their national homeland, could their nationalist yearnings be actualised. According to Zionism, only a territorialised Jewish people, engaged in common endeavours and sharing common values and practices could produce an authentic, unified national community and culture. Such a discourse thus renders invisible the multiplicitous nature of both Zionism and Jewishness that, as is clearly evident in Israel today, resists all efforts at total unity.[8]

As Deleuze makes clear, the reterritorialisation of Jews, or any other group, in their national homeland could not be exclusively liberating. Any socius, national or otherwise, is striated by lines that capture and arrest, as well as produce desiring energies. In Israel, minority voices of Palestinian Arabs, Mizrahi (Middle-Eastern) Jews, women, and gays and lesbians together have, in recent years, rendered these molarising grids increasingly visible.

Concepts such as mapping, multiplicity, minority, lines of flight and becomings shift our vision from the macro to the micropolitical, from the stratified state to the multiplicity of forces, from the organised society to proliferating lines of flight. In this way, Deleuze and Guattari call our attention to the complex and multiple lines comprising the state that Zionism helped bring into existence:

> One can't think about the state except in relation to the higher level of the single world market, and the lower levels of minorities, becomings, 'people' . . . below the state are becomings that can't be controlled, minorities constantly coming to life and standing up to it. (Deleuze 1995: 152)

Such a perspective results in a representation that diverges significantly from the majority arborescent representation of Israel as a logically consistent, rational system of ideas, values and institutions.

For Deleuze, minorities and becomings are key to understanding social dynamics. In his words, social fields are 'fleeing all over the place'. Accordingly: '[I]n constitutional states, it's not established and codified constitutional rights that count but everything that's legally problematic and constantly threatens to bring what's established back into question that counts' (Deleuze 1995: 153).[9] Rendering visible the multiplicity that characterises a state/nation, Deleuze and Guattari direct attention to the multiple, dynamic energies and lines of flight that majority representations eclipse. Through concepts such as majority/minority, they shift our attention away from numbers that play such an important role in liberal discourse and enable a reframing of social dynamics and power relations in terms of processes that produce them: 'What defines majority is a model you have to conform to . . . A minority has no model, it's a becoming, a process' (Deleuze 1995: 173). Whereas the dominant liberal view analyses majority/minority in terms of numbers, Deleuze represents the majority in terms of its power to produce and enforce a 'model you have to conform to', a face by means of which everyone is measured and judged. In such a reading, a minority, rather than being defined numerically and evaluated in that light, is viewed as being in tension with the majority. Consequently, what state apparatuses seek to represent as marginal phenomena positioned over and against the will of the majority, become, in Deleuze's terms, an essential part of the dynamic process by means of which a multiplicity is able to continue to become.

Accordingly, Israel, like any state, was from its inception a multiplicity. Notwithstanding the concealing effect of majority representations, numerous minority lines of flight such as Palestinian Arab citizens, Jews of Middle-Eastern origins (Mizrahi or Arab Jews), women, gays and lesbians were present from the very beginning. Rather than speak of the 'Invention and Decline of Israeliness', Deleuze and Guattari enable us to see that 'Israeliness' as such was always in process and always contested.[10] In their view, it is far more productive to see Israel, like any nation, as a multiplicity, an assemblage of individuals, collectivities, places, institutions, narratives, actions, events and subjectivities. This, in turn, renders problematic the drive of Israel, like all states, to privilege unity. Rendering visible and empowering minority voices, such an analysis assigns to them a significance obscured or concealed in virtually all (majority) representations:

> We think any society is defined not so much by its contradictions as by its lines of flight, it flees all over the place, and it's very interesting to try and follow the lines of flight taking place at some particular moment or others. (Deleuze 1995: 171)

Central to understanding of minority becoming is the concept of war machines:

> understood not as 'machines for war', but as free arrangements (*agencements*) [assemblages] oriented along a 'line of flight' out of the repressive social machinery that configures or codifies all processes and production within the extrinsic ends of a transcendent state oriented along the single 'static' line of a unitary history. (Deleuze 1988: 185 n. 5)

Rather than privilege continuity, Deleuze directs our attention to transformative processes that are rendered in terms of deterritorialisation and lines of flight.

Numerous writings produced in the Israeli academy offer concrete examples of the processes of which Deleuze speaks and increasingly provide support for an interpretation based on his concepts. Among the earliest articles to do this are several by literary critic and scholar, Hannan Hever. Hever is one of the few Israeli scholars consciously to apply Deleuze to the study of Israeli culture and society. Using such concepts as majority, minority and deterritorialisation, Hever proceeds to reframe the dominant representation of Israeli culture. He does this by applying these concepts to the writings of Israeli writer Anton Shammas, a cultural critic and the first Palestinian Arab citizen of Israel to write a Hebrew novel. Hever depicts Shammas as a minority writer who, through fiction and non-fiction, reveals the oppressive and marginalising mechanisms inscribed in Israeli culture. In Deleuze's terms, Shammas' minority writing helps to reveal the molarising effects of Israeli language and culture on Palestinian Arabs living within the borders of the state.

As Hever suggests, Shammas' writings also help to highlight the Israeli liberals' unwillingness to confront the presuppositions of their own discourse. In liberal Israeli discourse, the situation of the Palestinians is represented in terms of multiculturalism, equality and civil rights. Shammas' goal, however, is not simply to gain an equal place in the Israeli socius, but rather to open the way to a new Israeli becoming, a transformation beyond current limits of the socius. This is clearly revealed in Shammas' repeated efforts to formulate a new conception of Israeli citizenship that moves substantially beyond the boundaries established through zionist discourse.

In a debate with Israeli writer and liberal A. B. Yehoshua, Shammas challenged the Israeli practice of categorising citizens on passports as Arab or Jewish.[11] In the postzionist Israel envisioned by Shammas, a citizen would no longer be categorised in terms of Jew and Arab, but simply as Israeli. Shammas thus demanded of Israeli Jews 'that they change the rules of the game'. As Jews, he argued, they must 'reexamine the function that keeping old scores and accounts has in confusing the issues of their political and moral situation today' (Hever 1987: 57).

In Yehoshua's eyes, Shammas is comparable to a Pakistani who comes to England with a British passport and insists on being a partner in the creation of the British nationality, seeking to introduce Pakistani Muslim symbols and languages. To this, Shammas replied:

> Buli (the name by which Yehoshua is commonly known), the minute a man like you does not understand the basic difference between the Pakistani who comes to England and the Galilean who has been in Fasuta for untold generations, then what do you want us to talk about? (Grossman 1993: 254)

Responding to the further argument that to separate Israeli and Jewish is like trying to separate France from Frenchness, Shammas insisted that whereas 'France and Frenchness come from the same root, Judaism and Israeliness do not'. Thus, Shammas advocates 'the de-Judaization and de-zionization of Israel' (Grossman 1993: 256). In doing so, he seeks to redefine the word 'Israeli' so that it is inclusive of Palestinian citizens like himself. In contrast, in Yehoshua's transcendentalised vision of Israel: ' "Israeli" is the authentic, complete, and consummate word for the concept "Jewish".' Similarly, he regards Israeliness as 'the total, perfect, and original Judaism, one that should provide answers in all areas of life' (Grossman 1993: 253–4).

Rendering visible the molarising effects of the zionist state on its Palestinian citizens, Shammas effectively depicted the violence that the dominant Israeli culture perpetrates on its Palestinian population. In so doing, he posed a unique challenge to those on the Israeli-Jewish left, like Yehoshua, who frame the problems of Palestinians in Israel solely in the discourse of legal rights and political equality. This challenge effectively reveals the dilemma of Israeli liberals who take as given that there is no contradiction between Israel's claim to be both a Jewish state and a democratic state. To Shammas, however, only by transforming the 'character' of Israeli society and abandoning the dominant zionist conception of Israel as a Jewish state, and Israeli culture as basically Jewish culture, will Israel succeed in functioning as a truly democratic society.

Scholarly writings by Israeli social scientists provide additional examples that support Deleuze and Guattari's argument that: 'One of the fundamental tasks of the state is to striate the space over which it reigns' (Deleuze and Guattari 1989: 385).[12] Making visible the political and cultural effects of boundaries and spatial divisions in Israel, such writings reveal their molarising effects on Palestinians as well as Jews of Middle-Eastern origin. In the process, they render problematic the majority representation of Israel as a democracy.[13] Thus, while Jewish settlers who live outside the pre-1967 borders in the occupied territories are accorded full participation in the Israeli political system, such rights are denied to the Palestinian inhabitants of these territories. Such practices, effectively erasing any clear state borders, significantly expand the range of molarising forces in the everyday life of the society.

Several early contributions in the journal *Theory and Criticism*, a major site of postzionist critique, also highlight the power effects of such spatialising practices. Expanding on the arguments of critics who depict zionist settlement practices as colonialistic, these writings expand the scope of that critique by demonstrating the ways in which Israeli art, museums, art schools and artists' villages together with the discourse used to represent Palestinian space serve to exclude Palestinians and eclipse their presence in the land.[14]

Other studies argue that the concept of the 'Arab village', a primary tool for labelling Arab settlements, serves to objectify and fix Arab space, perpetuating a binary of modern/traditional and Jew/Arab (Eyal 1993: 41). In the period following the establishment of the state, the concept of the Arab village functioned as an object of study and control linked to the security needs of the state (Eyal 1993: 51–2). In these studies, differences between villages were eclipsed. Such studies demonstrate the ways in which spatialising practices feed into the prevailing majority discourse of 'Israeli separatism'.

As Deleuze and Guattari point out: 'It is a vital concern of every state . . . to control migrations and, more generally, to establish a zone of rights over an entire exterior, over all of the flows traversing the ecumenon' (Deleuze and Guattari 1989: 385).

In the case of Israel, studies of spatialising practices problematise the majority Israeli representation of territory, culture and national identity as essentially interconnected. Palestinian culture and society, transcending state boundaries, reveal the porous, smooth character of Israeli space. This, in turn, renders problematic the boundary lines and borders drawn by the state (Rabinowitz 2000, 2003). As a result of these borders, Palestinians have become what one scholar refers to as a 'trapped minority', torn between two national narratives and two national spaces (Rabinowitz 2001).

Notwithstanding the identification of Arab citizens of Israel with the Palestinian people, the basic terms the Israeli majority uses to label them conceal and erase this identification. The majority nomenclature of Arabs of Israel/Arviei Yisrael, Israeli Arabs/Aravim Yisraelim and simply Arabs/Aravim, conceals 'the contestatory nature of the land' (Rabinowitz

1993: 145). The use of the generic concept 'Arabs' to refer to Palestinian citizens of Israel shifts attention from the internal political conflict to internal cultural differences, thereby feeding into the liberal discourse of cultural pluralism. Yet Israeli Jews, when speaking of Arabs outside Israel, have no difficulty referring to their national identity (Jordanians, Egyptians, and so on) rather than their (Arabic) cultural identity.[15]

Such striating/labelling practices are by no means limited to Palestinian citizens of Israel. A growing number of studies highlights the impact of such practices on Israeli Jews of Middle-Eastern origin, labelled Sefardim during the state's first decades, but currently referred to as Mizrahi Jews.[16] Recent use of the concept 'Arab Jew' reflects the effort to demonstrate the ways in which the prevailing majority nomenclature is indicative of an ongoing effort to maintain a rigid separation between Jews of Middle-Eastern origin and the Arab societies and cultures from which they came (Shenhav forthcoming). The concept Arab Jew, going against the grain of majority discourse, helps to render visible both the molarising effects of that discourse as well as the complex historical and cultural interconnections between Jews from Middle-Eastern countries and Arabs. In the process, it helps to make visible the multiplicitous character of the Israeli nation, its culture and its history. On that note, perhaps the most blatant form of striation practised by the Israeli state is the wall currently being constructed to separate Israel from its Palestinian neighbours. Although framed through the discourse of security, recent writings have argued that the wall is best seen in the context of an ongoing system of violence (Azoulay and Ophir forthcoming).

Virtually all of the writings that I have cited have been labelled postzionist, primarily by defenders of Zionism.[17] In the 1990s, this term was widely applied by zionist critics to a small group of historians and social scientists who challenged and revised the majority representations of Israeli history and society. In the eyes of these critics, by calling into question the dominant interpretations, these scholars had moved beyond the boundaries of Zionism, embracing instead a postzionist position.

In Israel, majority scholarship refrains from critically analysing the zionist underpinnings of its own academic discourse (Kimmerling 1995).[18] Consequently, it stops far short of revealing the complex processes of subjectification within Zionism and in Israeli society. In most majority historical studies, for example, the 'return' of the nation to its homeland and the subsequent establishment of the state is represented as the outcome of natural historical processes. In this regard, they demonstrate the continuing force of Eric Hobsbawm's observation that: '[N]o serious historian of nations and nationalism can be a committed political nationalist . . . Nationalism requires too much belief in what is patently not so' (Hobsbawm 1990: 12).

However, among the generation of scholars that was born or entered adulthood after the establishment of the state of Israel in 1948, there were those, like Hever, who grew increasingly sceptical of the zionist axioms. In the wake of the ongoing occupation, the Yom Kippur War of 1973, the controversial 1982 invasion of Lebanon, and the first Palestinian Intifada that erupted in 1987, many of them came to doubt zionist premises. Strongly affected by the strength of increasing Palestinian nationalism and subsequent resistance efforts, they concluded that notwithstanding the majority narratives, the Israeli-Palestinian conflict stood at the centre of Israeli history and played a formative role in shaping Israeli society.[19]

Working in the 1980s with recently unclassified documents, scholars who came to be known as 'new historians' and 'critical sociologists' increasingly questioned official versions of Israeli history and social science.[20] It was to this group that the term 'postzionist' was first applied. However, another, theoretically informed type of postzionism influenced by the critical discourse of French post-structuralist theory among others produced a critique of Zionism that went far beyond conventional historical or sociological revisionism.[21]

Read through Deleuze's categories, postzionism may be best seen as a line of flight or war machine, which he characterised as having 'nothing to do with war but to do with a particular way of occupying, taking up, space-time, or inventing new space-times'. For Deleuze and Guattari: '[N]ot just revolutionary movements, but artistic movements too, are war-machines in this sense' (Deleuze 1995: 172). Viewing postzionism in this way enables an analysis that goes beyond the one I had previously posited. Whereas under the impact of Foucault, I spoke of postzionism, like Zionism, as discourse (1999, 2002 and forthcoming), I have increasingly come to see the inadequacy of this concept. As I see it, concepts such as line of flight or war machines, understood as transforming machines (Patton 2000), provide a far more cogent direction of analysis. Rather than position Zionism at the centre and define postzionism in relation to it, viewing postzionism as a line of flight renders more visible its creative, productive force. Represented in this way, postzionism is not solely a negative of critical project, but rather a productive, transformative process fuelled by a desire to transform Israeli society beyond the limits imposed by zionist boundaries. Although still regarded as Zionism's other, it emerges as a very different form of other, 'neither an object nor a subject (an other subject) but an expression of a possible world' (Deleuze 1995: 147).

With the exception of Hever's, none of the scholarly writings I have cited as contributing to the postzionist line of flight display any connection to Deleuze. Nonetheless, as I have sought to show, these writings help to fuel a Deleuzian analysis of Zionism and Israel. At the same time, framing these writings through a Deleuzian perspective has the effect of reshaping and connecting them so as to render more clearly their contribution to a postzionist line of flight.

Postzionists are frequently criticised for their failure to provide a detailed programme for the future. Such a refusal, however, is clearly consistent with Deleuze's perspective. As a process of becoming, postzionism cannot but refrain from proposing specific programmes. Instead, it invests its energies in making visible the ongoing processes of deterritorialisation and the lines of flight that continue to redefine and transform the Israeli socius. In the process, I would argue, postzionism helps to move these processes beyond the current majority imposed limits and open new and productive avenues of becoming, of becoming Israeli, of Israeli becomings.

# References

Alcalay, A. (1993), *After Jews and Arabs: Remaking Levantine Culture*, Minneapolis: University of Minnesota Press.

Almog, O. (2000), *The Sabra: The Generation of the New Jew*, Berkeley, Los Angeles and London: University of California Press.

Avineri, S. (1981), *The Making of Modern Zionism: The Intellectual Origins of the Jewish State*, New York: Basic Books.

Azoulay, A. and Ophir, A. (forthcoming), 'The Monster's Tail', in M. Sorkin (ed.) (forthcoming), *Against the Wall*, New York: New Press.

Benvenisti, M. (1986), *Conflicts and Contradictions*, New York: Dillard Books.

Benvenisti, M. (2000), *Sacred Landscapes: The Buried History of the Holy Land since 1948*, Berkeley, Los Angeles and London: University of California Press.

Deleuze, G. (1988), *Foucault*, trans. S. Hand, Minneapolis: University of Minnesota Press.

Deleuze, G. (1995), *Negotiations: 1972–1990*, trans. M. Joughin, New York: Columbia University Press.

Deleuze, G. (1997), 'Desire and Pleasure', in A. I. Davidson (ed. and intro.) (1997), *Foucault and His Interlocutors*, trans. D. W. Smith, Chicago: University of Chicago Press, pp. 183–92.

Deleuze, G. and Guattari, F. (1986), *Kafka: Toward A Minor Literature*, trans. D. Polan, Minneapolis: University of Minnesota Press.

Deleuze, G. and Guattari, F. (1989), *A Thousand Plateaus: Capitalism and Schizophrenia*, trans. B. Massumi, Minneapolis: University of Minnesota Press.

Deleuze, G. and Parnet, C. (1987), *Dialogues*, New York: Columbia University Press.

Evron, B. (1998), *Jewish State or Israeli Nation*, Bloomington and Indianapolis: Indiana University Press.

Eyal, G. (1993), 'The Discourse on the "Arab Village" in Israel' (Hebrew), *Theory and Criticism* 3 (winter): 39–55.

Foucault, M. (2004), *The Essential Foucault*, ed. P. Rabinow and N. Rose, New York and London: The New Press.

Gross, A. (1998), 'The Politics of Rights in Israeli Constitutional Law', *Israel Studies* V (3), (Fall): 80–104.

Grossman, D. (1993), *Sleeping on a Wire: Conversations with Palestinians in Israel*, New York: Farrar, Straus and Giroux.

Hertzberg, A. (ed.) (1970), *The Zionist Idea*, New York: Atheneum.

Hever, H. (1987), 'Hebrew in an Israeli Arab Hand: Six Miniatures on Anton Shammas's *Arabesques*', *Cultural Critique* 7: 47–76.

Hever, H. (1990), 'Hebrew in an Israeli Arab Hand: Six Miniatures on Anton Shammas's *Arabesques*', in A. R. JanMohamed and D. Lloyd (eds) (1990), *The Nature and Context of Minority Discourse*, New York: Oxford University Press, pp. 264–93.

Hever, H. (2002), *Producing the Modern Hebrew Canon: Nation Building and Minority Discourse*, New York: New York University Press.

Hobsbawm, E. (1990), *Nations and Nationalism since 1780: Programme, Myth, Reality*, Cambridge: Cambridge University Press.

Karsh, E. (1997), *Fabricating Israeli History: The 'New Historians'*, London and Portland: Frank Cass and Company.

Kemp, A. (1997), *Talking Boundaries: The Making of Political Territory in Israel, 1949–1957*, Ph.D. dissertation, Tel Aviv University.

Kimmerling, B. (1983), *Zionism and Territory: The Socio-Territorial Dimension of Zionist Politics*, Berkeley: University of California.

Kimmerling, B. (1995), 'Academic History Caught in the Cross-Fire: The Case of Israeli-Jewish Historiography', *History and Memory* 7 (1) (Spring/Summer): 41–65.

Kimmerling, B. (2001), *The Invention and Decline of Israeliness: State, Society, and the Military*, Berkeley: University of California Press.

Kimmerling, B. and Migdal, J. (1993), *Palestinians: The Making of a People*, New York: Free Press.

Landers, Y. (1994), 'The Sin that we Committed in Establishing the State' (Hebrew), *Davar HaShavua*, 18 March: 8–9.

May, T. (2005), *Gilles Deleuze: An Introduction*, Cambridge: Cambridge University Press.

Morris, B. (1988), *The Birth of the Palestinian Refugee Problem*, Cambridge: Cambridge University Press.

Motzafi-Haller, P. (1998), 'Scholarship, Identity and Power: Mizrahi Women in Israel', *Signs: Journal of Women in Culture and Society* 13 (2): 697–735.

Oz, A. (1983), *In the Land of Israel*, New York: Random House.

Patton, P. (2000), *Deleuze and the Political*, New York and London: Routledge.

Rabinow, P. and Rose, N. (eds) (2004), *The Essential Foucault*, New York and London: The New Press.

Rabinowitz, D. (1993), 'Oriental Nostalgia: The Transformation of Palestinians to "Israeli Arabs" ' (Hebrew), *Theory and Criticism* (Fall): 41–51.

Rabinowitz, D. (2000), 'Postnational Palestine/Israel: Globalization, Diaspora, Transnationalism, and the Israeli-Palestinian Conflict', *Critical Inquiry* (Summer): 757–81.

Rabinowitz, D. (2001), 'The Palestinian Citizens of Israel, the Concept of Trapped Minority and the Discourse of Transnationalism in Anthropology', *Ethnic and Racial Studies* 24 (1) (January): 64–85.

Rabinowitz, D. (2003), 'Borders and Their Discontents: Israel's Green Line, Arabness and Unilateral Separation', *European Studies: A Journal of European Culture, History, and Politics* 19: 217–31.

Rajchman, J. (2000), *The Deleuze Connections*, Boston: MIT Press.

Ram, U. (ed.) (1993), *Israeli Society: Critical Perspectives* (Hebrew), Tel Aviv: Breirot.

Ram, U. (1995), *The Changing Agenda of Israeli Sociology: Theory, Ideology, and Identity*, New York: SUNY Press.

Rosenthal, D. (2003), *The Israelis: Ordinary People in an Extraordinary Land*, New York: Free Press.

Rubinstein, A. (2000), *From Herzl to Rabin: The Changing Image of Zionism*, New York: Holmes and Meir.

Shafir, G. (1989), *Land, Labor and the Origins of the Israeli-Palestinian Conflict, 1882–1914*, Cambridge: Cambridge University Press.

Sharan, S. (ed.) (2003), *Israel and the Post-Zionists: A Nation at Risk*, Brighton and Portland: Sussex Academic Press.

Shenhav, Y. (forthcoming), *The Arab Jews*, Stanford: Stanford University Press.

Shimoni, G. (1995), *The Zionist Ideology*, Hanover: Brandeis University Press.

Shohat, E. (1988), 'Sephardim in Israel: Zionism from the Standpoint of its Jewish Victims', *Social Text* 19–20: 1–34.

Shohat, E. (1989), *Israeli Cinema: East/West and the Politics of Representation*, Austin: University of Texas Press.

Silberstein, L. J. (1999), *The Postzionism Debates: Knowledge and Power in Israeli Culture*, New York and London: Routledge.

Silberstein, L. J. (2002), 'Postzionism: A Critique of Israel's Zionist Discourse', *Palestine Israel Journal* 9 (2–3) (summer): 84–91, and (winter): 97–106.

Silberstein, L. J. (forthcoming), 'Postzionism as Critique: The Challenge to Jewish Studies', in A. Gotzmann and C. Wiese (eds) (forthcoming), *Modern Judaism and Historical Consciousness: Identities – Encounters – Perspectives*, Leiden and Boston: Brill Publishers.

Smith, D. (2003), 'Deleuze and the Liberal Tradition: Normativity, Freedom and Judgement', *Economy and Society* 32 (2): 299–324.

Swirski, S. (1989), *Israel: The Oriental Majority*, London: Zed Books.

Yiftachel, O. (1998), 'Nation Building and the Division of Space: Frontiers and Domination in the Israeli "Ethnocracy"', *Nationalism and Ethnic Politics* 4 (3): 33–58.

Yiftachel, O. (1999), 'Ethnocracy: The Politics of Judaizing Israel/Palestine', *Constellations* 6 (3): 364–90.

Yiftachel, O. (2000), 'Ethnocracy and Its Discontents', *Critical Inquiry* 26 (4) (summer): 725–7.

Zerubavel, Y. (1995), *Recovered Roots: Collective Memory and the Making of Israeli National Tradition*, Chicago: University of Chicago.

## Notes

1. While those critics who charge that Foucault retains a dualism of discourse and practice have disregarded Foucault's repeated insistence that discourse entails practice, the term 'discourse' does open the door to such misunderstanding. Moreover, whereas Foucault repeatedly emphasised the positive and negative dimensions of power, I am persuaded by Deleuze's argument that the category of desire more effectively reveals power's creative and productive dimensions (see, in particular, Deleuze 1997 and 1995: 83–118).

2. See in regard to the 'new Hebrew', Rubinstein 2000, Chapters 1–3. On the sabra, see Almog 2000.

3. See Silberstein 1999, Chapter 1. See also Hertzberg 1970 and Shimoni 1995. I find their use of the singular in their titles, *The Zionist Idea* and *The Zionist*

*Ideology*, to be indicative of a synthesising orientation that is commonly found in scholarly writings on Zionism.

4. For a perceptive analysis that renders problematic these categories, see Evron 1998.
5. For a lucid and persuasive description of the way in which order words actually functioned in Israeli culture see Benveniste 1986, especially Chapters 2 and 3. See also Silberstein 1999: 58–65.
6. The fact that these terms no longer carry the same connotations to most Israelis is a sign of the weakening hold of zionist discourse. See Zerubavel 1995. See also Silberstein 1999, Chapter 4.
7. In the ensuing discussion, I have benefited greatly from Patton's incisive study of Deleuze's political philosophy (Patton 2000) as well as from Smith's (2003) highly useful review essay.
8. On the conflicts that inform Israeli society see, for example, Oz 1983, Kimmerling 2001, and in a less academic but highly perceptive vein, Rosenthal 2003.
9. For discussions of the ways in which the Israeli judicial process functions to bring 'what is established back into question', see Yiftachel 1999 and Gross 1998.
10. The title of a highly significant study by sociologist Baruch Kimmerling (2001), whose work is commonly regarded as representative of a postzionist perspective.
11. These debates are effectively described in Grossman 1993.
12. See Yiftachel 1998, 1999, 2000. Neither Yiftachel nor Rabinowitz refer to Deleuze, nor am I implying that their critique is influenced by his writings. However, their analysis of Israeli spatialising practices provides useful examples of practices that in Deleuze's terms would be considered molarising. Important discussions of striating processes in Israel are Benvenisti 1986 and 2000.
13. This claim has been reiterated by Yiftachel in many of his writings.
14. See on this Kimmerling 1983 and Kemp 1997.
15. Rabinowitz (1993: 146) argued that the use by Israelis of the term 'Arabs' to refer to Israeli Palestinians makes it easier to preach 'transfer' to another Arab country.
16. See Shenhav (forthcoming) and Motzafi-Haller 1998. For early examples of critiques of the effects of Israeli striating practices on the Mizrahi minority and the ways in which these distort the Arab component in Mizrahiness, see Swirski 1989, Shohat 1988 and 1989, and Alcalay 1993.
17. For the background of this term and a discussion of its recent usage, see Silberstein 1999, Chapter 4. Uri Ram, a sociologist, was one of the first to embrace the term, calling for 'the formulation of a post-zionist sociological agenda'. According to Ram, whereas 'zionist sociology . . . promoted the idea of an identity among unequals and the exclusion of the others', post-zionist sociology was to be 'guided by the ideal of a society characterised by equality among non-identicals and the inclusion of the others' (Ram 1995: 206). An early criticism of postzionist scholarship is Landers 1994. I discuss some of the early critics and the postzionist responses in Silberstein 1999, Chapter 4. For more recent works critical of postzionism see Karsh 1997 and Sharan 2003.
18. For an analysis of Kimmerling's argument and its significance for the shaping of a postzionist critique, see Silberstein (forthcoming).
19. See Silberstein 1999, Chapter 4.
20. A commonly cited example of this kind of scholarship is Morris 1988. Although labelled a postzionist scholar, Morris has repeatedly proclaimed his Zionist affiliation. Other examples of important works labelled by critics as postzionist are Shafir 1989, Kimmerling 1983, and Kimmerling and Migdal 1993.

21. See Silberstein 1999, Chapter 6. Hever's writings (1990 and 2002) are import-
    ant examples of a theoretical informed, poststructuralist postzionist critique.

I wish to express my gratitude to the editors and to my colleagues Michael
Raposa and Ruth Knafo Setton for their careful reading of earlier drafts and
their most helpful suggestions.

# Chapter 9

# Affective Citizenship and the Death-State

*Eugene W. Holland*

I take it as an axiom of post-structuralist social theory that various determinations of social life – the economy, the family, gender, religion, ethnicity, sexuality and so on – are to be considered in principle independent of one another: not just relatively autonomous, but completely autonomous from one another, with no privilege being automatically assigned to any one instance over all the others. This axiom is perhaps most evident in Foucault, who took his teacher Althusser's notion of the 'relative autonomy' of social determinations (politics, economics, ideology and so on) one step further to insist on their absolute autonomy from one another (Foucault 1972). But it is also evident in Derrida's insistence that the structurality of structure be understood not to harbour any centre that would privilege one structural element or instance over the others (Derrida 1972, 1994). In Deleuze and Guattari, finally, the axiom appears under the rubric of immanence: determinations are immanent within the social field they determine, without any transcendent instance determining all the others (Deleuze and Guattari 1994). But it then becomes an empirical or conjunctural question as to how these various instances intersect and interact with one another in specific circumstances, for even absolute autonomy definitely does not entail complete isolation. So if one were able to show that, let us say, familial and economic determinations under certain circumstances in fact reinforce one another, that would be an important result of examining them in relation to one another, as parts of what we might call an undetermined or non-deterministic whole. What if the political terms 'Motherland' and 'Fatherland' are more than just quaint or colourful expressions, but actually express a deep-seated connection between affective investments children make in family members and the kinds of affective investments citizens make in the nation-states to which they belong? What if the private and public spheres that seem so distinct in modern societies secretly resonate with one another? Then tools developed for the analysis of 'family romance', of the affective life of the private sphere, could prove useful for the analysis of the affective life of citizens in the public sphere, and vice versa.

Schizoanalysis is uniquely positioned to provide tools for such an analysis of affective citizenship that would take into account the resonance between the public and private spheres. For one of the signal contributions of schizoanalysis is to show that in modern capitalist societies, socio-economic and familial determinations tend to be distinct from, yet mirror and thus reinforce one another: the privatisation of production coincides with the privatisation of reproduction, such that Oedipal relations foster and support capital relations and vice versa. This is more than a mere formal homology – although it can be expressed as such. Adding the figure of the child to a quotation from Marx, Deleuze and Guattari assert at one point in *Anti-Oedipus* that 'Father, mother, and child . . . become the simulacrum of the images of capital ("Mister Capital, Madame Earth, and their child the Worker")' (Deleuze and Guattari 1972: 265). The structures of the nuclear family and the capitalist economy thus mirror one another: just as capital separates the worker from the means of life (Mother Earth) and defers access to the goods and ensuing gratification until after work, pay-day, and/or retirement, so the Father separates the child from its means of life (the Mother) and defers access to the opposite sex and ensuing gratification until after puberty and the founding of a new family through marriage. Deleuze and Guattari insist that the nuclear family and Oedipal psychoanalysis are strictly capitalist institutions for this reason: the dynamics of both the nuclear family and standard therapeutic transference effectively programme the Oedipal psyche to accept and even relish the structure of capitalist social relations. They go so far as to say that capitalism delegates the social reproduction of subjects to the nuclear family, since in their view capital is a quantitative calculus and not the kind of meaningful system of representation required to foster subjectivity. But this is either an overly casual formulation, or it implies that the family and psychic life are mere effects of an economic cause – which flies in the face of the post-structuralist axiom with which we started.

In this connection, the analysis offered by the late Norman O. Brown in *Life Against Death* (1959) is especially important. Like Deleuze and Guattari, Brown focuses on the relationship between psychoanalysis and history ('The Psychoanalytic Meaning of History' is his sub-title), and like them, he is especially interested in the relations between the domestic and public spheres (or between the family and economics) in determining social conduct. But where Deleuze and Guattari tend to

favour sociohistorical determination (with capital 'delegating' the reproduction of subjects to the nuclear family), Brown insists on unilateral
psychological determination. In fact, he explicitly sets out to replace
what he considers to be inadequate historical (Hegelian, Marxist) explanations for society-wide human neuroses with a purely psychological,
Freudian explanation – albeit by reading Freud somewhat against the
grain and insisting that the repression of death (about which Freud said
relatively little) is at least as important as the repression of sexuality
(about which he said a great deal).

Now in order for Brown to parry effectively the historicising thrust of
schizoanalysis, he would have to specify some determining feature of
family life that escapes the historical variability of family forms that
Deleuze and Guattari insist on so strenuously and demonstrate so convincingly.[1] And he does so: it is prolonged infantile dependency, which is
understood as a biological condition that is invariably true of all family
forms (regardless of how extended or privatised they may be), and that
has direct and profound repercussions for the human psyche. The human
animal, Brown reminds us, is utterly dependent on adults for its very survival for an extended period of time after birth – much longer than most
other mammals. This period of dependency of human infants on (let's call
them) 'care-givers' (rather than mother, father or even parents – for it
makes no difference who) fosters exaggerated expectations for physio-
logical and psychological gratification, intense separation anxiety (since
separation from care-givers at this stage means death), and a consequent
repression or refusal of death. In effect, the repression of death leaves
humans fixated on all the impossible infantile projects they refused to let
die in the past, leaving them unable to live in the present and giving motive
force to an obsessive orientation toward the future. So the 'psychoanalytic
meaning of history' is that humans sacrifice 'that state of Being which was
the goal of [human] Becoming' (Brown 1959: 19) and compulsively rush
headlong into a future they can never attain.

Now from a schizoanalytic perspective, this analysis is suggestive
because it coincides with Deleuze and Guattari's analysis of capitalism,
which also entails a 'refusal of death' – what they call the subordination
of anti-production and the corresponding transformation of death into
an instinct (Deleuze and Guattari 1972 and Holland 2000). As in the case
of the Oedipus complex itself, Deleuze and Guattari don't deny the
(relative) truth-value of Freud's death instinct: both are understood to be
effects or products of the capitalist mode of production, rather than
indelible features of the eternal human psyche. Like the Oedipus
complex, the death instinct merely expresses the 'apparent objective

movement' of capitalist society; under capitalism, death does become an instinct. And this is because capital systematically sacrifices social expenditure in favour of accumulation. Economies, according to Deleuze and Guattari, always involve processes of both production and anti-production, both the production of resources for the maintenance of life and the wasteful or useless expenditure of such resources in ways that do not contribute to life, but in fact risk death (Deleuze and Guattari 1972, Holland 1999). In all other societies, anti-production prevails over production, but the advent of capitalism reverses this relation: as the imperative to produce surplus-value comes to dominate society, the risk of death through expenditure becomes subordinate to the overproduction and accumulation of means of life, and even more perversely, to the overproduction of further means of production. Of course, the repressed always returns – death returns, now as an instinct – but capitalism manages to yoke even the production of means of death to its own self-realisation and self-expansion, so that the arms race and weapons production usurp public spending and contribute massively to capital accumulation. Indeed, from this perspective, bombs are the perfect capitalist commodity and an ideal solution to capital's notorious crises of overproduction, inasmuch as they blow up and immediately call for the production of more bombs to replace them; the death that was refused within the bounds of a state now devoted not to glorious expenditure but merely to furthering capital accumulation gets projected and inflicted outside the bounds of the state through military expenditure in the service of what Eisenhower today would have to call the military/fossil-fuel/industrial complex.

These are two very powerful accounts of the state of death in the psychic and social registers, but each assigns causal priority to a different register. So how are we to understand the relation between them? Clearly, an obsessive psychological future-orientation in search of an impossible state of complete gratification gets captured by – or does it produce? – a society-wide consumerism that contributes directly to, and is indeed required for, the realisation of surplus value and the accumulation of capital, which in turn requires wage-suppression so that the drive for gratification is perpetually frustrated – whatever role our analysis assigns to the mediation of advertising, whether as expression of a psychic compulsion or as mechanism of an economic imperative: the least we can say is that they are mutually reinforcing. And no doubt the Solomonesque solution – a solution perfectly consonant with the poststructuralist principle stipulated above – would be simply to grant psychic compulsion and economic imperative equal determinacy.

The Freudian concept of *nachtraglichkeit* or 'deferred action', however, suggests a very different resolution: rather than conceiving of infantile dependency and all its repercussions as determining social conduct and economic dynamics in linear fashion, as Brown's analysis would have it, this concept suggests that it is the refusal of death in social life under capitalism in particular that enables the refusal of death as one infantile complex among many to take centre stage in contemporary psychic life. There may be an innate psychological tendency in humans to sacrifice the present for an infinitely-deferred and impossible future, but it is capitalism that creates the historical conditions for that tendency to flourish and indeed become a predominant dynamic of social life. The separation-anxiety over the loss of parental love (which early in life means losing access to nourishment supplied by parents or care-givers) mirrors and reinforces the separation-anxiety over the loss of one's job (which later in life means losing access to nourishment supplied by the market): part of what is anti-Oedipal about schizoanalysis is the way it reads Freud against Freud this way – or rather; Freud against his own Oedipus complex – by suggesting in line with Brown's analysis that, under capitalism anyway, separation anxiety is far more important than castration anxiety.

But this does not mean that market-induced separation-anxiety causes infantile separation-anxiety (for which biology is clearly the cause), nor that capitalism delegates the breeding of anxiety-ridden subjects to the family so as to prepare them for psychic life under market capitalism (which grants capitalism far too much totalising prescience and agency). I would prefer to say simply that the capital-economic and Oedipal-familial instances, which are in principle autonomous, turn out in fact to resonate with one another under certain conditions, and that they do so today in a mutually reinforcing way that makes the task of transforming Oedipal-capitalist social relations all the more difficult.

Now let us suppose that, in addition to these two instances of mutually reinforcing resonance, the economic and the familial, there were a third: let's call it the political, here construed narrowly to refer to affairs of the state. The state plays a key intermediary role between the abstract calculus of capital and the concrete reproduction of subjectivity, although it has not always played such a role. The shift from what Foucault calls the sovereign state to the biopower state – to a form of power ideally suited to industrial capitalism, as Foucault himself insists – (or what Deleuze and Guattari in *Anti-Oedipus* call the shift from barbarism to civilisation)[2] entails an important recalibration of the state's relation to other instances in society, most notably the economic.

Whereas the sovereign state had been a locus of transcendence imposing order from above (through overcoding), the biopower state has become subordinate to capital, and henceforth organises social processes in the service of capital (through recoding)[3]. Where the sovereign state was content to wield death and terror to impose order and merely extract whatever surplus was available for useless glorious expenditure, the biopower state in principle represses death so as to maximise the production of surplus appropriated by capital in order to reinvest and pursue further accumulation. But repressed death in fact returns, giving rise to a regime of biopower I call the Death-State.[4] The question then becomes: how do the particular flows of psychic and capital investment resonating in the domestic and economic spheres find another register of resonance in politics, in the Death-State?

Schizoanalysis approaches this question on the basis of a Nietzschean power-principle: libidinal investment in the state depends on the degree to which belonging to a state enhances citizens' feelings of power – or as sociologists might put it: loyalty-quotients to the state depend on the reward-structures offered to its citizens. Citizen loyalties have often been parsed along an axis of inclusion and exclusion: fellow-citizens are included within the bounds of the state, while non-citizens are more or less forcibly excluded; classically, the state on one hand provides for those included among its citizens, and on the other hand protects them from non-citizens who have been excluded, and feelings of power arise from both. More specifically, the modern nation-state has, at least since Fichte (1922), been understood in terms of these two aspects or layers: one aspect (which Fichte calls 'the nation') involves the feeling of belonging together with fellow-citizens in a shared, enclosed space and common culture. Feelings of connection with and responsibility for fellow citizens combine with trust that the Motherland as a community will provide for the wellbeing of its members. The other aspect (which Fichte calls 'the state') involves the sense of order imposed on the nation from above by the state, in order to bolster and ensure the web of relations comprising the community, but also to relate the nation as one people to other nation-states, and so that the Fatherland can protect the nation from threats to its wellbeing coming from outside its borders.[5]

So Motherland and Fatherland can be understood as dual aspects of the affective investment in nation-states, which operates on a continuum marked at the extremes by categories such as inclusion/exclusion, positive/negative, affirmative/defensive, constructive/destructive and immanent/transcendent. But each pole of fantasy-investment also involves a distinctive sense of justice, which we can call (following Iris Marion

Young) 'the social-connective' and 'the individual-retributive'. Whereas the former views questions of justice systemically rather than individualistically, and seeks corrective measures in systemic transformation through collective action involving perpetrators, intermediaries and victims alike, the latter seeks categorically to separate victims and perpetrators, and targets discrete individuals for blame in order to punish and/or exact retribution from them. Given these collective fantasies about the Motherland and the Fatherland, the question then becomes what conditions would induce investment in one more than the other, or even in one to the exclusion of the other? Critics have spoken, often in the context of a vaguely-defined globalisation, of the declining salience of the state to many of its citizens. But that is only half the story. It is the Motherland that has increasingly 'negative salience' for citizens, as we shall see, while the salience of the Fatherland on the contrary continues to increase. Indeed, it will be possible to argue that wounded feelings of abandonment by the Motherland fuel a vindictive rage to punish some foreign Other that is blamed for the betrayal, thereby provoking a compensatory and pathological overinvestment in the Fatherland as rewards from the Motherland diminish: these, in a nutshell, are the psychodynamics of the Death-State.

We can see why this would be the case by examining the state's relations with citizens in three major domains of social life – production, reproduction and anti-production – in each of which we see a pattern of decreasing rewards and loyalty-quotients. Starting with the domain of reproduction, it is clear that the nuclear family has suffered severely under neo-liberalism, so that families require not one but two, three and sometimes four jobs to support themselves. At the same time, the provision of social services in support of reproduction more broadly conceived – including most notably public education, but also civil amenities, public health and safety, urban and transportation infrastructures, and so on – has declined radically in quantity and quality. This is no doubt due to capital's successful reduction of its share of reproduction costs and their displacement onto beleaguered citizens, who now shoulder a proportionally larger share of the tax burden than ever before. But in any case the result is that citizens feel the Motherland is no longer functioning as public provider, and this feeling translates into diminished citizen-loyalty, if not outright resentment and/or a search for alternative and mostly private forms of 'provisioning' elsewhere. This is the context in which feelings of abandonment by the Motherland provoke compensatory investments in compulsive consumerism, among other things. Foreign policy based on expropriating scarce resources around the globe, meanwhile, is perfectly consonant with insistence on the private right to drive a Sports Utility Vehicle; in fact, one function of the Death-State is precisely to align a psychological compulsion to consume, instilled in subjects since prolonged infancy, with the economic imperative to expand production and consumption in the service of capital-accumulation – an imperative that often enough requires military action to fulfil.

In the sphere of production, the situation is more complicated, even if the resulting pattern is more of the same. In the context of 'global competition' and 'post-fordism', income guarantees and, more importantly, job security itself have been drastically curtailed. That is why what T. H. Marshall has famously called 'social citizenship' as the 'third stage' in the evolution of modern citizenship – otherwise known as the welfare state – was either not a stage but a variable within an older stage, or if it was a stage, is now over: for social citizenship itself is steadily getting stripped away (Marshall 1964). At the same time, the state is losing economic sovereignty in the face of a number of institutions, including most notoriously the International Monetary Fund and the World Trade Organisation, but also trade agreements such as NAFTA and GATT. Especially when it is clear that their government actively supports shipping their jobs overseas, citizens feel neither internally well-provided-for nor well-protected from external competition in the sphere of production – and their affective investment in the state diminishes as a result.

In the sphere of anti-production, things are more complicated still. Generally speaking, war is a prime mover of citizenship affect, as innumerable polls in recent decades have shown. Indeed, 'giving one's life for one's country' may be the ultimate sign of loyalty to the state. And yet, the 'citizen-soldier' is virtually nowhere to be found. War is fought instead with mercenary soldiers – and everyone, especially the politicians, knows what would happen if the draft were reinstated. What was once supposed to be positive affective investment in the Fatherland – the noble fight for freedom in World War II, for instance – has become a more or less purely instrumental exchange relation: I volunteer for the Army Reserves (expecting to sacrifice my weekends, not my life) in exchange for higher educational opportunities I otherwise couldn't afford.

At the same time, however, the Death-State needs war more than ever, and indeed, waging war has become its primary function. For even though wars no longer mobilise positive affective investment (willing sacrifice for a noble cause), they certainly mobilise negative affective investment – that is to say, investment based on trauma and fear. An unending war on some vaguely-defined 'terror' fits the bill perfectly: citizens are made to feel the need for the state-as-protector more than ever before, even if the protection it affords is illusory at best. War thus kills at least three birds with one stone: it solves the crisis of overproduction of economic goods by producing endless demand for more weaponry; by commandeering the lion's share of public expenditure, it provokes a compensatory libidinal investment in private consumerism; and it solves the crisis of underproduction of citizenship goods by producing endless demand for mere protection by the Fatherland and a willingness to sacrifice or indeed disparage almost any form of nourishment by the Motherland. It doesn't take a second George Orwell to see the second George Bush as Big Brother, for the dynamics outlined in *1984* have never stopped becoming true.

Theoretically speaking, we can consider the Death-State as one 'model of realisation' or regime of capital accumulation among others. According to schizoanalysis and so-called 'regulation school' theorists (Boyer 1990), the role of the modern state is to organise the contents of a given society so as to enable the accumulation and concentration of capital: such organisation includes, in the productive sphere, establishment and protection or expansion of markets (their regulation and/or deregulation); in the reproductive sphere, formation and training of labour power, purchasing power, and specific modes of citizenship; and in the anti-productive sphere, management of forms of non-productive expenditure (wars, advertising, and so on) conducive to the realisation of surplus value. At the same time that the state organises these (and other) contents of social activity, the authority-structures of various institutions can resonate with one another. We have already seen this to be the case regarding the formal structure and dynamics of the nuclear family, capital and the state itself; but what if other institutions were to resonate in tune with these? What if the authorities of church groups, school systems, civic groups, and so on begin to align themselves on the authority-structures of capital and the state? In principle, according to schizoanalysis, the greater the degree of resonance among social authorities in various institutions, the greater the tendency toward fascism in the social formation.[6]

In this context, the term 'Institutional state Apparatuses' coined by Althusser risks obscuring important differences in degree, if not a difference in kind. While a tyrannical or totalitarian régime simply imposes its authority top-down on other institutions via the force of the state and state institutions (government bureaucracies, military, police, et al.), the fascism identified by schizoanalysis designates a convergence of authority-structures from social institutions and instances that are in principle autonomous from one another and from the state. Of course, any concrete historical example of fascism will combine imposition and convergence in varying degrees. The Bush régime curtails academic freedom via direct imposition of its directives through the NEA, the NEH, and Title IV Area Studies programmes, while also making appeals to the convergence of its views with that of various fundamentalist Christian sects completely independent of the state apparatus. But what is truly distinctive about Death-State fascism is that George Bush is not making the trains run on time, as Mussolini did; he is not restoring the economic and symbolic wellbeing of a nation brought to its knees by military defeat and to the brink of bankruptcy by the Treaty of Versailles, as Hitler did. On the contrary, Bush is gutting public services of all kinds and spending the country into bankruptcy: his is a politics of fear rather than triumph, an almost exclusive appeal via the Fatherland rather than the Motherland – yet no less effective for being so. At the same time, and no doubt as a consequence, the appeal of Death-State fascism is to the mere survival of individuals in isolation, not to the advancement of the people as a whole: its rhetoric functions to atomise the population through fear-mongering rather than unify it through appeals to a greater social good (the way Mussolini and Hitler did). Once again, it is not T. H. Marshall's but George Orwell's vision that becomes truer under Junior Bush than ever before, inasmuch as the Death-State is predicated not on prosperity, growth and a burgeoning, inclusive 'social citizenship', but on austerity, retrenchment, terror and isolation.

The importance of schizoanalysis, then, lies ultimately in its ability to make correlations among the Oedipal psyche, the capitalist economy and the contemporary state. It is all too easy – but no less relevant or less true for being so – to construe the Junior Bush invasion of Iraq as an obsession with avenging his father's 'defeat' or compromise in the first Iraq war. But the correlations between family romance and state policy, between private-sphere psychology and public-sphere politics, go far deeper than that. In a context where both an all-pervasive, monopoly-controlled mass media and a grossly under-funded public education system utterly fail to provide citizens with the knowledge and critical reading and writing skills required to make mature and informed decisions about the complexities of global geopolitics, and cultivate instead a juvenile sports-culture and two-party electoral system where complex historical narrative and multi-sided debate give way to a simplistic us-against-them, winner-take-all mentality, citizens identify with a figure they feel is a lot like them: even a lazy, immature, ignorant, petulant and patently inarticulate puppet who takes pride in his intellectual mediocrity and his faux-cowboy swagger.

Here, the Junior Bush personality-profile is not irrelevant: intolerant of ambiguity, rigid in world-view, incapable of handling complexity, unwilling to entertain dissent or alternative points of view, requiring absolute loyalty and uncritical assent from those around him – for all too many North Americans, these are the personality-traits of a saviour (Jost et al. 2003). A citizenry more or less completely overwhelmed by events will react to situations they are ill-prepared to understand with a craving for simplicity and a puerile loyalty to a strong-man leader who promises to protect them; the Fatherland's retributive model of justice separating perpetrator from victim becomes even more totally Manichean, and converges with the religious credos of Christian fundamentalism regarding absolute 'good and evil'. This is the significance of 9/11, which couldn't have been more salutary for the Junior Bush régime if it had been planned for him by Bush Senior, the Saudi princes, and other members of the Carlyle Group oil cartel: for many Americans, it seemed to reduce the overwhelming complexities of the Middle East and long-standing US complicities with its most heinous monarchs and dictators to an absolutely clear-cut, black-and-white stance: 'We're good, they're evil, and if you're not with us, you're against us'. A staggeringly complex situation had by all appearances shrunk to fit the measure of the cowboy president who just happened to be in power to face it.

But such a citizenry feels not just overwhelmed by events apparently beyond its control and understanding, it also feels guilty for those same events. Schizoanalysis goes beyond merely denouncing the rank hypocrisy of claiming to defend our freedoms against attacks from abroad while curtailing those very freedoms at home, by diagnosing a virulent social pathology that is perhaps as widespread as it is complex and unacknowledged: punitive projective identification, whereby one projects onto and punishes in the other something one dislikes or fears about oneself. So it is that calls for defending the 'sanctity' of heterosexual marriage are strongest in states where divorce rates are highest; calls for protecting 'unborn children' are strongest in states and nation-states where spousal and child abuse rates are highest; calls for sealing the coastline against refugee boat-people are made by people who were themselves once refugee boat-people, as happened recently in Australia (Buchanan 2003); calls for vengeance are made at New York's 'ground zero' in the name of protecting the very state that perpetrated the original 'ground zero' at Nagasaki and Hiroshima in the first place (Davis 2001, 2002). Punitive projective identification is precisely what is at work in the officially-promulgated geopolitical fantasy according to which 'they' – Islamic fundamentalist militants – hate us for our freedom and for what they consider American secular decadence. But so do the Christian fundamentalists in the United States, who despise and decry any freedom of choice that goes beyond selection of toothpaste brands and touches on whether to bear children or not, to live free from ortho-dox religious doctrine and control, to choose marriage partners based on love rather than gender stereotypes, and so on – choices that they con-sider decadent and sinful. There is thus a fateful mirror-symmetry between the fundamentalist religio-political rhetoric of jihad and the fun-damentalist religio-political rhetoric of crusade, between the Bin Laden jihad against the United States and the Junior-Bush crusade against Iraq. We punish them for what Bush is doing to us: depriving us of our freedom and material wellbeing – even though the punishment only deprives them of their freedom, too, whether in direct subservience to American domination or to a strong-man saviour of their own devoted to protecting them from us.

The diagnosis schizoanalysis offers through conjunctural analysis of our present moment is not a rosy one. But the aim here is not to erect a new theory of 'the' state, but to produce the concept of an Event: the advent of the shrink-to-fit presidency of George W. Bush, and the emer-gence of a twenty-first-century form of fascism in the United States. It is important to take not passive consolation but active encouragement from the fact that the United States of America may be doing better than Nazi Germany at a similar stage of historical development: only about 20 per cent of eligible voters elected George Bush in 2004, and slightly more or less than half of those who did vote (depending on who's count-ing and even more on who got to vote in the first place) voted against him. To what degree Death-State fascism will approximate – or surpass – its twentieth-century predecessors remains to be seen, but its potency and dangers need to remain on our radar screens.

## References

Boyer, R. (1990), *The Regulation School: A Critical Introduction*, New York: Columbia University Press.

Brown, N. O. (1959), *Life Against Death: The Psychoanalytic Meaning of History*, Middletown: Wesleyan University Press.

Buchanan, I. (2003), 'August 26, 2001: Two or Three Things Australians Don't Seem to Want to Know About "Asylum Seekers" ', *Australian Humanities Review* 29 (May–June): http://www.lib.latrobe.edu.au/AHR/archive/Issue-May-2003/buchanan.html

Davis, W. A. (2001), *Deracination: Historicity, Hiroshima, and the Tragic Imperative*, Albany: State University of New York Press.

Davis, W. A. (2002), 'Death's Dream Kingdom: the American Psyche after 9/11', *CounterPunch* (6 January): http://www.counterpunch.org/davis01062002.html

Dean, M. (2001), 'Demonic Societies: Liberalism, Biopolitics, and Sovereignty', in T. B. Hansen and F. Stepputat (eds) (2001), *States of Imagination: Ethnographic Exploration of the Postcolonial State*, Durham: Duke University Press, pp. 42–64.

Deleuze, G. and Guattari, F. (1972), *Anti-Oedipus: Capitalism and Schizophrenia*, trans. R. Hurley, M. Seem and H. R. Lane, Minneapolis: University of Minnesota Press.

Deleuze, G. and Guattari, F. (1994), *What is Philosophy?*, trans. G. Burchell and H. Tomlinson, New York: Columbia University Press.

Derrida, J. (1972), 'Structure, Sign and Play in the Discourse of the Human Sciences', in R. Macksey and E. Donato (eds) (1972), *The Structuralist Controversy: The Languages of Criticism and the Sciences of Man*, Baltimore: Johns Hopkins University Press.

Derrida, J. (1994), *Specters of Marx: The State of the Debt, the Work of Mourning, and the New International*, New York: Routledge.

Fichte, J. G. (1922), *Addresses to the German Nation*, London and Chicago: Open Court Publishing Company.

Foucault, M. (1972), *The Archaeology of Knowledge*, New York, Harper and Row.

Hage, G. (2003), *Against Paranoid Nationalism: Searching for Hope in a Shrinking Society*, Annandale and London: Pluto Press and Merlin Press.

Holland, E. W. (1999), *Deleuze and Guattari's Anti-Oedipus: Introduction to Schizoanalysis*, New York: Routledge.

Holland, E. W. (2000), 'Infinite Subjective Representation and the Perversion of Death', *Angelaki: Journal of the Theoretical Humanities* 5 (2): 85–91.

Jost, J. T., Glaser, J. Kruglanski, A. W. and Sulloway, F. J. (2003), 'Political Conservatism as Motivated Social Cognition', *Psychological Bulletin* 129 (3): 339–75.

Marshall, T. H. [1949] (1964), 'Citizenship and Social Class', in T. H. Marshall (1964), *Class, Citizenship, and Social Development*, Garden City: Doubleday, pp. 65–122.

Mbembe, A. (2003), 'Necropolitics,' *Public Culture*, 15 (1): 11–40.

Poster, M. (1978), *Critical Theory of the Family*, New York: Seabury Press.

Protevi, J. (2000), 'A Problem of Pure Matter: Fascist Nihilism in *A Thousand Plateaus*', in K. A. Pearson and D. Morgan (eds) (2000), *Nihilism Now! Monsters of Energy*, London: Macmillan Press, pp. 167–88.

Young, I. M. (forthcoming), 'Responsibility and Structural Injustice', *Philosophy and Public Affairs*.

# Notes

1. On the historical variability of family forms and their effects on psychic structure and dynamics, see Deleuze and Guattari 1972, and Poster 1978.
2. See Deleuze and Guattari 1972, especially Chapter 3, and Holland 1999, Chapter 3.
3. On overcoding and recoding, see Holland 1999, Chapter 3; for more on the transition from the sovereign state to the biopower state, see Holland 2000.
4. For other reconsiderations of the relations of Foucault's biopower and death, see Mbembe 2003 and Dean 2001.
5. On fantasies of Motherland and Fatherland, see Hage 2003 and Davis 2001.
6. I refer here to the schizoanalytic concept of fascism, highlighted by Foucault in his preface to the English translation of *Anti-Oedipus* (1972); this is a philosophical

concept, not a social-scientific one: the relation of this concept to actual historical fascism in Germany, Italy or Spain would require much further investigation along lines only sketched here (in terms of imposition/convergence). The concept of fascism developed in *A Thousand Plateaus* is significantly different. See Protevi (2000) for a valiant attempt to construct a concept of fascist nihilism based on *A Thousand Plateaus*.

# Chapter 10

# Arresting the Flux of Images and Sounds: Free Indirect Discourse and the Dialectics of Political Cinema

## Patricia Pisters

In order to address the issue of contemporary political cinema I will propose that contemporary cinema should be conceived as a speech-act in free indirect discourse. I will depart from Deleuze's observation that in the time-image the whole of cinema becomes a free indirect discourse, operating in reality (Deleuze 1989: 155). But I will also propose a more polemical reading of Deleuze's cinema books, arguing that there is a dialectical shift between the movement-image and the time-image, or, between First, Second and Third Cinema.

### Cinema and the Masses

As Walter Benjamin wrote in 'The Work of Art in the Age of Mechanical Reproduction', film, because of its mechanical reproduction and therefore its relation to the masses, is fundamentally related to politics (Benjamin 1999a). When Benjamin wrote this article, two main political currencies were dominant. On the one hand, fascism used cinema to give the people a feeling of strength and beauty born of a remythologisation of the present, while at the same preserving property relations and power structures. Fascism rendered politics aesthetic.[1] Communism, on the other hand, Benjamin argued, responded by politicising art. Eisenstein's Russian revolution films like *Potemkin* (1925) and *October* (1928) Benjamin considered fine examples of such politicised art.

From this one can conclude that, in a way, cinema is always political: either it makes the masses 'absent minded' as in fascism, or it can be used as a weapon in the emancipation of the people in the communist tradition. Although in contemporary audiovisual culture it is no longer possible to make these oppositional distinctions (I will come to that later) I will take the communist approach of cinema as a political weapon for the emancipation of the masses as a starting point for my discussion of political film. In the 1960s this form of cinema was named 'Third Cinema'. Let me first map out briefly the concept of Third Cinema, before looking at Deleuze's observations about this type of cinema which he calls 'the modern political film'.

## Third Cinema and the People

In the 1960s, in the wake of independence struggles and movements of decolonisation all over the world, a new type of post-colonial cinema emerged. In a manifesto from 1969, Fernando Solanas and Octavio Gettino called this type of cinema 'Third Cinema'. Filmmakers in Argentina themselves, Solanas and Gettino argued for a militant type of cinema to decolonise culture from the former colonisers. 'We have to film with a camera in one hand and a rock in the other,' they wrote (Solanas and Gettino 2000: 278). Third Cinema refers to the minority political position of the third-world as it is explicitly addressed in these films. But they also coined the term as an aesthetic opposition to what they call First Cinema (Hollywood) and Second Cinema (European Art cinema).

First Cinema is Hollywood genre cinema, what Deleuze calls 'the action-cinema of the movement-image', in which the action is followed through one or two central characters that meet a challenge that is over-come in the course of the actions (Deleuze 1986: 141–77). Protagonists of First Cinema films find themselves caught in at least two duels (one roman-tic and one other type of duel like a physical struggle with their milieu, or a political duel with opponents, or a psychological duel with a hostile family, and so on). Second Cinema is auteur cinema, often an idiosyncratic reworking of classical genres, sometimes with non-professional actors. Here, there is more attention to the socially less fortunate but the stories are also universal, talking about the human condition in general. The seamless montage (continuity editing) of the action-image has become 'montrage' of the long take and deep staging; or it now provides irrational cuts that make it difficult to distinguish between the actual and the virtual. This type of cinema is broadly categorised by Deleuze as modern cinema of the time-image (Deleuze 1989). In his book *Political Film* Mike Wayne gives several characteristics for Third Cinema (Wayne 2001). It is a cinema that considers history as a Marxist dialectic process of change and con-tradiction. The raising of political consciousness is also very important. There is always a critical engagement with the minority position. And finally Third Cinema always speaks from a position within the culture it speaks for. Films now regarded as Third Cinema are discussed by Deleuze as time-images, which he distinguishes from classical political film (Deleuze 1989: 215–24).

Wayne does not refer to the emancipation of 'the people' but clearly this issue is addressed in many of the early Third Cinema films. We find the hopes of Che Guevara for a united South America for the people in the films of Solanas and Gettino; in Egypt, Yussef Chahine, directs the film *Saladin* (1963) to commemorate Nasser's nationalisation of the Suez Canal; in Algeria, the liberation struggle of the FLN is reflected in many of the films produced right after independence, like *The Battle of Algiers* (1967): and in Africa the hopes of new nations find their parallels in the organisation of African film associations and festivals. In all these early Third Cinema expressions, the idea of 'the people' as a united force that can be represented and addressed is very strong.

## 'The People are Missing' and Cinema as Speech-Act: Imagined Communities

But this expectation of a new people would not last very long. The military juntas that arose in several third-world countries in the decolonisation period, the Six Day War, and many élitist and dictatorial state régimes in the new nations soon caused a feeling of profound deception throughout the third-world. Civil wars, poverty and migration followed: the people fell apart. So Third Cinema, in fact, very soon turned out to be based on this condition of the absence of the people. As Deleuze says in *The Time-Image*: 'If there were a modern political cinema, it would be on this basis: the people no longer exist, or not yet . . . the people are missing' (Deleuze 1989: 216).

In classical political cinema, such as Eisenstein's films or the early Third Cinema films, the people exist; they can be represented and addressed. In the modern political film of the time-image, however, the people are missing: it is no longer possible to represent or address the people. As Deleuze argues, the status of film changed. Films become speech-acts that act upon reality, that help the people to 'become', to invent themselves in the stories that are being told.[2]

> Not the myth of a past people, but the story-telling of a people to come. The speech-act must create itself as a foreign language in a dominant language, precisely in order to express an impossibility of living under domination . . . [T]hird world cinema has this aim . . . to constitute an assemblage which brings real parties together, in order to make them produce collective utterances as the prefiguration of the people who are missing. (Deleuze 1989: 223–4)

The idea of a speech-act in cinema that can produce 'a people' might be compared in some sense to Benedict Anderson's idea of the 'imagined community'. Reflecting on the origins of nationalism, Anderson argues that the nation is an imagined political community that was made possible by two forms of imagining that were significant in Europe in the eighteenth century: the novel and the newspaper (Anderson 1983: 25). The novel and the newspaper made it possible for a large group of people who do not know each other to share the same 'clocked', calendrical time (Anderson calls 'homogeneous empty time'). Anderson illustrates his point by referring to a novel by Balzac, which presents several characters that do not know each other and yet are embedded in the same society. At the same time these characters are embedded in the minds of the omniscient readers who now can imagine this world as a shared reference. While Anderson clearly speaks of the nation, he also acknowledges that in fact 'all communities larger than primordial villages of face-to-face contact (and perhaps even these) are imagined. Communities are to be distinguished, not by their falsity/genuineness, but by the style in which they are imagined' (Anderson 1983: 6).

Following Anderson's logic of the people as an 'imagined community' it is plausible to argue that cinema is the twentieth and twenty-first century's means of creating imagined communities. However, this poses a difficulty for the distinction Deleuze makes between the ways the people pre-exist and are addressed in the movement-image, as opposed to the way the people are imagined and invented in the time-image. In fact Deleuze himself gives some examples of speech-acts in silent cinema (Deleuze 1989: 233). Possibly the distinctions between these types of images in respect to their political dimensions are not that easy to make. I will return to this point.

## Free Indirect Style

As indicated by Anderson, style (in film and literature) can be considered a distinctive characteristic of different types of community. So perhaps the difference between the two types of political cinema can be sensed in matters of style. A classical style of the movement-image moves between two poles: the 'subjective' (direct presentation of the events through the point of view of a character) and the 'objective' (indirect presentation of the events through the camera from a more distant point of view). In *The Movement-Image* Deleuze argues that the final goal of the cinema is to reach a more diffuse and supple status that could be characterised as semi-subjective or free indirect. The free indirect style is actually the basis of cinematographic perception, but cinema had to go through a 'slow evolution before attaining self-consciousness' (Deleuze 1986: 74–5). With the advent of the time-image after World War II and in the modern political film after colonial independence struggles, free indirect discourse becomes the dominant style.

Free indirect discourse is a term derived from Russian linguistics.[3] It refers to a style of reporting in which the reporter and the reported fuse together. In a direct style the difference between reporter and the reported (narrator and character) is clear. An example would be: 'My father rose, took my hand and said: "Do not get involved in politics." '[4] In a free indirect style this sentence would be: 'I should not get involved in politics.' Free indirect discourse creates the impression the narrator is superseded by his character. As John Marks indicates, Flaubert developed this conception of language as a literary technique (Marks 1998: 106). It is as though Flaubert has ceased to speak and Madame Bovary has begun to speak for herself. Where the author was, there the character is, and in the best worked instances, of which Flaubert is clearly an example, the author disappears into their characters, in a process of double becoming. This ambiguity of the status of the linguistic utterance, somewhere between the narrator and the character, is also central to understanding free indirect discourse in cinema.

Free indirect discourse in cinema was theorised initially by Pasolini in his 1965 speech 'Cinema of Poetry' (Pasolini 1988). Just prior to writing this essay, Pasolini had made *Il Vangelo Secondo Matteo*; during the making of this film the question he had to ask himself was the following: how could he, as an atheist Marxist, make a film about Christ through the eyes of a religious person?[5] As Deleuze explains, Pasolini discovered how to go beyond the two elements of the traditional story, the objective indirect story from the camera's point of view and the subjective direct story from the character's point of view, by the form of free indirect discourse:

> In the cinema of poetry the distinction between what the character saw subjectively and what the camera saw objectively vanished, not in favor of one or the other, but because the camera assumed a subjective presence, acquired an internal vision, which entered into a relation of simulation with the character's way of seeing . . . The author takes a step towards his characters, but the characters take a step towards the author: double becoming. (Deleuze 1989: 148, 222).

Like in linguistics, the relationship between the one who is talking (the narrator/the camera) and what is being said in the image (the character) is rather ambiguous; it is unclear where one begins and the other ends. Pasolini himself gives the example of Antonioni's *Il Deserto Rosso* (1964) in which the neurotic experience of the world of the main character blends with the cinematographic style of the director. Equally ambiguous is the relation between fiction and reality. As Deleuze and Guattari indicate in *What is Philosophy?* free indirect styles create an 'acentred "plane of composition", instituting counterpoints between the heterogeneous elements of "characters, current events, biographies, and camera eyes"' (Deleuze and Guattari 1994: 188).[6] Objective and subjective, reality and fiction lose their distinction. As Deleuze indicates, we should no longer talk about 'a cinema of truth but of the truth of cinema' (Deleuze 1989: 151). In free indirect discourse the camera makes itself felt through salient techniques (like obsessive framing, zooming, or the dissociation of image and sound, as I will demonstrate in the next section). As Deleuze points out: '[W]e are caught in a correlation between a perception-image and a camera-consciousness which transforms it (the question of knowing whether the image was objective or subjective is no longer raised)' (Deleuze 1986: 74). As I said before, Deleuze argues that, with the time-image, the whole of cinema becomes a free indirect discourse:

> It is under these conditions of the time-image that the same transformation involves the cinema of fiction and the cinema of reality and blurs their differences; in the same movement, descriptions become pure, purely optical and sound, narrations falsifying and stories simulations. The whole of cinema becomes a free, indirect discourse, operating in reality. (Deleuze 1989: 155)

What does this dominance of the time-image and free indirect discourse mean for contemporary political cinema?

## Aesthetics of Free Indirect Discourse in the Time-Image

In *The Skin of Film*, Laura Marks (2000) analyses a range of modern political films that belong to the category of Third Cinema (which she refers to as 'intercultural cinema') and are clearly time-images in a Deleuzian sense. One of these films is *Lumumba, Death of a Prophet* (1992) made by Raoul Peck. Patrice Lumumba was the first leader and prime minister of independent Congo in 1960. But he was soon dismissed by President Kasa-Vubu and in 1961, with the complicity of the US, he was murdered. General Mobutu then took power. The circumstances of Lumumba's death (and the involvements of Belgium and the United States who considered him a dangerous communist) have been hushed up for a long time. With this film Peck gives a voice to Lumumba.

Telling a story in free indirect discourse is possible through several aesthetic techniques. One way to make subjective and objective, fiction and reality, past and present more ambiguous is by disconnecting sound and image. A voice tells us something, and at the same time we see something else. In this way the voice digs up layers of the past or adds aspects of the future that cannot be seen directly. This strategy is widely used in *Lumumba*: we see images of Brussels, while in voice-over Peck tells the story of Lumumba. By using image and sound autonomously (or 'heautonomously' as Deleuze calls it) image and sound start to speak to each other and influence each other. Lumumba's ghost becomes visible in Brussels in 1992. The past speaks in the present in a free indirect way, neither completely subjective (there isn't a character in the film whose point of view we follow) nor completely objective (the voice of the filmmaker is clearly present commenting in a personal way).

As a filmmaker, Peck moreover relates to Lumumba in a free indirect way. The film is also Peck's story. At the beginning of the 1960s, Peck's family moved from Haiti to Congo to help build the country. His mother was secretary of the government for several years. By using both home movies and news footage, Peck infuses official history with non-official history in a free indirect discourse. In one scene we see Super 8 home movie images of Peck's father, who films a few boys in the garden of their house. Peck's voice-over then tells us: 'My father is trying his new camera. He has found some actors. Among them a future psycho-analyst, a truck driver, a lawyer, two business men, a filmmaker and a male nurse.' Here the voice takes the images of the past to the future. We also see Peck's mother looking at her children. And when Peck tells us: 'My mother says . . .' the images switch to a picture of Lumumba with the Belgian king, Boudoin and President Kasa Vubu. Meanwhile Peck continues, 'that Lumumba was dismissed by the one he himself installed'.

Official historical images are alternated with home movies and stories about the political situation by his mother. Image and sound, filmmaker and his character (Lumumba), official and unofficial history, now come together in a free and indirect way. The film is a perfect example of what Deleuze calls a 'modern political film of the time-image' because it presents simultaneously several layers of time and functions as a speech-act, an act of fabulation that helps to 'invent' (the history of) a people. It is also a typical Third Cinema film in that it deals with the contradictions and conflicts of history, aims at the raising of political consciousness, clearly takes a minority perspective and speaks (mostly) from within Congolese culture.

## Reality and Fiction: A Free Indirect Relation

And yet, Peck felt the need to retell the story differently, in a more classical way. He precisely felt this need in order to make Lumumba's story, the story of the people of Zaire, accessible to a larger audience, an audience that is necessary in order to construct an 'imagined community'.[7] In 2000, therefore, he made a First Cinema version of those events as a political thriller, *Lumumba*. Now we engage with the story mainly through the eyes of Lumumba, played by Eriq Ebouaney. And parallel to the political story, we also witness Lumumba's family life, and his relationship with his wife and kids whom he has to leave behind. The scene just described now looks very different. When Kasa Vubu dismisses Lumumba, the latter is in his office at home. He gets the message of his removal through the radio. Immediately he leaves the house, telling his pregnant wife, who is doing the laundry, that he is going to parliament. There he tries to dismiss Kasa Vubu in turn. But he no longer has the support of the army, which has been paid off with American dollars. In the next scene he is put under arrest by General Mobutu.

Aesthetically, in the cinematographic language we have an alternation between direct discourse (subjective images from the point of view of Lumumba) and indirect discourse (objective images where the camera is at a distance and shows what happens to Lumumba). However, I would like to argue that free indirect discourse has become important for this type of Hollywood genre cinema as well. So taking Deleuze's argument that time-images are free indirect discourses that operate in reality one step further, not only time-images, but also contemporary movement-images like First Cinema films, have to be considered as free indirect discourses, as speech-acts that operate in reality. Aesthetically these images might follow a classic path, but in terms of their content, First Cinema equally relates fiction and reality in a free indirect way. Or perhaps it is possible to say that now that with the time-image cinema has become self-conscious, this also affects contemporary movement-images. Latently there from the beginning, free indirect discourse as 'zero degree' of the perception-image takes its full effects in contemporary cinema.[8] Consequently we have to accept that movement-images are also speech-acts that act upon reality and as such are important for the constitution of 'a people'. It is no longer the privilege of the time-image. As I demonstrated above, this too was part of cinematographic power from the beginning, but becomes more evident in contemporary cinema.

## Dialectics of Contemporary Political Cinema

But we have to acknowledge that there are clearly differences between the various types of cinema and their political perspectives. In order to analyse these perspectives and see how the free and indirect relations between reality and fiction are coloured, we should consider the relations between movement-image and time-image, not only in clear opposition to each other, but in a dialectical way. Here I concur with Mike Wayne who has proposed a dialectics between First, Second and Third Cinema which I would like to translate in a Deleuzian perspective. Connecting Deleuze to any kind of dialectics might not appear a logical step to make. As Ian Buchanan points out in *Deleuzism*, it has become an axiom of Deleuze and Guattari studies to say that they are anti-dialectical:

> Deleuze and Guattari never stop saying that they are anti-dialectical, it is a kind of mantra with them. But in going along with them on this we do ourselves a profound disservice, I believe, because we neutralize one of the most effective tools we have for mobilizing their work towards positive political ends and consequently fall tendentially into a paradigm of pure description of the adjectival kind. More importantly it assumes that there is only one kind of dialectics, which is patently not the case. I would agree wholeheartedly with anyone that said that Deleuze and Guattari's approach was not dialectical if that meant synthesizing, but would disagree strongly if instead it meant historicizing – which is to say, creating the means to 'distance' the present as an 'event' from itself as 'mindless immediacy' of 'flux' – and as Jameson has amply demonstrated one conception of dialectics does not imply the other (Buchanan 2000: 46)

As Buchanan demonstrates, Deleuze and Guattari in their construction of concepts never cease to refer to specific (historical) *contexts*, planes of immanence that function as perspectives on a particular problem. Another (and related) dialectical characteristic in the work of Deleuze and Guattari is that their concepts are always constructed from *concrete material* reality. As Buchanan argues, this is dialectical 'because it attempts to think the ground *as* ground, which is to say as prephilosophical, and at the same time conceptualize that ground as something philosophers construct by fiat (the very antithesis of a ground) and impose on the world a new way of framing it' (Buchanan 2000: 57). A final dialectical characteristic that is important in respect to a dialectical reading of contemporary political cinema is to recognise that in a

Marxist spirit, the past is not something that prevents the future, but rather provides the building blocks for the *transformation* of the present into the future.

As Fredric Jameson indicates in his article 'Marxism and Dualism in Deleuze' (1997), in an axiomatic world, it might even become more important to consider Deleuze in a dialectic way. It is useful to recall that in *A Thousand Plateaus* Deleuze and Guattari mention four axiomatic fluxes: the flux of energy-matter, the flux of population, the flux of food products and the flux of the urban (Deleuze and Guattari 1988: 468). I would like to add another flux, although that could be considered as part of the energy-matter flux, namely the flux of audio-visual images. It is a flux that becomes increasingly complex.

Axioms are operational, they are a set of rules put into effect.[9] Jameson discusses the most important axiom, capitalism, which always surmounts its contradictions by adding new axioms. And, as Jameson adds: 'There can be no return to any simpler axiomatic or purer form of capitalism; only the addition of ever more rules and qualifications' (Jameson 1997: 398). By same token, we cannot go backwards aesthetically either: it is no longer possible to have pure forms of the movement-image (First Cinema) or the time-image (Second and Third Cinema). In cinema too, new rules, influences and qualifications are constantly being added as the medium pushes up against seemingly insurmountable aesthetic limits, only to discover new techniques, new technology, new ways of telling stories, thus reviving the aesthetic once more. And we cannot escape a certain dualism or dialectics between the different types of images. Jameson puts it even more strongly when (speaking about the dualism between state and nomads in Deleuze and Guattari's work) he argues that: '[A] certain dualism might be the pretext and the occasion of the very "overcoming" of Deleuzian thought itself and the [dialectic] transformation into something else . . .' (Jameson 1997: 414). He adds that perhaps the best way to read the opposition between the nomads and the state is to see it as 'reterritorialization by way of the archaic, and as the distant thunder, in the age of axiomatic and global capitalism, of the return of the myth and the call for utopian transfiguration' (Jameson 1997: 414).

Political cinema has a utopian mission in the invention of a people and it operates sometimes by reterritorialisation and deterritorialisations between First, Second and Third Cinema, or between movement-images and time-images. Here it is important to note that Deleuze himself considered classical cinema of the movement-image in itself as a form of Hegelian (not Marxist) dialectical thinking. Illustrating his point with the dialectical montage of Eisenstein he argues:

Three relationships between cinema and thought are encountered together everywhere in the cinema of the movement-image: *the relationship with a whole which can only be thought in a higher awareness, the relationship with a thought which can only be shaped in the subconscious unfolding of images, the sensory-motor relationship between world and man, nature and thought.* (Deleuze 1989: 163)

The modern cinema of the time-image develops new relations with thought which Deleuze characterises as:

the obliteration of a [organic] whole or of a totalising of images [synthetic moment], in favour of an outside which is inserted between them [something that is unsummonable, inexplicable, undecidable, impossible or incommensurable]; the erasure of the internal monologue as whole of the film, in favour of a free indirect discourse and vision; the erasure of the unity of man and the world, in favour of a break which now leaves us with only a belief in this world. (Deleuze 1989: 188)

The restoration of 'a belief in this world' is what has become the task of modern filmmakers – and this is what critical thinking implies with respect to cinematographic modernity (and which could be called dialectical in a Marxist sense). Now, my point is not that what we witness today in contemporary cinema is the fusion or synthesis of Hegelian and Marxist dialectics, but that there are dialectical movements and moments between movement-images and time-images that influence each other. By analysing the precise dialectic movements it becomes possible to distinguish the various political perspectives on material history.

Of course, not all political perspectives are equal, or equally powerful and effective, and we need tools to see in which ways exactly the dialectics between different types of cinema work. By considering film a speech-act that operates as free indirect discourse in reality, we can start unpacking the political dimensions of a variety of perspectives. And it becomes possible to define a new ethics of the image that tries to map the different speaking positions/perspectives, and the ways in which these speaking positions colour the relationship between fiction and reality. Consequently, we don't necessarily need a time-image, or even a Third Cinema film, to discover the minority perspective necessary for political film in the communist tradition. And vice versa, not all First Cinema films propose fascist absent-mindedness of the people, even though historically the movement-image gave way to the time-image because of the fascist misuse of classical cinema (Deleuze 1989: 264).

It is impossible to give a simple code or model of analysis that can be applied to each film in a similar way. Although we have some conceptual tools, like the movement-image, the time-image and categories of First, Second and Third Cinema, the dynamics or dialectics between all these elements always changes. It is important to disentangle both the virtualities within the image (the past, present, the future) and the forces behind the image (the money flows, who made or supported the image). In order to put these thoughts to work I want to conclude with a few examples of contemporary films that propose dialectical transformations of political cinema.

### *The Interpreter*: First and Third Cinema

Undoubtedly, *The Interpreter* (Pollack 2005) is an example par excellence of a work of First Cinema. A big budget Hollywood film, a political thriller (with little direct interest in politics), with big stars – Nicole Kidman and Sean Penn in leading roles – it meets all the classic criteria of the type. Kidman plays an interpreter/translator for the United Nations who overhears plans for the murder of President Zuwani of the fictional African country, Matobo. Sean Penn is a security officer assigned to protect her. Much of the film is shot as an action-image around this murder plan, with the obligatory parallel subplot centred on the relationship between Kidman and Penn. Pure entertainment, indeed. And yet it would be too easy to dismiss the film as a nonpolitical film on these grounds alone. Two elements relate *The Interpreter* to Third Cinema practice. First of all Sylvia Broome, the Kidman character, is a white African, born and raised in Matobo, whose life has been profoundly and personally affected by the civil war. She lost her parents and sister in a landmine accident; she herself was involved in protest movements and killed a boy in self defence. After this she decided to drop the weapons and work as an interpreter for the United Nations. So she is not an innocent tourist who just happens to be in the wrong place at the wrong moment.[10] There is a critical engagement with the minority perspective that Sylvia Broome in the film translates in terms of UN diplomacy.

Secondly, the film refers to the historical political situation in many African countries, without representing one particular country. The African country is called Matobo; the president, who from a liberator turned into a dictator, is called Edmund Zuwani. Zuwani breaks all resistance to his politics by labelling it 'terrorism' and he gets support in the West for doing so. It is a fictitious country, a fictitious president, and Kidman speaks Matoban, a fictitious language developed especially for the film. But it is not difficult to recognise figures like Mobutu (Congo/Zaire), Mugabe (Zimbabwe), or other African dictators and their relations to Western governments who often supported them. So in this way political history is referred to by what Georg Lukács has called 'typicality'. According to Lukács typicality is:

> the convergence and intersections of all . . . the most important social, political, moral and spiritual contradictions of a time. . . . Through the creation of a type and the discovery of typical characters and typical situations, the most significant directions of social development obtain adequate artistic expression. (Lukács, cited in Wayne 2001: 36)

Typicality is one of the key ways of politicising narrative in Third Cinema.[11] Also the Kidman character, as interpreter for the United Nations, can be considered as typical. Throughout the film numerous references are made to the profession of interpreter. Kidman propagates the UN ideal of transnational dialogue. The fact that Sydney Pollack got permission from Kofi Annan to film (for the first time ever) in the actual United Nations building, does not come as a surprise. In many ways, the politics of this film is 'safe', unthreatening to the dominant order, and not likely to raise the eyebrows of suspicious powerbrokers. Yet it is also the case that concealed behind the approved exterior there lurks a radical potential for a translation of 'tame' First Cinema into highly politicised Third Cinema. In his essay 'The Task of the Translator' (1999b), Benjamin argued that for a good translation, the interpreter has to let languages influence each other mutually. Here it is the relation between political discourses that is at stake. The languages move toward each other and there is a certain ambiguity between the literal and the free interpretation of the words. This mutual influencing of languages, and all the cultural connotations that belong to it, is thematised in *The Interpreter*. This happens both at the level of the profession of the translator, and on a higher level of transnational influences in a globalised world, symbolised in the United Nations.

## *Viva Laldjerie*: Second and Third Cinema

*Viva Laldjerie* (Nadir Moknèche 2004) is a characteristic example of Second Cinema. Distributed in the Art House Circuit, it tells the story (based on a real situation) of a mother and daughter who live in a hotel room in contemporary Algeria. The film belongs to the category of Second Cinema because on the one hand, its story isn't told in the forceful and direct manner of a Hollywood film, and on the other hand, the historical and political references are indirect. It is careful to exclude even the use of typical characters and allegorical references that might point to the (recent) political situation in Algeria. The focus is on the relationship between the characters and on the more general human condition.

And yet, *Viva Laldjerie* is a political film. Its Third Cinema characteristics are, however, quite subtle. At the beginning and end of the film, we are presented with images of a crowd walking in the streets of Algiers, as if the director wanted to frame his fictional story of the women in a free and indirect way to these people of Algiers. The women are not representative of Algerian women today. Indeed, after the screening of the film at the International Film Festival in Rotterdam, the director was heavily criticised for that. But, as I have already argued, representative cinema of the old-fashioned political type is no longer possible in the modern political film: 'the people are missing'. As such, the expectation that the women should be 'representative' is misplaced and politically distracting. It has become impossible to represent the multiplicity and fragmentation of people as 'the people'. The title of the film, 'Viva Laldjerie', nevertheless not only refers to the slogan shouted at football games, it also recalls that classical revolution film *The Battle of Algiers* where 'Viva Algeria' is shouted in the demonstrations against the French.

The political dimension that the director gets across with this film is the fact that these women continue to live, despite the traumatic experiences of the civil war in the 1990s, which have inflicted profound wounds on Algerian society. The film is fiction and has to be seen as a speech-act that refers to Algerian society in a free and indirect way. By refusing to represent people or nation, the film contributes to the creation of a people that is becoming, (re)inventing itself, by opening a space, what Deleuze calls a 'plane of immanence', for that important political transformation to occur. It was precisely this 'plane of immanence' that, during the civil war, when it was dangerous and even impossible to make films or images of any kind, was lacking.[12] Algerians had the feeling of being completely forgotten by the rest of the world, as if they did not exist. Now images, and 'imaginary communities' seem to re-emerge. But no single film can take the 'burden of representation' (Hall 1996). As Deleuze says:

> The speech-act has several heads, and, little by little, plants the elements of a people to come as the free indirect discourse of Africa about itself, about America or about Paris. As a general rule, third world cinema has this aim: through trance or crisis, to constitute an assemblage which brings real parties together, in order to make them produce collective utterances as the prefiguration of the people who are missing (and, as Klee says, 'we can do no more'). (Deleuze 1989: 223–24)

## *Tangier, le Rêve des Brûleurs* (*Tangier, the Burners' Dream*): Third and First Cinema

Leila Kiliani's film *Tangier, the Burners' Dream* (2002) is a contemporary Third Cinema film that is shown at smaller festivals but does not get regular distribution on the big screens. In a Deleuzian sense, it is a true modern political film in which the filmmaker (who creates beautiful images) and her characters (two communities of illegal refugees in Tangier who tell their stories, their dream of crossing the ocean) find each other in a free indirect discourse. The characters are often filmed at night or dawn, framed by the intense colours of the city of Tangier or against the backgrounds of the sea or the harbour. Sometimes their voices are in voice-over and sometimes they are embodied. When we hear their voices in voice-over they are shown in the image as silhouettes, as distant figures; or we just see the border, the Spanish coast on the other side of the ocean. These images and sounds are truly poetic, and the way the images are alternated with the concrete bodies and stories is very powerful because this turns the personal stories also into a larger story about marginality. The characters are clearly comfortable with the camera: they choose what they tell, they decide what the filmmaker will show in the end. As a Third Cinema film it refers to the contemporary political situation of the closure of Europe's borders, it presents the perspective of the 'burners' who get time and space to tell their stories and dreams, and it is told from within the cultural knowledge of Tangier, which is the home town of the director. But at the same time the film is also a sort of Western: the burners continue to survive because, like cowboys, they want to conquer the frontier: 'Even if they would built a fence until the sky, we would find ways to climb over,' one of the burners says.[13] This Western element is present not only in their stories but is also emphasised in the *mise-en-scène* in which the border, as indicated above, is an important element. In some instances, the images are also full of suspense. In several stories, for instance, of how to get across by hiding under trucks or in dustbins, the close-ups of trucks, cars and wheels, combined with appropriate music, make our hearts beat faster. And our perception of cars is changed (remember how Hitchcock changed our perception of birds). Here we have First Cinema elements in a Third Cinema film. And it is precisely this dialectical reversal that provides the difficult existence of these people with another, more heroic dimension through which we can view their lives, allowing them also to see themselves in a more dignified light.

## Conclusions

The significance of free indirect discourse to political cinema should be understood on three levels. First of all, it is important to see that, contrary to the case with classical political film, it has become impossible to represent a people. This perhaps seems obvious, but for many filmmakers, especially Third World filmmakers, or minority filmmakers in the West, it is still very difficult to shake off 'the burden of representation'. But from Deleuze we learn that in the modern political film, the relationship between filmmakers and their characters is a free indirect one. And political films have to be considered as fabulations and speech-acts that contribute to the invention of a people; they are not representative of an entire people (or nation).

Secondly, not only time-images but also contemporary movement-images have to be considered as free indirect discourses that operate in reality. The relation between the films and reality is often ambiguous (and in any case never direct). It is useful to analyse the dialectical shifts between First, Second and Third Cinema elements in order to understand some of the political dimensions of the different perspectives. It is necessary to take both elements within the films, as well as forces behind the films, into account. And instead of asking: is this a true representation? we should ask: who wants this to be true, what interests are at stake? Of course the power relations between all the different agents in First, Second and Third Cinema are not equal – but neither are they fixed. And the minor position can find expression in unexpected places.

Thirdly, in a globalised, transnational world, money, goods, people and images travel at ever-increasing speeds and in greater quantities. This makes it necessary to think the invention of 'a people' (the becoming of a people) both on a national and transnational level. Intercultural films, accented films, films that deal with migration explicitly refer to this. But also, more directly, 'national' cinemas acknowledge that the people to come will be constructed out of many different stories. In all these stories the relationship between the West and other parts of the world is a complex and free indirect one. In varying dialectic dynamics these relations that started, amongst others, with colonialism, always crystallise differently in increasingly complex transnational networks.

Deleuze's concept of the rhizome and rhizomatic thinking is one that does justice to this complexity. A supplementary and perhaps more visual metaphor could be added: the geometrical figure of the fractal. Like the rhizome, this is not just a metaphor, but also a concrete pattern and material reality.[14] Arjun Appadurai proposes to take the fractal as a figure of thought for thinking the complexity of transnational cultural formations (Appadurai 1996: 46). In order to understand the whimsical multiplicity of contemporary cultural formations, classical geometric forms, like circles and squares with fixed measures and oppositional sides, are no longer adequate (or only in abstractions). Fractals are new geometrical figures that can be calculated only by computer. They are figures in endless 'repetition with difference'. A detail of the figure presents the same shapes as the complete figure, though it is not necessarily identical. Most importantly, fractal formulae create unpredictable but not arbitrary effects. The free indirect relation between people and images, between reality and fiction, can be imagined as a fractal formula with capricious, unpredictable, but not arbitrary dynamics.

And filmmakers produce with their films fractal imaginary landscapes. They produce speech-acts that influence reality. In 'The Work of Art in the Age of Mechanical Reproduction', Walter Benjamin compared the filmmaker with a camera to the surgeon with a scalpel. Like the surgeon who cuts deep into the patient's body, the filmmaker penetrates (operates in) reality's flesh. As we know, every operation involves risks. The instrument can be wrong (a knife that is too blunt), the remedy can be worse than the disease, or unexpected side effects can occur. All of which points to the importance of making good, effective diagnoses to begin with, so that the complexity of contemporary culture and politics is not reduced to a clash of civilisations, but the complex dynamics between many different (his)stories and coloured perspectives become visible.

# References

Adorno, T. and Horkheimer, M. (1997), 'The Cultural Industry: Enlightenment as Mass Deception', in T. Adorno and M. Horkheimer (1997), *Dialectics of Enlightenment*, trans. J. Cumming, New York: Continuum, pp. 120–67

Anderson, B. [1983] (1991), *Imagined Communities: Reflections of the Origin and Spread of Nationalism*, London and New York: Verso.

Appadurai, A. (1996), *Modernity at Large: Cultural Dimensions of Globalization*, Minneapolis and London: University of Minnesota Press.

Austin, J. L. (2004), 'How to Do Things with Words?', in H. Bial (ed.) (2004), *The Performance Studies Reader*, London and New York: Routlegde, pp. 147–53.

Barbrook, R. (2001), 'The Holy Forts', in P. Pisters (ed.) (2001), *Micropolitics of Media Culture*, Amsterdam: Amsterdam University Press, pp. 159–75.

Benjamin, W. (1999a), 'The Work of Art in the Age of Mechanical Reproduction' in *Illuminations*, trans. H. Zorn, London: Pimlico, pp. 211–44.

Benjamin, W. (1999b), 'The Task of the Translator', in W. Banjamin (1999b), *Illuminations*, trans. H. Zorn, London: Pimlico, pp. 72–82.

Buchanan, I. (2000), *Deleuzism: A Metacommentary*, Edinburgh: Edinburgh University Press.

Deleuze, G. (1986), *Cinema 1: The Movement-Image*, trans. H. Tomlinson and B. Habberjam, London: The Athlone Press.

Deleuze, G. (1989), *Cinema 2: The Time-Image*, trans. H. Tomlinson and R. Galeta, London: The Athlone Press.

Deleuze, G. and Guattari, F. (1988), *A Thousand Plateaus: Capitalism and Schizophrenia*, trans. B. Massumi, London: The Athlone Press.

Deleuze, G. and Guattari, F. (1994), *What is Philosophy?*, trans. G. Burchell and H. Tomlinson, London and New York: Verso.

Hall, S. (1996), 'New Ethnicities', in D. Morley and K. Chen (eds) (1996), *Critical Dialogues in Cultural Studies*, London and New York: Routledge, pp. 441–9.

Jameson, F. (1997), 'Marxism and Dualism in Deleuze', in I. Buchanan (ed.) (1997), *A Deleuzian Century?*, (a special edition of) *The South Athlantic Quarterly* 96 (3), Durham: Duke University Press, pp. 393–416.

Khaili I, B. (2005), 'Syncrétiques Attitudes', in D. Pax and C. Béghin (eds), *Glauber Rocha*, Paris: Edition Magic Cinema, pp. 76–80.

Marks, J. (1998), *Gilles Deleuze. Vitalism and Multiplicity*, London and Sterling, Pluto Press.

Marks, L. (2000), *The Skin of Film: Intercultural Cinema, Embodiment and the Senses*, Durham and London: Duke University Press.

Pasolini, P. (1988), 'The Cinema of Poetry', in *Heretical Empiricism*, trans. B. Lawton and K. L. Barnett, Bloomington: Indiana University Press.

Pisters, P. (2001), *Micropolitics of Media Culture: Reading the Rhizomes of Deleuze and Guattari*, Amsterdam: Amsterdam University Press.

Solanas, F. and Gettino, O. (2000), 'Towards a Third Cinema: Notes and Experiences for the Development of a Cinema of Liberation in the Third World', in R. Stam and T. Miller (eds) (2000), *Film and Theory; An Anthology*, Malden and Oxford: Blackwell Publishers, pp. 265–86.

Wayne, M. (2001), *Political Film: The Dialectics of Third Cinema*, London and Sterling: Pluto Press.

# Notes

1. Adorno and Horkheimer (1997) argued similarly in their essay on the cultural industry.
2. 'Speech-act' refers to the performative quality of certain linguistic expressions. The most famous example given by Austin is the wedding vow: 'Yes I do' implies an actual change of civil status. As such words and films can act upon reality. See also Austin (2004).
3. Deleuze refers to *Marxism and the Philosophy of Language* by V. N. Volosinov, which he attributes to M. Bakthin (1973, New York: Seminar Press).
4. This is a sentence inspired by the novel *Ali and Nino* by Kurben Said (1937).
5. In her article 'Syncrétiques Attitudes' (2005), Bouchra Khalili I analyses the free indirect discourse in the work of Pier Paolo Pasolini and Glauber Rocha.
6. In his account on free indirect discourse and Deleuze John Marks also refers to this passage (see Marks 1998: 106 and 152–6).
7. By accessible I mean both in terms of its style and especially in terms of purchasing video or DVD copies. Many Third Cinema films for which it is so important to get an audience are extremely expensive and difficult to get hold of. Even to the point that a danger of elitism, that is a danger that threatens a strict and pure application of Deleuze as well. See Barbrook 2001.

8. Deleuze calls the perception-image a 'zeroness' before Pierce's firstness (Deleuze 1989: 31–2).
9. See also Ian Buchanan 'Treatise on Militarism', in this volume.
10. *Black Hawk Down* (Ridley Scott 2001) and *Missing* (Costa Gravas 1985) are films that portray American characters in a third-world country who seem to get involved 'by accident' in a third-world situation. *Black Hawk Down*, about the failed mission of the US Special Forces in Mogadishu in 1993, doesn't give any insights into the civil war in Somalia. Just like *Missing* does not give any Chilean perspective on the coup d'état by Pinochet in 1973. It is possible to criticise these films for that reason. It is important to know that *Black Hawk Down* was made with the support of the Pentagon and hence presents the facts from an American perspective. *Missing* focuses, indeed, on a couple of Americans in Chile while ignoring the rest of the population, but it actually criticises the American support in the dictatorial coups in South America. These films are not Third Cinema films. They do not speak from within a third-world culture although the stories are set there. This doesn't make the films less political, though (here I disagree with Mike Wayne). They still present a free indirect relation to reality that can influence reality from an American perspective (which as the two examples show, is also not one single perspective).
11. Other ways to politicise are by allegory and satire (Wayne 2001: 129).
12. In the documentary *Guerre Sans Images* (Mohammed Soudani and Michael von Graffenried 2002), this absence of images during the civil war is the central focus.
13. A contemporary Second Cinema (with First Cinema elements) film situated in Tangier, *Les Temps Qui Changent* (André Téchiné 2005) shows, several times, groups of immigrants waiting for their boat but they are barely noticed by the main characters Catherine Deneuve and Gerard Depardieu, who are occupied with their own love affair. They are noticed, however, and not completely left out of the picture (as is the case in many First Cinema films that deal with a love story between white stars) but are nonetheless very marginal within it. In this way the film seems consciously to acknowledge that most Westerners are not concerned with these people. At the time of writing, there are news reports of hundreds of 'illegal' African immigrants rushing border fences of the Spanish enclave Mellila in Northern Morocco. Western news media start to present images and stories of the immigrants. Perhaps, if the desperate and heroic actions of these people are accompanied by their stories in all kinds of media forms, concrete action will be taken to improve their situation.
14. In fact, Deleuze and Guattari give the fractal as an example of a smooth (nomad) space in *A Thousand Plateaus* (Deleuze and Guattari 1988: 486).

# Chapter 11

# Information and Resistance: Deleuze, the Virtual and Cybernetics

## John Marks

The main aim of this essay is to bring out some important distinctions between the work of Deleuze and Guattari and what has come to be known as 'cybertheory' or 'cyberculture'. After looking briefly at some of the themes that characterise the imaginary of cyberspace, the essay will assess the significance of the cybernetic inheritance of much contemporary cybertheory, since, as several commentators have claimed, cybertheory is founded upon the informational and communicational paradigm that emerges out of cybernetics in the post-war era. The essay will then move on to look at the way in which Deleuze's concept of the 'virtual' can be distinguished from Pierre Lévy's attempt – taking Deleuze's concept as a starting point – to conceptualise a general dynamic of *virtualisation* which is at work in contemporary societies. The closing section of the essay will focus on Deleuze's resistance to the informational/communicational paradigm.

It is in many respects not surprising that Deleuze and Guattari's work has been identified with aspects of cyberculture. For one thing, they seek to undermine the *molar* organisation of the organism, with its clearly defined and delineated body, in favour of a *molecular* plane of disorganisation. In an apparently analogous way, cybertheory often talks in terms of disrupting or even transcending the limits of the body. Also, the dissemination of the work of Deleuze and Guattari has coincided with the growth of the Internet as a ubiquitous, global social practice. During this time, a number of commentators have claimed Deleuze and Guattari as nothing less than prophets of cyberspace. Neil Spiller, for example, has recently identified *A Thousand Plateaus*, and in particular the opening section on the rhizome, as 'the philosophical bible of the cyber-evangelists' (Spiller 2002: 96).

It is also undeniable that the concept of the rhizome as a proliferating multiplicity which has no organising dimension or centre suggests metaphorical and analogical links with the Internet as a global system.[1]

The Internet functions and develops in ways that correspond closely to the six principles of the rhizome set out by Deleuze and Guattari in *A Thousand Plateaus*: connection, heterogeneity, multiplicity, asignifying rupture, cartography and decalcomania (Deleuze and Guattari 1987: 3–25). At the most straightforward level, the Internet has no central point of organisation and no precise point of origin, although it can arguably be traced back to an experiment called the ARPANET in the late 1960s.[2] Like the rhizome, the Internet is best thought of as being composed of lines rather than points, and in principle these lines are connectable in infinite ways. The use and development of the Internet does not refer to a pre-existing programme, and the individual user can navigate their way around the Net by means of hyperlinks in a way that cannot be predetermined or predicted by an editor, author or librarian. As well as there being no model or blueprint for the Net, no clear boundaries can be drawn that would indicate where it begins and where it ends. It is a *multiplicity*, in the sense that it is a network of networks, the dimensions of which are continually proliferating and undergoing transformations. In this sense the Internet is, notwithstanding the increasing corporate colonisation of cyberspace, a 'flat', immanent rhizomatic structure: it is, apparently, a 'smooth' rather than a 'striated' space. This freedom of movement and access, as well as the inherent flexibility of the Net as a rhizome, has led some commentators to focus on the creative potential of the Internet for the construction of new forms of subjectivity and media-activism (See Videcoq et al. 2005: 11–14). For some working in this area, the Internet seems to offer the resources for the sort of transversal linkages and possibilities for resistance that might characterise what Guattari termed 'post-media' society (See Guattari 1996: 263). The Internet has emerged, for example, as a mode of communication and dissemination that has become constitutive of transnational rhizomatic political groupings.

However, the argument here will be that, although there are elements in Deleuze and Guattari's work that undeniably connect with the creative and liberating aspects of cyberspace, there is also much which indicates a resistance to, and a critique of, what might be termed the 'imaginary' of cyberspace. For example, the *smooth* space within which the 'body without organs' operates is, for Deleuze and Guattari, a kinetic space of intensities located alongside the *striated* space of organisation (Deleuze and Guattari 1987: 479). For cybertheory, on the other hand, it often seems the world itself is in the process of becoming *smoother*. As Deleuze and Guattari state quite clearly in *A Thousand Plateaus*, we should 'never believe that a smooth space will suffice to save us' (Deleuze and Guattari 1987: 500). Whereas cybertheory often seems to claim that the manifest, everyday reality within which we live and transact our business is increasingly constituted by a series of smooth continuums, Deleuze and Guattari seek to locate and explore a set of intensive forces which form the temporary and contingent actualisations that we conventionally identify as bodies, organisms, species, and so on. Of course, Deleuze was not unaware that contemporary societies are characterised by their dependence upon information technology and computers (Deleuze 1995: 180). However, the theory of creative *involution* that Deleuze and Guattari elaborate in *A Thousand Plateaus* views body, brain and world as a complex whole which has a material density. Ultimately, it is the material complexity of Deleuze and Guattari's plane of immanence that is missing in much cybertheory.

## The Imaginary of Cyberspace

In order to deal with the issue of cyberspace, it is necessary to consider briefly what Tim Jordan has recently termed the 'virtual imaginary', which is to say the way in which cyberspace has been figured in the collective imagination (Jordan 1999: 179–207). Jordan points to two sides of this imaginary: the 'heaven' and 'hell' scenarios for cyberspace. First, there is a utopian dimension, which manifests itself in a general sense as a focus on new, 'virtual' communities. In more extreme terms, this utopian dimension may express itself as the 'cyborg' fantasy, according to which life is freed from previous material constraints – such as the body – and is reconfigured as flows of *information*. Second, there is the dystopian figure of the 'Superpanopticon', extrapolated from Michel Foucault's concept of discipline, according to which all the social transactions of everyday life – which would previously have remained private, or at the very least isolated in their significance – will be translated into an ongoing digital record and profile of the individual. In addition to this, there is the fear that developments in the field of the human genome will provide the means for writing a normalising genetic profile for each individual.

In this way, the cyborg fantasy depends upon blurring the boundaries between human and machine. This raises the possibility of transcending the body, and thus achieving a disembodied version of immortality, as well as bringing together individual human minds in some sort of higher, collective consciousness. Consequently, the 'heaven' scenario for cyberspace is frequently formulated in 'rhapsodic' terms by its proponents:

> There we have it, the ultimate dream of humanity. The moral of this myth of
> the electronic frontier is that freed from our bodies, our Is will be able to

mingle, join and finally create the heaven that rests within us now only as a dimly perceived potential. Cyberspace offers the ultimate fantasies of both individual immortality and collective transcendence. The body's dominance over the mind is the stranglehold broken by complex computer systems. The mind comes to dominate the body, to the extent that the mind will pick and choose its bodies. Made into the informational codes that live so well in cyberspace, all the Is finally have a chance to become We. Cyberspace allows the becoming of a transcendental community of mind. (Jordan 1999: 187)

Jordan's characterisation of the cyberspace imaginary highlights a number of key themes. Firstly, a preoccupation with *communication* and *transparency* runs throughout positive and utopian assessments of cyberspace. The fact that cyberspace, particularly in the shape of the Internet and the World Wide Web, facilitates communication and the dissemination of information is seen as an essentially positive phenomenon. Cyberspace seems to offer the possibility of ever-increasing transparency in social relations and the potential for a new, more open 'cyberdemocracy'. Secondly, cyberspace is one of the most important focal points for the conviction that biology, technology and social structures are converging in revolutionary and potentially liberatory ways: both the heaven and hell scenarios tend to imply some sort of paradigm shift. As will be shown, one of the most influential expressions of the perceived convergences between biological systems and machines is the notion of a evolving 'world-brain' or 'noosphere'; a collective human consciousness and intelligence. Unsurprisingly, this concept is often formulated, whether implicitly or explicitly, in a religious mode. This shift towards an episteme based on information and communication feeds into a subsequent cultural and intellectual preoccupation with themes of flexibility, flux and creativity at the *molecular*, rather than *molar* level. Thirdly, emerging from these themes is what N. Katherine Hayles has termed the 'concept of virtuality': the cultural perception that information and materiality are discrete concepts, and that material objects are interpenetrated and defined by information patterns (Hayles 2000). Jordan identifies this as a pervasive concept in both the positive and the negative formulations of cyberspace, when he claims that they both rely upon the conviction that 'everything is made of information or can be turned into information' (Jordan 1999: 181). For cyberspace enthusiasts, this conception of information as virtuality evokes the tantalising Gnostic dream of freeing humanity from the burdens of bodily existence.

Finally, there is the issue of the links between cyberspace and advanced capitalism, given that many cyberspace enthusiasts also seem to embrace the free-market ethos of globalised neo-liberal capitalism.

The most obvious expression of this cybercapitalism is *Wired* magazine. The magazine's executive editor, Kevin Kelly, for example, perceives a direct analogy between the use of cybernetic feedback loops to improve production and efficiency in the post-war steel industry, and the neo-liberal theories of Hayek and the Austrian school of economics (Kelly 1994: 121–2). For Kelly, the emerging global network economy is rhizomatic, and should be thought of as a constantly evolving, decentralised system that proliferates in a quasi-biological manner:

> As networks have permeated our world, the economy has come to resemble an ecology of organisms, interlinked and coevolving, constantly in flux, deeply tangled, ever expanding at its edges. As we know from recent ecological studies, no balance exists in nature; rather, as evolution proceeds, there is perpetual disruption as new species replace old, as natural biomes shift in their makeup, and as organisms and environments transform each other (Kelly 1998: 108).

In this way, then, in recent years, Deleuze and Guattari have found themselves co-opted into this alliance between cyberspace and cutting-edge capitalism. In his recent assessment of Deleuze's work, *Organs Without Bodies*, Slavoj Žižek goes so far as to claim that it may well be justified to call Deleuze 'the ideologist of late capitalism' (Žižek 2004: 184).[3] He implies that Deleuze does not fully work through the consequences of the 'spectral materialism' that is entailed by the information revolution, biogenetics and quantum physics (Žižek 2004: 25). He goes on to suggest that, particularly in his work with Guattari, Deleuze may in some ways be seen to endorse the Gnostic fantasies of cyberspace that are such an important part of late 'digital' capitalism (Žižek 2004: 184–7). In this way, Žižek suggests that there is a 'pro-capitalist' aspect, as he puts it, in the work of Deleuze and Guattari themselves (Žižek 2004: 193). There is a close correlation, he claims, between Deleuze's Spinozist commitment to the impersonal circulation of affects and the affective dynamics of late capitalism (Žižek 2004: 183–4). Others have also argued that Deleuze and Guattari's work is in some ways in tune with the particular phase of late or advanced capitalism that has coincided with the recent growth of information and computer technologies. Without going so far as to claim that such a tendency is inherent in the work of Deleuze and Guattari, Richard Barbrook has drawn direct parallels between 'Deleuzoguattarian' Net enthusiasts and what he terms 'Californian hi-tech neo-liberalism' (Barbrook 2001: 173).

As far as Žižek is concerned, the 'proto-capitalist' aspect of Deleuze and Guattari's work is developed most fully in the recent Swedish bestseller *Netocracy*, by Alexander Bard and Jan Söderqvist (2002). Žižek is aware that Bard and Söderqvist claim that the 'netocratic' society that is currently emerging is actually *post*-capitalist. For them, Deleuze, as a key inheritor of what they call the 'mobilistic' tradition, offers ways of grappling this new reality (Bard and Söderqvist 2002: 110–11). This mobilistic, or 'eternalistic' mode of thought is the only one that will help us to think through the consequences of the new 'netocratic' society that is replacing capitalism. Just as capitalism replaced feudalism so, they claim, 'informationalism' is in the process of replacing capitalism. The Internet has emerged as the definitive model of the new social reality in which information and knowledge finally replace capital. However, for Žižek, there is no critical edge to Bard and Söderqvist's use of Deleuze and Guattari:

> What they are actually claiming is that the netocrats, today's élite, realize the dream of yesterday's marginal philosophers and outcast artists (from Spinoza to Nietzsche and Deleuze). In short, and stated even more pointedly, the thought of Foucault, Deleuze, and Guattari, the ultimate philosophers of resistance, of marginal positions crushed by the hegemonic power network, is effectively the ideology of the newly emerging ruling class. (Bard and Söderqvist 2004: 193)[4]

## Cybernetics: Information, Control and Communication

Although the Internet has been the most significant recent factor in the development of cybertheory, there are historical influences on this way of thinking that should not be underestimated. Hayles, for example, identifies the post-war emergence of molecular biology and information theory – or *cybernetics* – as the two key discursive influences on the notion that the body's materiality can be reduced to informational patterns (Hayles 2000: 69–73). As far as molecular biology is concerned, following Watson and Crick's discovery of the double-helix structure of DNA in 1953, right through to the present-day publicity given to the Human Genome Project, DNA has emerged as an object that ties together life and information in new ways. In short, as well as having considerable scientific impact, the notion that 'life' is encoded within the sequencing of the four nucleotides that make up the genes in the human genome has made its way into the public consciousness. Cybernetics, for its part, had its origins in research into military weapons systems and emerged as a body of thought in the post-war era and had a significant technical and social impact in Europe and North America. Over time, the term 'cybernetics', initially coined by Norbert Wiener, came to define a field of study that takes in communication and feedback control processes in biological, mechanical and electronic systems.

For Wiener, cybernetics as a discipline corresponded to a significant epistemic shift that was taking place: the focus of technological progress and scientific understanding was no longer either matter or energy, but rather *information*. If the seventeenth and early eighteenth centuries are the age of clocks, followed by the age of the steam engine, then the second half of the twentieth century is the age of the control and communication of information (Wiener 1961: 39). If, according to the second law of thermodynamics, there is a tendency for entropy to increase in closed systems, information seemed to offer an explanation for the fact that small islands of order, such as living systems, might be able to counter this general trend towards disorder: they could process information. Wiener, along with figures such as Claude E. Shannon and Warren Weaver, sought to establish 'natural' laws for the transmission and circulation of information, which would be applicable to both biological and technological systems. As such, cybernetics has provided fertile ground for theories of artificial intelligence and has contributed significantly towards the notion of a convergence of technology and biology that, as discussed already, cyber-enthusiasts such as Kevin Kelly have taken up. Wiener predicts that 'messages between man and machine, between machines and man, and between machine and machine' will play an ever-increasing role in the functioning of modern societies (Wiener 1954: 16). For Hayles, the distinction that information theory draws between *signal* and *message* is the crucial factor in the separation of information from materiality. A message as such has no material presence, and it is purely *pattern* until it is encoded in material form – printed text, electrical pulses, and so on – as signal (Hayles 2000: 73–4). In short, information is defined as pattern rather than presence and, as Hayles points out, this separation is expressed most strikingly in Wiener's claim that it would one day be possible to telegraph a human being (see Wiener 1954).

Wiener published his most influential work in the Cold War period and a constant theme is the necessity of 'free' communication as a guarantee of democracy and truth in the face of anti-communist censorship in the United States and the totalitarian Soviet state. Philippe Breton takes up this theme at some length, arguing that Wiener's cybernetics is an expression of a generalised utopian philosophy of 'communication' that emerges in response to both the horrors of the World War II and the rise of totalitarian régimes with state-controlled economies (Breton 1997: 49–60). Breton emphasises that the move towards the notion of a society built around the central value of 'communication' occurs in reaction to the 'modern barbarism' that unfolds in the thirty-one-year period that includes the two World Wars (1914–45). The mass destruction of two wars, and in particular the Holocaust and the drift towards total war focused quite deliberately on civilian populations, seems to represent the collapse of Enlightenment values. The concentration upon communication is, in one sense, a wholly predictable response to a situation in which established values have collapsed and need to be rebuilt along consensual lines. Also, communication seems to provide the obvious antidote to forms of organised state 'irrationality', such as the Nazi's 'Final Solution' which depended so heavily on obfuscation and secrecy. In this way, 'communication' seems to offer a guarantee against the potentially murderous consequences of secrecy, as well as being a 'neutral' alternative to the major ideologies of the first half of the twentieth century. According to Breton, this utopian vision of a 'society of communication' demonstrates strong parallels with nineteenth-century anarchist thought by virtue of its focus on the potential for spontaneous self-regulation within small communities (Breton 1997: 60–1). This is the historical context within which cybernetics seeks to deal with the problems of control and communication (See Wiener 1954: 17).

In the narrative that Breton presents in *Le culte de l'Internet* (2000), the project for a new society organised around communication is based upon an *informational* model of the world. According to this 'radical ontology of the message', the world is divided between, on the one hand, forms, ideas and messages and, on the other hand, disorder, entropy and chance (Breton 2000: 36). As contemporary historians of information, such as Philippe Breton (1997) and Ronald E. Day (2001) point out, the great fear of cybernetics in general, and Wiener in particular, was of entropy and noise within communications systems. Information must be disseminated, but it must also be subject to laws of *communication* and *control*. As Day points out, Wiener's cybernetics is both a technical model, drawing on the logic of systems engineering, and also constitutes a social and communicational utopia (Day 2001: 49). That is to say, cybernetics is both a science and an industrial social practice that seeks to discover general laws of communication, and to ensure mankind's survival in the face of 'nature's tendency to degrade the organised and destroy the meaningful' (Day 2001: 50). Day also emphasises that Wiener's humanism is a reaction to what he perceives not only as a threat from the forces of nature, but also the 'nonrational' elements of humans themselves (Day 2001: 51). Day shows that Wiener's fear of chaos in the shape of disordered, entropic communication means that he inevitably attempts to naturalise the technical model of cybernetics as a social utopia. Cybernetics will help 'man' to survive in the face of nature's tendency towards entropy (Day 2001: 49–50). It is a matter of uncovering 'natural' laws which will protect man against irrationality and entropy. As far as Day is concerned, the central premise upon which the communicational utopia prescribed by cybernetics is founded is what he calls the 'conduit' metaphor of communication:

> According to this model or metaphor, information is the flow and exchange of a message, originating from one speaker, mind, or source and received by another. Analogous to theories of production and exchange in liberal capitalism, information, here, is understood as created by the 'free' will of one person and is then transferred through the 'medium' or market of public language into the ear and mind of another person, at which point the second person acknowledges the correct value of the original intention by his or her performative actions. (Day 2001: 38)

Cybertheory develops when the communicational utopia of the postwar period comes into contact with technologies such as the Internet. The belief that information and communication will protect society from the spectre of irrationality and guarantee a certain level of social transparency, together with the conviction that information allows us to transcend the body, act as foundational tenets for those who see a utopian promise in cyberspace. This utopian vision manifests itself in the conviction that cyberspace is the avatar of a 'noosphere', the convergence of human intelligence to form a collective 'mind sphere'. As Michael Heim points out, the concept of the noosphere has its origins in the work of the French Jesuit palaeontologist Teilhard de Chardin. The concept of a convergent networking of minds from which a new stage of spirit emerges is significantly influenced by Hegel's dialectical idealism (Heim 2000: 35–6). In developing the idea of the noosphere Teilhard sought to bring together the emerging science of evolutionary biology with a theology of divine forces. Just as matter converges to form larger units like living organisms, so individual minds must also converge into some larger thinking entity. In short, evolution points towards the emergence of a global consciousness: an envelope of thinking substance (Teilhard de Chardin: 1964). There is, as far as Teilhard is concerned, an 'evident kinship' between the human brain, with its billions of inter-connected nerve-cells, and the apparatus of social thought. In bringing together an evolutionary perspective with a theory of technology, Teilhard comes close to imagining an entity like the Internet. He summarises the process in the following way: 'psychic centration, phyletic intertwining and planetary envelopment: three genetically associated occurrences which, taken together, give birth to the Noosphere' (Teilhard 1964: 159). It is already the case, in the late 1940s, that there is a network of radio and television communications that link humanity in what Teilhard calls an 'etherised' universal consciousness (Teilhard 1964: 167). However, he is also aware of the new technology of computers:

> [But] I am also thinking of the insidious growth of those astonishing electronic computers which, pulsating with signals at the rate of hundreds and thousands a second, not only relieve our brains of tedious and exhausting work but, because they enhance the essential (and too little noted) factor of 'speed of thought', are also paving the way for a revolution in the sphere of research. (Teilhard 1964: 167)

## Pierre Lévy: A 'Nomad' Planet

The key preoccupations of cyberspace and cybertheory can be traced throughout the work of the French sociologist and 'philosopher of cyberspace' Pierre Lévy. Significantly for the discussion here, Lévy draws explicitly and extensively on the work of Deleuze and Guattari. Lévy defines cyberspace as being comprised of the new medium of communications that is constituted by the global interconnection of computers, as well as the 'oceanic universe of information' that this network holds (Lévy 2001: xvi). He does not deny that cyberspace and telecommunications are currently producing a 'deluge' of information. However, the positive potential of cyberspace means that it is no longer necessary to mount a 'rescue operation', to hold a watertight sample of crucial data, in the spirit of Noah. Instead, this new flood creates the conditions for a fluid circulation of messages that is ultimately beneficial:

> It sweeps everything along in its path. Fluid, virtual, simultaneously gathered and dispersed, it is impossible to burn this library of Babel. The innumerable voices that resonate through cyberspace will continue to call and respond to one another. In this deluge, the floodwaters will never wash away the signs that have been engraved. (Lévy 2001: xv)

A number of concepts and themes drawn from Deleuze and Guattari, and subsequently transformed, are incorporated into Lévy's work: the nomadic, deterritorialisation, the molar and the molecular, and the virtual. In *Collective Intelligence: Mankind's Emerging World in Cyberspace*, Lévy claims that cyberspace is one important element of the increasingly 'nomad' planet that we now inhabit (Lévy 1997: vii-xii). Although this new 'nomadism' may intersect with the familiar co-ordinates of spatial displacement, it is more a question of new 'textures of humanity'. Lévy suggests that many of the stable epistemological co-ordinates that were previously taken for granted are now in the process of becoming more flexible and mutable: 'Even if we manage to achieve a condition of personal immobility, the landscape will continue to flow around us, infiltrate us, transform us from within' (Lévy 1997: xxv). Lévy also formulates this nomadism as a general move from the *molar* to the *molecular*. Whereas the mass, *molar* production and management of life, matter and information entailed a relatively high level of entropy, the new *molecular* technologies – nanotechnology, genetic engineering, digital information technologies – allow for more precise and less wasteful control (Lévy 1997: 42). Genetics, nanotechnology and the development of cyberspace are transforming our relationship to our bodies, reproduction, health, knowledge and community (Lévy 1997: 39–55).

Lévy's *Becoming Virtual* (1998) draws explicitly on Deleuze's concept of the 'virtual'.[5] Lévy takes as his starting point Deleuze's statement in *Difference and Repetition* (1994) that the virtual is not opposed to the real. Inspired by this, he seeks to counter what he sees as the general tendency of philosophy to analyse the passage from the virtual to the actual. Instead, we should focus on the *real* status of the virtual:

> The virtual should, properly speaking, be compared not to the real but to the actual. Unlike the possible, which is static and already constituted, the virtual is a kind of problematic complex, the knot of tendencies or forces that accompanies a situation, event, object, or entity, and which evokes a process of resolution: actualization. (Lévy 1998: 24)

An entity both produces and is constituted by its own virtualities: they constitute its 'problematic', the tensions, constraints and projections that animate it. In one sense, Lévy claims, actualisation is the 'solution' to the 'problem' of the entity, in that it is a transformative and productive process. Having established this broadly Deleuzian framework, Lévy sets out what he sees as some of the key features of the process of *virtualisation*. This is not, Lévy claims, a process of *derealisation* – reality is not transformed into a collection of possibilities – but rather a 'displacement of the centre of ontological gravity of the object considered' (Lévy 1998: 26). Instead of actualising itself as a 'solution', the entity remains within a problematic field. In focusing on opening up activity to a 'more general problematic', virtualisation has the effect of making existing boundaries and distinctions more fluid (Lévy 1998: 27). Lévy offers as a contemporary example what he calls the virtualisation of a company, which moves from assembling its workforce in a precise location or series of locations to use of 'telecommuting'. In this way, Lévy claims, the spatiotemporal co-ordinates of work are turned, in the *virtualised* company, into a continuously renewed problem as opposed to a stable solution.

For Lévy the key modality of the virtual is that it is 'not there', in that its components cannot be located precisely within spatial or temporal co-ordinates. He suggests that this means that, in the case of a virtual community freed from the constraints of geographical location, the affective and associative aspects of this community are, if anything, amplified (Lévy 1998: 29). Any individual, community, act or piece of information that is virtualised in this way *deterritorialises* itself. As the contemporary world virtualises itself, there is a proliferation of types of space and durations. In navigating this complex, rhizomatic network of space-times, we are returned to the condition of *nomads*:

> The contemporary multiplication of spaces has made us nomads once again. But rather than following tracks and migrations within a fixed domain, we leap from network to network, from one system of proximity to the next. The spaces metamorphose and bifurcate beneath our feet, forcing us to undergo a process of heterogenesis. (Lévy 1998: 31)

Lévy goes on to describe how this process of heterogenesis applies to the virtualisation of the body. He is keen to emphasise that by the virtualisation of the body he does not mean some sort of disembodiment or dematerialisation. Instead, he wants to emphasise how the ontological gravity of the body has shifted. He suggests that we now need to think of the individual body as a temporary actualisation of a vast 'technobiological hyperbody' (Lévy 1998: 44). The virtualisation of the body is accomplished by a range of technologies which deterritorialise and socialise it. The body is inserted into a continuum which allows it to escape itself. Implants and prostheses blur the boundaries between the animal and the mineral, and human organs and bodily fluids, such as blood, now constitute deterritorialised networks. The individual body is exteriorised and subsequently transformed by this shared 'flesh and blood'. In this way, Lévy defines virtualisation as a form of 'desubstantiation'.

The main problem with Lévy's use of the virtual is that the *metaphysical* and *ontological* significance that the concept has in Deleuze's thought is largely jettisoned in favour of a historical argument that outlines a continuing ontological shift. In historical terms, Lévy claims that the ongoing *virtualisation* of bodies, text and economy constitutes an ontological transformation of the human – 'une *poursuite de l'hominisation*'. For Lévy, the Internet is a key instrument in this process. His arguments are familiar: classic media forms have instituted a clear separation between the emitters and receivers of messages, and have imposed a 'crude' form of hierarchical organisation on messages; conversely one-to-one media connections (such as telephones) have facilitated reciprocal communication, but have not allowed for a global vision or the construction of a common context. In contrast to the straightforward diffusion of messages, the Internet offers a form of continuous interaction that each individual can modify or stabilise at any time. The Internet is the partial objectivisation of the virtual world: a rhizomatic space populated by nomads. However, for Deleuze, the virtual is not a realm that we can enter as part of a historical process of development. It is, rather, a concept that serves to divert our attention from the world of finished products to the open, *intensive* world of divergent processes.[6]

The problems associated with Lévy's transformation of the concept of the virtual are encapsulated in *Becoming Virtual: Reality in the Virtual Age* (1998), which presents an unrecognisably 'smooth' cybernetic reading of Deleuze and Guattari. Day outlines two main ways in which Lévy's use of the notion of the 'virtual' deviates from the concept as set out by Deleuze and Guattari. Firstly, the perception and prediction of virtualisation on a global scale effectively turns Deleuze's philosophy of immanence into a form of Hegelianism. The virtual, in Lévy's hands, is appropriated for a quasi-Hegelian synthesis of individual and collective thought. Secondly, Lévy's 'anthropology' privileges the virtual as a manifest historical and social space, rather than an 'event' in the Deleuzian sense. Rather than being an analytical and problematising concept, the virtual is reified spatially and historically. As Day argues, Lévy analogises Deleuze and Guattari's notion of 'desire' to that of 'information', and argues that new digital technologies work against Oedipal capitalisation in favour of new 'entrepreneurial' forms of existence. Effectively, as Day suggests, Lévy sets up an equivalence between a Deleuzian philosophy of immanence and a neo-liberal ideology of entrepreneurship. The only element of control that this new, open 'Universal' of cyberspace needs is more transparency, since the current market is the 'still imperfect embryo' of a general system for the evaluation and remuneration of individual acts by everyone else' (Lévy 1998: 88). As Day suggests, Lévy effectively territorialises the virtual. His point of departure may be Deleuze and Guattari, but his ultimate aim is to resuscitate Teilhard de Chardin's evolutionary notion of the noosphere; the 'thinking layer' which achieves consistency in the twentieth century.[7]

Lévy describes *World Philosophie* (2000) as a 'love-song to the contemporary world'. The year 2000 has arrived, and he declares that he has decided to opt for 'humanity'. In sweeping historical terms, he talks of an initial dispersion of humanity which is followed, from the fifteenth century onwards, by the gradual reconnection of humanity with itself, a process which is now reaching its apogee with the rise of the Internet and a genuinely global capitalism. Information technology and biotechnology are leading us into a 'noolithic' revolution. The 'hollow' concept of nationality is rapidly fading in importance and human beings are gradually being brought together in a generalised condition of 'nomadism'. When he begins to talk of the Cold War as a 'moment of hesitation' before a general move towards global reconnection, it becomes clear that a version of the 'end of history thesis' informs much of the book.

In fact, the global society that Lévy describes in such ecstatic terms rapidly comes to resemble a version of the emerging 'control society' set out by Deleuze, only described with not a hint of the latter's 'joyous pessimism' (see Deleuze 1995: 177–82). Lévy celebrates a world in which consumption replaces production as the dominant paradigm. *World Philosophie* portrays the global economy in terms of a continuous expansion of the 'virtual'. Marketing, business, commerce and 'ideas' are the continuous, 'smooth' forms that are replacing the world of state, industry, economy and natural resources. Lévy relishes the continuous modulation that is 'business', in which each individual becomes an 'enterprise' and life-long learning and 'personal development' replace what was previously understood as education. Cyberspace facilitates the convergence of *homo economicus* and *homo academicus*, with the result that universities are becoming businesses and businesses are becoming universities. The global market encourages 'creativity', and money is simply a 'unit of epistemological measure'. Universities sell education and qualifications to students, whilst selling their research to public or private organisations. The market, for Lévy, generates co-operation, and he borrows from cognitive neuroscience in order to claim that collective intelligence emerges from a process of 'competitive co-operation' that is homologous to the neo-Darwinist notion of genes in 'competition' and the cognitive evolution of the brain.

Philippe Breton puts forward a stinging critique of Lévy in *Le culte de l'Internet* (2000). Essentially, Breton sees the embrace of the Internet by evangelists like Lévy as proof of a 'latent religiosity': a religiosity in which he perceives currents of Gnosticism, puritanism and Buddhism conjoined with a form of ecstatic liberalism. He locates the 'cult' of the Internet within a 'cult of information' that has its origins in the cybernetic visions of the 1940s. Breton's position is humanist, in that he is disturbed by what he sees as the 'debiologisation' – the hollowing out of the corporeal reality and complexity, the essential *depth* and *integrity* – of the human. From a humanist phenomenological perspective, Breton argues that 'informational' man is robbed of interiority, and the body is seen as nothing more than a source of entropy, a point of resistance to the process of communication. For Breton, the recurrent images that are associated with this world of ecstatic communication are of 'transparency', 'light', 'clarity' and 'openness'. All that is 'hidden', 'secret' or 'private' is seen as constituting an obstacle to the free flow of communication. In the face of what he considers to be Lévy's combination of free-market values and cybernetic mysticism, Breton defends humanist values of interiority and privacy, and he opposes a general theory of 'embodiment' to the computational models of cognitive neuroscience and evolutionary psychology.

## Communication, Information and Thought

Of course, Deleuze's work is also opposed to the sort of communicational utopia that Lévy proposes. However, Deleuze does not seek to defend the integrity and interiority of the human subject in the same way that Breton does. Instead, he sees the human as a 'fold', a point of resistance in circuits of communication and information. Deleuze's aversion to 'communication' has an obvious contemporary force and relevance. In *What is Philosophy?* (1994), Deleuze and Guattari talk of the 'inter-subjective idealism' of markets, and claim that all the 'debaters and communicators' of contemporary life are fuelled by *ressentiment*, setting their empty generalisations against one another. For Deleuze and Guattari, *philosophy*, as opposed to communication, is, on the one hand, too sure of itself to engage in debate and communication, and on the other hand, has more 'solitary paths' to pursue (Deleuze and Guattari 1994: 28–9).

As well as expressing a commitment to philosophy as an antidote to the general communicational/confessional drift of contemporary culture, Deleuze's choice of terminology when he talks of 'control' and 'communication' has a more precise historical dimension. In using these terms, he points to the revival of cybernetics as a way of theorising and justifying emerging forms of neo-liberalism that has been discussed at length in this essay. So, for Deleuze, contemporary control societies, in which 'instant communication' plays a key role, correspond to 'cybernetic' machines (Deleuze 1995: 175). Whereas industrial, disciplinary societies concentrated on the organisation of life and production, creating a network of sites and institutions – prisons, hospitals, factories, schools, the family – within which individuals were located, trained and punished, control societies are structured according to principles of continuous variation. The individual in a contemporary control society is in a constant state of *modulation*. In control societies the dominant model is that of the business, in which it is more frequently the task of the individual to engage in forms of competition and continuing education in order to attain a certain level of salary. Unlike cyber-enthusiasts such as Lévy, Deleuze is to a large extent averse to the prospect of control societies in which we are constantly coerced into forms of communication and obliged continually to reinvent and account for ourselves. Deleuze suggests that the move towards continuous assessment in schools is extended to society in general, with the effect that much of life takes on the texture of the gameshow or the marketing seminar. We are denied the privilege of having nothing to say, of cultivating the particular kind of creative solitude that Deleuze values:

> Maybe speech and communication have been corrupted. They're thoroughly permeated by money – and not by accident but by their very nature. We've got to hijack speech. Creating has always been something different from communicating. The key thing is to create vacuoles of noncommunication, circuit breakers, so we can elude control. (Deleuze 1995: 175)

Rather than encouraging a real social engagement with the prepersonal, control societies threaten to turn the individual into an object with no resistance, no capacity to 'fold' the line of modulation. Although the body without organs lacks the discreteness of what we conventionally know as an individual, that is not to say that it does not have resistance. It is, on the contrary, a zone of intensity. It may be traversed by forces, but it is not simply a relay for those forces. It is for these reasons that John Rajchman identifies the 'intelligence of the virtual' – in the Deleuzian sense of the term – in *thought*; that is to say the capacity to distinguish between real and false problems and to resist *doxa* (Rajchman 1998: 407).

In conclusion, although Deleuze and Breton obviously share a distrust of 'communication societies', Deleuze's position cannot be reduced to a humanist defence of interiority and embodiment. What Deleuze, along with Guattari, does present us with in his later work, is the sketch of a new philosophical approach to the brain and its interaction with the world. In *The Deleuze Connections* (2000) Rajchman emphasises that Deleuze rejected computer models of the mind, along with the reductive 'Darwinism of the cognitive'. As Rajchman says, Deleuze's language of connection, rhizome and network may well sound like talk of neural nets or the Internet, but we should proceed with caution (Rajchman 2000:

11). In his work on cinema, Deleuze starts to talk about an uncertain, probabilistic brain that he felt was suggested in contemporary microbiological research. This 'lived' brain opens up the potential for new pathways and connections, and conforms to Deleuze's expressive materialism rather than the reductive materialism of computational or cognitive models:

> It's not that our thinking starts from what we know about the brain but that any new thought traces uncharted channels directly through its matter, twisting, folding, fissuring it. . . . New connections, new pathways, new synapses, that's what philosophy calls into play as it creates concepts, but this whole image is something of which the biology of the brain, in its own way, is discovering an objective material likeness, or the material working. (Deleuze 1995: 149)

Deleuze talks of the brain as a 'screen', and claims that the way in which cinema can stimulate thought is *molecular*, in that it physically creates new molecular pathways in the brain (see Deleuze 1986). As Rajchman emphasises, the central problem that Deleuze addresses in much of his later work, including the books on cinema, is that of *resistance* in a world saturated with information, which constantly incites us to acts of communication. The most enigmatic expression of this theme is found in a short piece on the cinema of Straub and Huillet (Deleuze 1998). Here, Deleuze defines being 'informed' as being told what to believe, or rather to act as if we believed. (One inevitably thinks here of the ubiquity of the 'mission statement' in contemporary business and institutional culture.) We are back in the territory of cybernetics – the flow of information as a protection against irrationalism, noise and the destructive tendencies of 'nature' – and it is significant that Deleuze refers in passing to the Holocaust and National Socialism. 'Counterinformation', he suggests, achieves nothing; it is only when it becomes an act of *resistance* that it becomes useful:

> The work of art has nothing to do with communication. The work of art strictly does not contain the least bit of information. To the contrary, there is a fundamental affinity between the work of art and the act of resistance. There yes. It has something to do with information and communication as acts of resistance. (Deleuze 1998: 18)

Ultimately, it seems unjustifiable to read Deleuze and Guattari as cyber-enthusiasts *avant la letttre*. Deleuze's materialist ontology – developed in both his own work and with Guattari – may constitute a useful resource in thinking through the stakes of an increasingly networked society, but it is not a blueprint for a utopian, disembodied cyberspace.

Instead, it serves as a stimulus to analyse the precise nature of the *actual*, promoting a critical evaluation of what we are ceasing to be as we encounter new constellations of forces.

# References

Barbrook, R. (2001), 'The Holy Fools: Revolutionary Elitism in Cyberspace', in Pisters P. (ed.) (2001), *Micropolitics of Media Culture: Reading the Rhizomes of Deleuze and Guattari*, Amsterdam: Amsterdam University Press, pp. 159–75.

Bard, A. and Söderqvist, J. (2002), *Netocracy: The New Power Elite and Life after Capitalism*, trans. N. Smith, London: Pearson Education.

Breton, P. (1997), *L'Utopie de la communication: le mythe du village planétaire*, Paris: La Découverte.

Breton, P. (2000), *Le culte de l'internet: une menace pour le lien social?*, Paris: La Découverte.

Day, R. E. (2001), *The Modern Invention of Information: Discourse, History, and Power*, Carbondale and Edwardsville: Southern Illinois University Press.

DeLanda, M. (2002), *Intensive Science and Virtual Philosophy*, London and New York: Continuum.

Deleuze, G. (1986), 'Le cerveau, c'est l'écran', *Cahiers du cinéma* 380 (février): 25–32.

Deleuze, G. (1994), *Difference and Repetition*, trans. P. Patton, New York: Columbia University Press.

Deleuze, G. (1995), *Negotiations: 1972–1990*, trans. Martin Joughin, New York: Columbia University Press.

Deleuze, G. (1998), 'Having an Idea in Cinema', in E. Kaufman and K. J. Heller, (eds) (1998), *Deleuze and Guattari: New Mappings in Politics, Philosophy, and Culture*, trans, E. Kaufman, Minneapolis and London: University of Minnesota Press, pp. 14–19.

Deleuze G. and Guattari, F. (1987), *A Thousand Plateaus: Capitalism and Schizophrenia*, trans. B. Massumi, Minneapolis: University of Minnesota Press.

Deleuze G. and Guattari, F. (1994), *What is Philosophy?*, trans. H. Tomlinson and G. Burchell, London: Verso.

Deleuze, G. and Parnet, C. (1996), *Dialogues*, Paris: Flammarion.

Guattari, F. (1996), 'Remaking Social Practices', in G. Genosko (ed.) (1996), *The Guattari Reader*, Oxford: Blackwell, pp. 262–72.

Hayles, N. K. (2000), 'The Condition of Virtuality', in P. Lunenfeld (ed.) (2000), *The Digital Dialectic*, Boston: MIT Press, pp. 68–94.

Heim, M. (2000), 'The Cyberspace Dialectic', in P. Lunenfeld (ed.) (2000), *The Digital Dialectic*, Boston: MIT Press, pp. 25–45.

Jordan, T. (1999), *Cyberpower: The Culture and Politics of Cyberspace and the Internet*, New York and London: Routledge.

Kelly, K. (1994), *Out of Control: The New Biology of Machines, Social Systems and the Economic World*, London: Fourth Estate.

Kelly, K. (1998), *New Rules for the New Economy: 10 Ways the Network Economy is Changing Everything*, London: Fourth Estate.

Lévy, P. (1997), *Collective Intelligence: Mankind's Emerging World in Cyberspace*, trans. R. Bononno, New York and London: Plenum Trade.

Lévy, P. (1998), *Becoming Virtual: Reality in the Digital Age*, trans. R. Bononno, New York and London: Plenum Trade.

Lévy, P. (2000), *World Philosophie*, Paris: Odile Jacob.

Lévy, P. (2001), *Cyberculture*, trans. R. Bonnono, London and Minneapolis: University of Minnesota Press.

Rajchman, J. (1998), 'Y-a-t-il une intélligence du virtuel?' in E. Alliez (ed.) (1998), *Gilles Deleuze: une vie philosophique: Rencontres Internationales Rio de Janeiro – São Paulo 10–14 juin 1996*, Le Plessis Robinson: Insitut Synthélabo, pp. 403–20.

Rajchman, J. (2000), *The Deleuze Connections*, Cambridge and London: MIT Press.

Spiller, N. (ed.) (2002), *Cyber-Reader: Critical Writing of the Digital Era*, New York: Phaidon.

Stivale, C. (1998), *The Two-Fold Thought of Deleuze and Guattari: Intersections and Animations*, New York: Guilford Press.

Teilhard de Chardin, P. (1964), *The Future of Man*, trans. N. Denny, New York: Harper and Row.

Videcoq, E., Holmes B. and Querien, A. (2005), 'Les trois plis du média-activisme', *Multitudes* 21 (été): 11–14.

Wiener, N. (1954), *The Human Use of Human Beings: Cybernetics and Society*, 2nd edn, Boston: Houghton Mifflin.

Wiener, N. (1961), *Cybernetics: Or Control and Communication in the Animal and the Machine*, 2nd edn, Cambridge: MIT Press.

Wise, J. M. (1997), *Exploring Technology and Social Space*, London: Sage.

Žižek, S. (2004), *Organs Without Bodies: Deleuze and Consequences*, New York and London: Routledge.

# Notes

1. See Wise 1997 and Stivale 1998.
2. Widely seen as being the precursor of the Internet, the ARPANET was created by the United States Defense Advanced Research Project Agency. It is often claimed that it was designed as a means of developing a military information and communications network that would be able to function in the event of nuclear conflict, although it was initially the case that the ARPANET linked universities and research centres. As the project evolved and was gradually transformed into what we know today as the Internet, it was instrumental in the development of key functions such as e-mail, telnet remote computer control, and file transfer protocol.
3. Žižek claims in *Organs Without Bodies* that there are essentially two 'logics' within Deleuze's work: one that runs through his single-authored publications on philosophy, film and literature; and one that can be attributed to his co-authored work with Guattari. The first logic – the line of Deleuze 'proper' according to Žižek – is that of the 'sterile flow of surface becoming'; the pure effect of corporeal causes (Žižek 2004: 21). The second logic – the 'guattarized' Deleuze – conceives of bodily entities as the product of the 'pure flow of Becoming' (Žižek 2004: 22).
4. Žižek misrepresents somewhat Bard and Söderqvist's use of Deleuze and Guattari in *Netocracy*. Although their claim that 'netocracy' will actually replace capitalism is somewhat sweeping and certainly hard to sustain, it is at the same time unfair to suggest that they employ Deleuze and Guattari solely in order to lend theoretical legitimacy to new forms of capitalism. On the contrary, for all that is contentious in *Netocracy*, Bard and Söderqvist do argue that it is naïve to assume that the 'new economy' associated with cyberspace will lead to the emergence of a transparent, conflictless social realm of digital capitalism. Instead, they argue it will be a question of new forms and new conflicts that emerge in the 'informationalist' régime. What remains enigmatic in their account

is the precise status of 'mobilistic' philosophy. Ultimately they seem to suggest that this philosophy may spawn netocratic 'class traitors' who will resist the appropriation of knowledge and information by an entrepreneurial élite.

5. Lévy's book is cited as a footnote in the appendix 'L'actuel et le virtuel' to the 1996 Flammarion edition of Deleuze and Parnet's *Dialogues* (1996).

6. In recent years, Manuel Delanda has argued in persuasive terms – particularly in *Intensive Science and Virtual Philosophy* (2002) – that the virtual is the concept that takes us to the heart of Deleuze's ontology of the intensive.

7. Although Lévy is careful to distinguish his concept of collective intelligence from the 'molar becoming', as he puts it, of Hegelian philosophy, he also acknowledges that an 'essential affinity' exists between the two approaches (Lévy 1997: 223).

# Chapter 12

# The Joy of Philosophy

*Claire Colebrook*

Why philosophise? Why think? What is the function, purpose or point of philosophy in a world directed more and more towards efficiency, out-comes and economy of effort? Why suspend action and life for the sake of an idea? It is possible to answer these questions, via Deleuze, with two mutually exclusive sets of answers. The first 'Platonic' path would stress the incompleteness of actual life. Existing life, the life of the organism that strives to maintain its own being (to remain as it already is), perceives and responds to a given world. However, that world can only be said to *be*, to be actualised, because there is some condition or logic beyond being. What exists beyond beings is the Idea: a thing can only exist *as* this or that actual being because it instantiates or actualises some form. For Plato such forms – the logic that is the truth and proper being of the world – require a turn away from the physical and sensible life that fluctuates through time, to those forms from which time unfolds. This Platonic logic has a curious status in contemporary continental philosophy. On the one hand, there is Heidegger's classic critique of this logical turn whereby Plato establishes a being which will become the proper object or paradigm for human self-development (Heidegger 1998: 166). This critique of a separate or higher being that is other than this world is anticipated by Nietzsche, who will diagnose the belief in a 'higher world' or ideal of man as a failure of life and will. Nietzsche is, however, equally virulent in his attacks on a scientific restriction to matter or a utilitarian calculation of life. Heidegger, Nietzsche and Deleuze will all insist that while the Platonic appeal to a pre-given norm is an abandonment of thinking, there can be no question of a simple and positivist restriction to the immedi-ately apparent. On the other hand, then, in addition to overturning the Platonism that will establish a model or transcendent norm for appear-ance – a ground or origin of simulation – there is also in Deleuze a resis-tance to a simple reversal of Platonism. Philosophy is neither a turning away from this world, nor an exorcism of all the illusions, phantoms and desires that take thought beyond the self-evident.

The task of philosophy, in this immanentist tradition, will be to maintain the question, problem or meaning of life beyond any living organism. The post-Nietzschean resistance to *Lebensphilosophie*, utilitarianism, scientism and positivism insists upon the decision, act, will or force – the desire – which will posit some being as the foundation upon which thinking may be grounded. Thus, when Foucault criticises the nineteenth-century turn to 'life' as the table or a priori upon which all beings (including 'man') might be known (Foucault 1970: 128), he argues that literature will open up a radical outside, a beyond life that is not a logic, foundation or condition of life. Those forms of twentieth-century philosophy, such as phenomenology or structuralism, that present man as a being who speaks and thereby discloses the world, are manifestations of a more general failure to think about the division or fold between what we see (things) and what we say (words). Always, some border or logic has been established between life on the one hand and its articulation on the other. From the point of view of vitalism or *Lebensphilosophie* 'man' speaks because he must live; speech flows from man's need to labour and to maintain social equilibrium. Against this surrogate foundationalism or what Foucault refers to as an 'empirico-transcendental' doubling, literature takes language away from the purposive, self-sustaining, striving organism and creates its own syntheses and logics irreducible to developing life (Foucault 1970: 305). For Deleuze, both following and criticising Foucault, the forces of language that take literature beyond the life of speaking man are accompanied by the forces of silicon that take bodily life beyond biological matter and the forces of genetics that take life beyond the self-maintenance of the organism:

> The forces within man enter into a relation with forces from the outside, those of silicon which supersedes carbon, or genetic components which supersede the organism, or agrammaticalities which supersede the signifier . . . What is the superman? It is the formal compound of the forces within man and these new forces. It is the form that results from a new relation between forces. Man tends to free life, labour and language *within himself*. The superman, in accordance with Rimbaud's formula, is the man who is even in charge of the animals (a code that can capture fragments from other codes, as in the new schemata of lateral or retrograde). It is man in charge of the very rocks, or inorganic matter (the domain of silicon). It is man in charge of the very being of language (that formless, 'mute, unsignifying region where language can find its freedom' even from whatever it has to say). As Foucault would say, the superman is much less than the

disappearance of living men, and much more than a change of concept: it's the advent of a new form that is neither God nor man and which, it is hoped, will not prove worse than its two previous forms. (Deleuze 1988: 132)

In his writings on Bergson, Deleuze goes even further with this idea of thinking forces *beyond* the already actualised. From composed unities it is possible to discern the differential forces from which identities have emerged, and then, in turn, to think difference or genesis in itself; this would not be the differentiation of actuality which plays itself out in the world, but the difference that makes that differentiation possible. In this sense, difference *as virtual* is what truly is:

[T]he virtual is the mode of that which does not act, since it will act only by differentiating itself, by ceasing to be in itself, even as it keeps something of its origin. Precisely, however, it follows that the virtual is the mode of *what is*. (Deleuze 2004: 44)

In some respects, then, philosophy could be considered Platonic (Deleuze 2004: 42): in addition to the actual multiplicity of what is we are also obliged to think those forces that have composed the given. Those forces cannot be traced back to *a* being from which logic emerges. In this sense we could see Deleuzian philosophy as retrieving the Platonic turning away of the soul from the already given or the actual, but nevertheless refusing to insist on a 'one' from which the given would emanate. The answer, then, to why we philosophise would not take the form that runs from Plato, through Aristotle, to Kant: 'I ought because I can.' In this tradition of transcendence, if there is a power or soul capable of forming an idea of what is not given, of what might be, or what potentially is, then one can no longer remain within the point of view of mere (nutritive or perceptive) life. One must philosophise, think theoretically, not to maintain the pleasure of what one *is*, but to become what one ought to be, to realise one's proper potentiality. Such an imperative to philosophise would be exclusively human, grounded on the soul's intrinsic potential (Irwin 1988).

For Deleuze, however, the imperative to think the forces which take life beyond communicative speech, biological matter and the organism are necessarily inhuman. To philosophise is to become-imperceptible – no longer a being who masters the world but one who feels the very joy of life in an intuition that is no longer directed towards the realisation of some external end: 'Intuition is the joy of difference' (Deleuze 2004: 33). 'We' philosophise, not to arrive at who we are, not to realise our ownmost powers, but because life is desire. Life is the potentiality for force and synthesis that pays no attention to the already formed.

Before going on to examine how this might relate to the social force, role and function of philosophical thinking we might consider another incommensurable way in which Deleuze's thought can answer the question of why one might philosophise. The first, Platonic, answer that we have already considered might be labelled as 'discontinuist'. That is, there are certain life drives and functions located in self-maintaining organisms such that each being in the world maintains its own point of view and its own world. However, *human* beings have an additional capacity, not only of self-maintenance and perception of a world – noticing and adapting to relevant differences – but also of intuiting the world as such, not from this point here and now for me, but as it would be for all time, for any subject whatever. Essences are for Plato the forms that remain the same and allow for particular instantiation and perception. A being is what it is because it participates in an unchanging form, and we know this being as the type of being it is because our soul is capable of intuiting such forms. Much later Husserl will maintain the importance of categorical intuition, the capacity to intuit, through change and variation, the *meaning* or ongoing identifiability of a perceived thing; and Heidegger will also insist that *Dasein's world* is perceived *as* this or that. From Plato to Heidegger human perception is not the immediate grasp of an outside, but a relation to a world oriented by sense. By contrast, if the animal is 'poor in world', this is because it may perceive its own environment but not have a *sense* of what that perceived being might have beyond its immediate existence. Deleuze will maintain that each perception has its world, and will even maintain the problem of essences. But essences are no longer forms that allow a human perceiver to grasp what would be true for any subject whatever. Essences are singularities, a power to be perceived, to open up divergent worlds; to perceive an essence is to perceive how something might be encountered not only by other styles of perception (becoming-animal) and not only beyond purposive cognition (becoming-woman) but also beyond any located point of view (becoming-imperceptible). We intuit or perceive this flux or variation not as it is for me and my sensory motor apparatus but as it might be for other perceivers, at other times, in other encounters, through other relations. We philosophise, then, to release the human brain from its biological home, allowing *mind* or connections and syntheses beyond the self, to open up from the world to the cosmos.

However, much work in philosophy, neurophilosophy and popular neuroscience appears to be uncannily Deleuzian in positing a *continuist* or extensional framework for the relation between the embodied mind and the (once seemingly elevated) activities of philosophical and artistic thinking. To get a sense of this we can see how both neurophilosophy and Deleuzism have sounded the death-knell of the linguistic paradigm. If it were the case, as highly simplified structuralist accounts once suggested, that in order to think (and in order to have an 'I' who thinks) I must be subjected to some system of differences, then there would be a *digital* break between language and world. We would not experience a quality, label it, build up more and more labels and then have a shared language. On the contrary, in order to perceive a quality *as* capable of being labelled (as repeatable, differentiated, marked out, perceivable beyond the here and now, or iterable) I must already be working within some differential network, already have a proto-language or traced difference. The *human* condition is one of being subjected to a system of differences, of being placed in the position of having to interpret. While we imagine, necessarily, that there is some presence beyond those referring differences, we are always within the mediated system of difference, capable of imagining the origin retroactively, only after the event. Such an account would preclude, or mark as incomplete and illegitimate, any biological, evolutionary, materialist, physicalist or neurological narrative of the emergence of language. Just as Nietzsche argues that any philosopher who claims to intuit the truth of the world has illegitimately to negate and despise the rich flux of the world, he also argues that any reference in language to the sensation that causes the literal word and then metaphor, will itself be a displacement and metaphor. But it is just this pre-linguistic naïvety (or liberation) that seems to be allowed by the 'turn' to Deleuze, for whom Nietzsche is anything but an advocate of the prison house of language.

For Deleuze, the challenge of Nietzsche's philosophy of immanence is not to abandon oneself to one's linguistic point of view, or to maintain one's self as a narrative construction. Rather, Nietzsche's philosophy is one of life as a field of 'pre-individual singularities' (Deleuze 1990: 107). The liberating manoeuvre is not to see language as the system through which one perceives life, but to redefine life in such a way that something like *analogical* rather than digital language is thinkable. If life were a substance possessed of certain intrinsic properties, qualities and forms, and brains were perceptive mechanisms for organising those qualities into categories and concepts, then thinking and language would be digital. This would yield an equivocal ontology, with life's differences and qualities on the one hand, and then an arbitrary system of sounds and structures that allow us to map those differences on the other. The linguistic turn in both analytic and continental philosophy would have a primarily critical force: we know the world through our form of life, conventions and categories, and we cannot and should not try to find the *meaning* of some quality in life or substance itself, outside of use, context and relations. The idea of analogical language is, however, not only crucial to Deleuze's understanding of art; it also allows us to negotiate sections of Deleuze and Guattari's *Anti-Oedipus* and *A Thousand Plateaus*. Historically, before the digital code of 'the' system of signifiers which is, in principle, translatable, repeatable and purely arbitrary, Deleuze and Guattari describe the emergence and expression of difference in what now might be called the emerging or extended mind. Rather than a mind or body that must take its place in a system in order to have an 'I' and a world of stable and conceptual identities, we can think of connected, acting, moving, adapting and desiring bodies that do not have to know or represent their environment (or others) precisely because they exist and live only as already connected and involved with their territory or *Umwelt*.

In the beginning is the machine, not the organism: not a self-enclosed being that somehow has to attach itself to an outside world, but a series of connecting operations or functions that allows the relatively stable point of the living being to maintain its own life. Bodies are coupled to environments – eating, breathing, adapting movements to spaces, creating territories by moulding themselves to relevant differences, and relevant differences to themselves. Certainly, we do not need the Levi-Strauss myth of how we became social, whereby we abandon a life of immediate needs and submit to a system of delays. As Deleuze and Guattari argue in *Anti-Oedipus*, before systems of exchange and negotiation there is a pure abundance of the gift, a flowing outwards of life to difference and connection (Deleuze and Guattari 1983: 160). Bodies are already composed of sympathies; it is better, then, to begin with the concept of the system, rather than the self-contained organism. Accordingly, just as social systems *extend* sympathies – the partial attachments one has for the bodies of one's territory need to be captured by the image or figure of a body beyond the immediate network – so systems of writing and communication extend the expressive and inscriptive tendencies of primitive cultures. Deleuze and Guattari are quite clear in *Anti-Oedipus* that they do not see the entry into language as the submission to system, the outside of which can only be imagined as a dark and undifferentiated 'beyond'. Just as they reject the notion of a subject who speaks as the proper image of thought, so they also undertake a genealogy of writing and the emergence of a general sense of humanity. In this respect, Deleuze and Guattari's work might be aligned with recent work in neuroscience and cognitive science that rejects earlier models of the self and focuses instead on both mind and speech as emergent properties, not located 'in' a self, but distributed systemically among self, environment, bodies and others (Hansen 2000).

Consider the argument for emergent language made by V. S. Ramachandran, who offers an eloquent and persuasive criticism of the mind as a computational function and instead looks at human art and cognition in terms of broader neural and bodily systems (Ramachandran 2003). According to Ramachandran it is best to begin with an account of a tool-using, functional and active human body and ask how and why language might have developed; what functions was it 'bootstrapped' to? Ramachandran argues that language attaches itself to cross-activation areas of the brain. For example, while synaesthesia may be rare in the population – seeing certain numbers as having a certain colour – we all have some connection between visual recognition of shapes and certain sounds, so there is a connection in the brain or cross-activation of visual and auditory areas. This gene for cross-activation capacity survives, he argues, because it is useful, and we can see this clearly in the cognitive function of metaphor. But the development of such cross-activations also allows for abstraction, permitting us to give one sensory form to a quality from another field. Language is enabled by and develops these neural networks and does so because it extends and furthers human functioning. Language is neither an arbitrarily imposed system that differentiates the world (for it is built upon pre-existing cross-referencing tendencies), nor is it some innate grammar or system (for what characterises language is its plasticity and adaptability). Indeed, the complexities of syntax may well be derived from our capacity as tool-using animals. Just as I attach this stone to this piece of wood to cut this tree to make this plinth, so I can attach this verb to this clause to this conjunction to build up a complex grammar. Ramachandran even speculates that the sense of self is also an emergent property, derived from purposive, engaged and life-furthering action. Well before modern 'subjects' it would have been useful to imagine other bodies as having purposes and intentions; by doing so we would then be able to anticipate possibly hostile or co-operative actions. The sense of one's own self would be a refraction of this imagined other self and might be derivative from a more original unity, the distinction between self and other – ultimately – being a fiction or illusion.

To a limited extent – and these limits are all important – we can align such 'emergentist' accounts with Deleuze and Guattari's description of deterritorialisation, where the tool is a deterritorialisation of the hand, and speech a deterritorialisation of the mouth. Contrary to the idea that one speaks by situating oneself within an arbitrarily imposed code that differentiates and organises a perceiving brain, Ramachandran begins from a functioning, responsive body adapting to its environment. Certain sounds begin in concert with physical movements; we clench our teeth with effort, for example. When Deleuze in his book on Francis Bacon describes an analogical language that would paint the scream (rather than the horror that elicits the scream), he seems to support this idea that bodies issue in expressive movements, sounds and contortions that are *neither* actions that a subject undertakes to alter their world *nor* signs that would denote some object or action in the world (Deleuze 2003). Before representation or symbolism, and prior to but not disengaged from action, there are affective responses. Certain bodily sounds and movements are adjustments of the body that express what is beyond the body; we are not given the object itself but the force it elicits from the body. A scream is not a symbol for some horror, but it is the way horror expresses itself in the perceiver, and to paint such screams is not to attach a signifier to the event but to paint the genesis of the body's responses *from which* the organised, relational and detached codes of a language might emerge. Approaching Deleuze in this way allows us to situate his intuitionism, expressionism, empiricism and philosophy of desire in a broader late twentieth-century critique of mind and the cognitive paradigm.

Art would be crucial in overcoming the emphasis on representation and cognition and would instead give form to the body's basic responses to the problems of life; a reading of art would allow us to discern those forms through which we make our way in the world, and artists would be those who are most skilled in manipulating and maximising the pre-digital mappings of the human brain. Thus Ramachandran produces a list of universal criteria for art, which explains why art is not a copy of reality but a deployment of the same neural mechanisms that enable recognition; we have, for example, capacities for facial recognition which allow for the discernment of high degrees of specificity and individuality. A Picasso canvas that distorts the facial form, playing with its symmetry, taps directly into and extends *beyond reality* those neural potentials. Susan Greenfield (2000) has also suggested that while our everyday recognition and mastery of the world requires meaning, or the establishment of regular neural networks, artists have the capacity to release perception from those synaptic habits, allowing for the influx of renovated perception and experience. Such accounts are modern neurological versions of a tendency in Kantian aesthetics: we have certain powers that enable us to know and categorise the world, and while art is not *knowledge* of the world it nevertheless takes the *forms* that enable recognition and then plays with or extends their subjective employment. While art is thereby liberated from function and representation, it nevertheless originates from powers that had some type of function *and* can be explained as pleasurable precisely because it draws upon the brain's original adaptive powers.

If we were to align Deleuze with such movements that would release mind from its home in the subject then we would no longer see philosophy as an exercise in the virtual in its most radical sense – an exercise in thinking potentiality beyond the given, beyond the organism and beyond a life that is defined in terms of fecundity and self-enjoyment. And indeed there have been criticisms of Deleuze and Guattari's attempts to take the concept of life beyond the borders or relative stability of the organism (Hansen 2000; Hayles 2001). Exemplary of this tendency to play down Deleuze's critique of the lived is Manuel DeLanda's (2002) ongoing project of describing the virtual as integral to physical processes. Less emphasis would be placed then on *transcendental* empiricism, or the capacity for immanent life to yield a sense or image of itself, in favour of a return to 'life' understood in its purposive, productive and material processes. Rather than privileging philosophy's capacity to create a concept that *surveys* being – say, the Spinozist striving for a third kind of knowledge, or perception *sub specie aeternatis*, 'time in its pure state' – one would focus on Bergson's legacy that stresses the capacity for human life to intuit worlds or durations beyond its own organism. Indeed, in thinking about the social place and force of philosophy, the organism becomes a crucial image and concept. On the one hand we can begin our account from an image of self-furthering life, an organism that is nothing other than an assemblage of enabling responses to its world, and we could then see philosophy (as many have done) as one of those practices that maintains a sense of who we are, our world and what we can do. On the other hand, while acknowledging philosophy's traditional dependence on some image of thought, and its tendency to trace its transcendental claims from some already given or empirical form, we might say that philosophy nevertheless is the potential to think *beyond* both the image of organised life, and beyond a commitment to a life that is defined against death (a life that would not already include the redundant, inert, non-relational, destructive, wasteful and fruitless).

If we were to take the former path – recognising philosophy as an enabling practice grounded in the life of the human organism – we would set ourselves against the tendency to begin philosophy from a mind that must come to *know* a world. It is no surprise that those who defend the notion of the extended mind and celebrate the recent achievements of science in overcoming the computational paradigm also draw on the phenomenological tradition. Husserl has criticised the 'natural attitude' that would assume mind as some point within the world. The idea of intentional consciousness – that consciousness is an engagement, relation or comportment and not a thing – has underpinned not only Heidegger and Merleau-Ponty's insistence on a world that is *lived* before it is known and represented, but has also been appealed to by those working in cognitive science and artificial intelligence (Searle 1983; Wrathall and Malpas 2000; Dreyfus and Hall 1982; Clark 1997; Maturana and Varela 1998). While drawing upon philosophy, such scientific movements are also critical of the traditional philosophical elevation of mind. There is nothing special, mysterious or spiritual about the mind; there are biological, systemic, neurological and physical processes of which mind is one expression among others. We can, then, see Deleuze as part of a tradition of embodied cognition, going further than post-structuralists such as Derrida who would be critical of philosophy's supposed transcendent detachment from life; for Deleuze would actually account for the emergence of systems from life (Protevi 2001). To read Deleuze this way we would have to downplay those moments, particularly with reference to art, where Deleuze and Deleuze and Guattari are critical of phenomenology's appeal to the 'lived' (Deleuze 1997: 1; Deleuze and Guattari 1994: 178).

Today, not surprisingly, those defending the notion of an extended mind refer to Heidegger and Merleau-Ponty who insist that the body is purposively engaged in its world and only subsequently falls into the Cartesian error of thinking the world is 'out there' to be represented (Clark 1997). In terms of the ethics and social force of philosophy – philosophy's place in the world – what one would avoid is the Cartesian hyperbole defended by Jacques Derrida (Derrida 1978). Against Foucault's history of reason, Derrida argues that reason could not be given a birth or genesis, for any attempt to do so would itself be working within reason. The Cartesian gesture of hyperbolic doubt is just this *idea* or utopian spirit of philosophy: from within reason to doubt all that is given, to think as if one were deprived of all foundation and certainty. Without any such foundation the task of thinking presents itself as radically undecidable and therefore burdened with the responsibility *to think*. Against this capacity for thinking to imagine, if not achieve, a position without ground, the recent turn to 'life' would domesticate thinking to one more way of being in the world. Nowhere is this tension more evident than in looking at the different ways in which the Spinozist legacy might be mobilised. Both in the philosophy of Hardt and Negri and in the neuroscience of Antonio Damasio, Spinoza is a philosopher whose opposition to transcendence means that all thinking, movement and action should ultimately express the self-furtherance, wellbeing or home-ostasis of humanity (Hardt and Negri 2000) or the self (Damasio 2003). For Deleuze, however, the joy of philosophy lies not only in the over-coming of the self and the organism, a becoming-imperceptible, but the creation of dissonance and divergence – points of view or world that, far from expressing one life through diverse monads, create lives and worlds that are incommensurable. Whereas Hardt and Negri argue for a phi-losophy that might be returned to a self-unfolding humanity, Deleuze insists that philosophy will take us beyond the human *and* beyond all those concepts of life that were thought of in terms of self-maximisation. True thinking and true philosophy can only be achieved in affirming vio-lence, stupidity and malevolence – the capacity to create aberrant, destructive and demonic connections (Deleuze 1994).

Those in favour of a vitalist or materialist Deleuze stress the pre-cognitive – affective, neuronal, processual – forces that are not thought's own, demoting philosophy from its once privileged position of a reflective theory upon other knowledges. Such an approach would need to avoid looking too closely at Deleuze's aim to think 'time in its pure state' or to form a philosophy that works with those moments in the arts that allow affects to stand alone, to be released from the 'lived'. To align Deleuze with the recent return to 'life', we would have to ignore or play down those moments in Deleuze and Deleuze and Guattari that celebrate an architec-tonic paradigm: in contrast with a life that unfolds from itself Deleuze and Guattari stress the primacy of architecture precisely because architecture does not simply unfold from life, but stands alone and releases itself from the unfolding of the lived, creating an infolding – 'Art begins not with flesh but with the house. That is why architecture is the first of the arts' (Deleuze and Guattari 1994: 196). This would not be a Heideggerian being-for-the-world, an openness or comportment to being, but the creation of infold-ings or new worlds. A vitalist Deleuze, strangely, would be closer to the Heidegger who is critical of art or philosophy as the production of some external poetic object, closer to the Heidegger who wants to think a pre-Aristotelian notion of life as that which moves from itself. But the whole point of philosophy, stated both explicitly in *What is Philosophy?* and *Difference and Repetition* and implicitly in Deleuze's entire oeuvre, is not the maintenance or self-furtherance of life in its organic form, in the form of the lived, but the creation of concepts or styles of thinking that will do violence to cliché. To think time in its pure state is not to think the processes of material or physical life *in general*, for a concept is not a gen-erality but the extraction of an intensity. To think difference as such would require thinking difference beyond a difference of this or that living being: '[W]e shouldn't enclose life in the single moment when individual life confronts death' (Deleuze 2001: 29). As in *Anti-Oedipus*, the real locus of philosophical thought should not be the border between life and death, the former being good, the latter being evil, but the difference between life and the organism (Deleuze and Guattari 1983: 329). Perhaps, then, it is not surprising that when Deleuze wants to arrive at a thought of 'a' life – not *this* determined life – he considers not a self-animating, willing or purposive body, but a *corpse*. Referring to the scene in Dickens' *Our Mutual Friend* where Riderhood – 'a disreputable man, a rogue' – lies dying, Deleuze argues that it is the *loss* of distinction between subject and object that yields a pure haecceity or singularisation. Here, we are not given a quality or potential as it connects to, relates to, or unfolds a determined life; we are given pure potentiality. The ethics of such an encounter lies not in a body that maximises itself or gives a norm to itself, but in the capacity to think what is not one's own, what is not immediately human or worthy of sympathy:

> The life of the individual gives way to an impersonal and yet singular life that releases a pure event freed from the accidents of internal and external life, that is, from the subjectivity and objectivity of what happens: a 'Homo tantum' with whom everyone empathizes and who attains a sort of beatitude. It is a haecceity no longer of individuation but of singularization: a life of pure immanence, neutral, beyond good and evil, for it was only the subject that incarnated it in the midst of things that made it good or bad. (Deleuze 2001: 28–9)

Two Deleuzes then: first is the 'Platonic' Deleuze who emphasises the power of the virtual and its difference and distance from organic life, and then there is a vitalist, physicalist Deleuze whose philosophy makes sense only when its vocabulary is traced back to its scientific origins. But Deleuze's and Deleuze and Guattari's work already harbour a theory regarding such seeming binaries. It is not a question of elevating the molecular over the molar, the virtual over the actual; for the real opposition is not between these two tendencies, but in the way we think about the difference of tendencies. The incorrect, *moralising* path would be one of good and evil: life is original, productive, creative and positive (either an actuality that unfolds virtually, or a virtual realm that allows for the actual). One would then aim to avoid or expunge all the rigidities, opacities, redundancies and accidents which deflect life from its proper self-unfolding. But the radical path, beyond good and evil, is to think of philosophy not as the task to discern the proper path of life, but to think positively about the production of perceived borders between life and death, between the actual and the virtual, between what we take to be our own and what is negated as chaos or non-being. This is why Deleuze (1994) produces the term '?being', to create a new problem: philosophy is not the discernment of what properly is, but the creation of concepts that produce new existents, new orientations.

Why, then, philosophise? Today, the dominant answer, if there is any justification at all, is because we live. Philosophy helps us understand the world and life from which we emerge. Philosophy either helps us form an image, law or norm for ourselves, or philosophy is critical – helping us overcome the illusion or image of a lawful, cognitive and representing self. Through philosophy we become self-critical and self-founding. By contrast, Deleuze's thought has little to do with destroying the illusional, speculative grandeur of art and philosophy. Far from domesticating thinking within life or language, far from limiting thought to critique, reflection and communication, art and philosophy destroy the limits of the self: both the self-maintaining organism and the self-legislating subject. Philosophy does not come after the event but is the event. Studying the history of philosophy is a destruction of the present, not because we recognise that things might be otherwise, but because to *think* philosophically is to activate the potential, within life, to break with the image of life, the image of that which strives to maintain and preserve itself. It is the capacity to say no to all that cannot be lived, thought and willed beyond the now, beyond the present, beyond ourselves.

# References

Clark, A. (1997), *Being There: Putting Brain, Body, and World Together Again*, Cambridge: MIT Press.

Damasio, A. R. (2003), *Looking for Spinoza : Joy, Sorrow, and the Feeling Brain*, Orlando: Harcourt.

DeLanda, M. (2002), *Intensive Science and Virtual Philosophy*, London: Continuum.

Deleuze, G. (1988), *Foucault*, trans. S. Hand, London: Athlone Press.

Deleuze, G. (1990), *The Logic of Sense*, trans. M. Lester, ed. Constantin Boundas, New York: Columbia University Press.

Deleuze, G. (1994), *Difference and Repetition*, trans. P. Patton, New York: Columbia University Press.

Deleuze, G. (1997), *Essays: Critical and Clinical*, trans. D. W. Smith and M. Greco, Minneapolis: University of Minnesota Press.

Deleuze, G. (2001), *Pure Immanence: Essays on A Life*, trans. A. Boyman, New York: Zone Books.

Deleuze, G. (2003), *Francis Bacon: The Logic of Sensation*, trans. D. Smith, London: Continuum.

Deleuze, G. (2004), *Desert Islands and Other Texts: 1953–1974*, ed. Lapoujade, D., trans. M. Taormina, Los Angeles: Semiotext(e).

Deleuze, G. and Guattari, F. (1983), *Anti-Oedipus: Capitalism and Schizophrenia*, trans. R. Hurley, M. Seem and H. R. Lane, Minneapolis: University of Minnesota Press.

Deleuze, G. and Guattari, F. (1987), *A Thousand Plateaus: Capitalism and Schizophrenia*, trans. B. Massumi, Minneapolis: University of Minnesota Press.

Deleuze, G. and Guattari, F. (1994), *What is Philosophy?*, trans. H. Tomlinson and G. Burchill, London: Verso.

Derrida, J. (1978), *Writing and Difference*, trans. A. Bass, Chicago: University of Chicago Press.

Dreyfus, H. and Hall, H. (1982), *Husserl, Intentionality, and Cognitive Science*, Cambridge: MIT Press.

Foucault, M. (1970), *The Order of Things: An Archaeology of the Human Sciences*, London: Tavistock.

Greenfield, S. (2000), *The Private Life of the Brain*, London: Allen Lane.

Hansen, M. (2000), 'Becoming as Creative Involution?: Contextualizing Deleuze and Guattari's Biophilosophy', *Postmodern Culture* 11 (1): 000.

Hardt, M. and Negri, A. (2000), *Empire*, Cambridge: MIT University Press.

Hayles, N. K. (2001), 'Desiring Agency: Limiting Metaphors and Enabling Constraints in Dawkins and Deleuze/Guattari', *SubStance* 94/95 30 (1–2): 144–59.

Heidegger, M. (1998), *Pathmarks*, ed. W. McNeill, Cambridge: Cambridge University Press.

Irwin, T. (1988), *Aristotle's First Principles*, Oxford: Clarendon Press.

Korsgaard, C. M. (1996), *Creating the Kingdom of Ends*, Cambridge: Cambridge University Press.

Maturana, H. R. and Varela, F. J. (1998), *The Tree of Knowledge: The Biological Roots of Human Understanding*, trans. R. Paolucci, rev'd edn, Boston and London: Shambhala.

Protevi, J. (2001), *Political Physics: Deleuze, Derrida, and the Body Politic*, London: Athlone Press.

Ramachandran, V. S. (2003), *The Emerging Mind*, London: Profile Books.

Searle, John R. (1983), *Intentionality: An Essay in the Philosophy of Mind*, Cambridge: Cambridge University Press.

Wrathall, M. A. and Malpas, J. (2000), *Heidegger, Coping, and Cognitive Science*, Cambridge: MIT Press.

# Notes on Contributors

Rosi Braidotti is Distinguished Professor in the humanities at Utrecht University. During the academic year of 2005–6 she will be a Leverhulme Trust visiting professor at the law school of Birkbeck College in London. Her last book is *Metamorphoses* (Polity Press, 2002). Forthcoming in February 2006 is her new book: *Transpositions: On Nomadic Ethics*, Polity Press.

Ian Buchanan is Professor of critical and cultural theory at Cardiff University. He is the author of *Deleuzism* (Edinburgh University Press, 2000) and *Michel de Certeau* (Sage, 2000).

Claire Colebrook teaches English literature at the University of Edinburgh. She is the author of *New Literary Histories* (Manchester University Press, 1997), *Ethics and Representation* (Edinburgh University Press, 1999), *Gilles Deleuze* (Routledge, 2002), *Irony in the Work of Philosophy* (Manchester University Press, 2003), *Understanding Deleuze* (Allen and Unwin, 2003), *Gender* (Palgrave Macmillan, 2004), *Irony: The New Critical Idiom* (Routledge, 2004) and *Deleuze: A Guide for the Perplexed* (Continuum, 2005).

Verena Andermatt Conley teaches in the Department of Romance Languages and Literatures and in literature at Harvard University. Recent publications include, *The War Against the Beavers: Learning to Be Wild in the North Woods* (University of Minnesota Press, 2003) and *Littérature, politique et communisme: lire 'Les lettres françaises'* 1942–1972 (Peter Laws, 2004). She is currently interested in the transformations of space and subjectivity in recent French thought.

Eugene W. Holland has published widely on Deleuze, critical theory and modern French literature and culture. His work has appeared in anthologies and in journals such as *boundary 2*, *October*, *sub-stance*, *South Atlantic Quarterly* and *L'Esprit Createur*. He is the author of *Baudelaire and Schizoanalysis* (Cambridge University Press, 1993) and the *Introduction to Schizoanalysis* (Routledge, 1999). Dr Holland is Professor of French and comparative studies at the Ohio State University.

John Marks is Reader in Critical Theory at Nottingham Trent University. He is the author of *Gilles Deleuze: Vitalism and Multiplity* (Pluto, 1998), and co-editor, with Ian Buchanan of *Deleuze and Literature* (Edinburgh University Press, 2000). He is currently editing a special issue of the journal *Paragraph* dealing with Deleuze and science, and he is working on a book dealing with the cultural and philosophical mediation of molecular biology in post-war France.

Adrian Parr teaches in the College of Design, Architecture, Art and Planning at the University of Cincinnati. She is the editor of *The Deleuze Dictionary* (Edinburgh University Press, 2005), and the author of *Exploring the Work of Leonardo da Vinci* (Edwin Mellen, 2003).

Paul Patton is Professor of philosophy at the University of New South Wales. He is the author of *Deleuze and the Political* (Routledge, 2000) and editor (with John Protevi) of *Between Deleuze and Derrida* (Continuum, 2003). His current research interests include political philosophy, especially post-structuralist and contemporary liberal political theory, and the Rights of colonised indigenous peoples.

Patricia Pisters is Professor of film studies in the Department of Media Studies of the University of Amsterdam. Her teaching and research interests focus on questions related to multiculturalism, interculturality and the media, mainly looking at North African cinema and Arab media. Her publications include: *Micropolitics of Media Culture: Reading the Rhizomes of Deleuze and Guattari* (ed., Amsterdam University Press, 2001); *The Matrix of Visual Culture: Working with Deleuze in Film Theory* (Stanford University Press, 2003) and *Shooting the Family: Transnational Media and Intercultural Values* (ed. with Wim Staat, Amsterdam University Press, 2005).

Laurence J. Silberstein is the Philip and Muriel Berman Professor of Jewish Studies in the Department of Religion Studies, Lehigh University, and Director of the Philip and Muriel Berman Center for Jewish Studies. He is the author of *The Postzionism Debates: Knowledge and Power in*

*Israeli Culture* (Routledge, 1999) and *Martin Buber's Social and Religious Thought: Alienation and the Quest for Meaning* (New York University Press, 1989). He has edited and co-edited several books in Jewish cultural studies including *The Other in Jewish Thought and History: Constructions of Jewish Culture and Identity* (with Bob Cohn) (1994), *Mapping Jewish Identities* (2000); and (with Laura Levitt and Shelley Hornstein), *Impossible Images: Contemporary Art after the Holocaust* (2003), all published by New York University Press.

Kenneth Surin is based in the Literature program at Duke University, where he is also Director of the Center for European Studies.

Nicholas Thoburn is a lecturer in the School of Social Sciences at the University of Manchester. He is the author of *Deleuze, Marx and Politics* (Routledge, 2003).

# Index